PRAISE FOR
Mind over Monsters:

"Sarah Rose Cavanagh's *Mind over Monsters* is the book we need now—now, when the teen mental health crisis has reached alarming proportions. With thoughtful nuance, clear-eyed observation, and a sure grasp of the evidence, Cavanagh delivers a message to parents, teachers, and everyone else who cares about adolescents: what young people need from us is compassionate support *and* invigorating challenge. Her book is both reassuring and inspiring—a must-read for everyone who knows and loves a teenager."

—Annie Murphy Paul, author of *The Extended Mind:
The Power of Thinking Outside the Brain*

"Most current rhetoric about teaching and learning tends to frame challenging students and acting with compassion as mutually exclusive enterprises. But, as Sarah Rose Cavanagh reminds us in this beautifully written defense of humane teaching, that dichotomy has always been a false choice. Challenge without compassion is simply hazing, but compassion without challenge atrophies the vast potential and possibilities in our students. Neither is sufficient for our moment, Cavanagh shows us. Rather, "compassionate challenge" is the best way to do this work while still honoring and preserving our humanity. The crises we face are monstrous problems indeed. *Mind over Monsters* neither evades nor surrenders to this bleak reality but gives us the tools to create learning spaces offering both sanctuary and liberation. It is an essential book."

—Kevin Gannon, author of *Radical Hope: A Teaching Manifesto*

"Sarah Rose Cavanagh makes clear the value diverse faculty bring to the classroom, student learning, and campuses, articulating constructs that are deeply aligned with the research on the excellent teaching practices of diverse faculty."

—Chavella T. Pittman, PhD, founder of Effective & Efficient Faculty

"Like a conversation with a smart, hopeful, and passionate friend, Sarah Rose Cavanagh artfully shares her journey with anxiety and mixes in interviews with diverse students and experts. Educators, parents, and students will appreciate her call for learning environments that provide a sense of security and belonging so students can safely engage in risk and overcome their fears."

—Kelly Hogan and Viji Sathy, authors of *Inclusive Teaching: Strategies for Promoting Equity in the College Classroom*

"This is an important book. It makes a valuable contribution to the literature on teaching and learning, tackling an urgent mental health crisis and how we can build the learning environments that will help students overcome that crisis and thrive. As a bonus, readers will find Cavanagh's writing witty and imaginative, giving us insights that can transform college experiences."

—Ken Bain, president of the Best Teachers Institute and author of *What the Best College Teachers Do*

"There's a lot of bluster and a lot of people convinced they have the 'one true thing' about how we should be supporting the mental health of young people. But these issues are complex, not simple. I personally count on Sarah Rose Cavanagh as someone who will grapple with these complexities, while still providing a clear pathway toward helping people thrive."

—John Warner, author of *The Writer's Practice: Building Confidence in Your Nonfiction Writing*

MIND

SUPPORTING YOUTH MENTAL HEALTH

OVER

WITH COMPASSIONATE CHALLENGE

MONSTERS

SARAH ROSE CAVANAGH

BEACON PRESS
BOSTON

BEACON PRESS
Boston, Massachusetts
www.beacon.org

Beacon Press books
are published under the auspices of
the Unitarian Universalist Association of Congregations.

27 26 25 24   8 7 6 5 4 3 2 1

This book is printed on acid-free paper that meets the uncoated paper
ANSI/NISO specifications for permanence as revised in 1992.

Text design and composition by Kim Arney

Library of Congress Cataloging-in-Publication Data is available for this title.
ISBN: 978-0-8070-9339-9
e-book: 978-0-8070-0758-7; audiobook: 978-0-8070-0768-6

For William Fitzgerald Cavanagh

father, poet, lifelong guardian
of childhood at Nazareth Home for Boys,
the tall one who brings home stray kittens

And Stephen King,

who helped me conquer
my monsters from a very young age

It's no good *telling* the student that he isn't to be held responsible for the content of his imagination, he needs a teacher who is living proof that the monsters are not real, and that the imagination will not destroy you.

—KEITH JOHNSTONE, *Impro*

Monsters, I've argued, are creatures of historical context and cultures get the monsters they deserve, the vengeful ghosts they have raised.

—SCOTT POOLE, *Monsters in the Classroom*

CONTENTS

MONSTER NIGHT

W HEN I WAS BUT A FEW YEARS OLD, I was preternaturally fixated on a book about monsters. It was called *Monster Night at Grandma's House*. My family's early photo albums are littered with pictures of me plopped on the laps of various adults, the book propped up in such a way that the large jagged letters that form the title are clearly visible. In all of them, I look very serious under my 1980s bowl-cut helmet of blond hair. Determined.

Published a few weeks before I was born, *Monster Night* was the first book for young children by the acclaimed young-adult novelist Richard Peck. When my own quite determined daughter was born, I found a copy on eBay and bought it, excited to read it to her. But after paging through the old, beloved pages, I quietly tucked it away on a shelf for a few years.

The story itself isn't the problem, as it is a classic hero's journey writ small. A young boy named Toby sleeps over his grandmother's house and is terrified by the noises he hears at night. He bravely faces down a perceived monster, tracking it throughout the house until he falls asleep in the swing chair on the front porch, waking to the soft light and chirruping birds of morning. It is a lesson about facing your fears, about sitting with your discomfort, about knowing your strengths. A laudable tale.

So why did I tuck it away without reading it to my daughter? Because it is also terrifying—I didn't think at a few years old she was ready for how frightening it is. Peck is a talented author who writes with rich sensory detail, and the artist Don Freeman's illustrations are haunting. Little Toby lies alone on the upper floor of the house, eyes squeezed so tightly shut that he sees stars, while bugs hit the screen next to his head that sound for all the world like fingers of various sizes scratching to get in. A monster enters the room with hot, fiery breath, and the creak as he steps on the floor is so loud that all the finger-bugs scatter. As Toby tracks the monster through the house, he steps on warm floorboards still glowing with the heat of the monster's giant paws. The reader knows that Toby's fears are unfounded, that the monster has been swirled into existence from the sounds of an old house in midsummer, Toby's own shadow, and his very rich imagination. But it still works on a visceral level.

As Toby endures his monster night, he experiences a host of symptoms familiar to anyone who has suffered from anxiety. He has a delightful supper with his grandmother, but as the hours creep on and dusk falls, he begins to anticipate bedtime with increasing physical discomfort. At the end of bath time, he pulls on his pajamas with a face contorted in such a way we know there are a thousand "what-ifs" swirling in his mind. His breath comes shorter. His heart pounds. In the thick of the night, he sees stars, his flesh crawls, his skin flashes hot and then cold.

Like Toby, many of our young people suffer from surges of anxiety even in safe settings. Anxiety and depression are the most common mental health struggles among youth, constituting some 40 percent of all diagnoses among those ages ten to nineteen. But unlike Toby, many youths' fears are not resolved in a effective or timely manner. The Centers for Disease Control and Prevention estimates that a full 13–20 percent of children ages three to seventeen in the United States meet criteria for a mental, emotional, or behavioral disorder in any given year, their symptoms severe enough to warrant clinical attention. The story is even worse for teens, and young women and youth from marginalized identities appear to be particularly suffering. In 2019, suicide was the second leading cause of death among adolescents, with the highest suicide rates among women of all races, Black youth, and young people identifying as LGBTQIA+ (and intersections of these various identities can combine to amplify these vulnerabilities). Rates of suicidal ideation and behaviors among transgender youth are especially alarming.

Since 2019, the elongated COVID-19 crisis, ongoing struggles for racial justice, and worsening climate emergencies have presented new mental health challenges for everyone, but particularly for youth. One large, nationally representative analysis in the United States found higher depression symptoms in people of all ages during the initial pandemic lockdown than before, with a more than threefold worsening of depression symptoms in general. An analysis of all available studies on mental health symptoms in college students in the early aftermath of the pandemic revealed significant increases in depressive symptoms in American, Canadian, and European students.

Blame for this mental health crisis among youth has been laid at the feet of changes in parenting practices, of greater willingness to discuss and diagnose mental health symptoms, of economic and social developments that lead to wide disparities in life opportunities, and of everyone's darling scapegoat of the moment: the smartphones in their pockets. No matter what the cause, we need solutions—but no one can agree on the best approach. Major stakeholders argue over whether we need greater care and concern or, ironically, less, whether so-called coddling might in fact be driving up rates of mental health problems. Despite these troubling statistics and lack of understanding or consensus regarding causes and solutions, adolescent mental health is not well studied and does not receive adequate research funding.

It is not just depression and anxiety that are on the rise. You also can't escape news of college campuses embroiled in moral outrage and anger, feelings and events that are painted with very different brushes depending on who is delivering the news. Some voices claim these students are acting in righteous civic engagement, unwilling to suffer inequity any longer and eager to make change in their worlds. Others claim these students are pampered from birth until they no longer can tolerate challenge to their ideas, that well-meaning people are losing their jobs after sharing their thoughts on Halloween costumes, that respected academics can no longer feel safe being invited to elite campuses without being possibly pelted with abuse both verbal and (at times) physical.

This cauldron of fear and sadness and anger might be less worrisome if these negative emotions were tempered with equally high levels of positive, arousing experiences. After all, isn't youth the heyday of the blood? Don't we expect our young people to be running on high emotion all the time? But dismayingly, there are also signs that our youngest generations are also running low on hope and high on burnout, and too few of them are regularly engaging in healthy rejuvenating activities. In a viral article about millennial burnout, journalist Anne Helen Petersen reflects on the ill effects of being raised in a freelance culture where everything from employment to fitness to nutrition to meditation must be optimized, lest one topple from one's precarious social standing. She writes that it "takes things that should be enjoyable and flattens them into a list of tasks, intermingled with other obligations that should either be easily or dutifully completed." Activities that should be revitalizing instead deplete.

In terms of other positive rejuvenating activities, while Americans in general are notoriously sleep deprived, the statistics for college students are especially worrisome—one assessment reported only 11 percent of college students get adequate sleep during the school year. And though popular culture loves to paint the college years as a dizzying parade of hookups and threesomes, evidence suggests that even sex is on the decline among young people. Dubbing this decline a "sex recession," journalist Kate Julian investigates potential causes and, like the epidemic of sadness and anxiety, finds no easy answers—just possibilities ranging from easy availability of pornography to changing sexual norms in the wake of #metoo to the same overprotective parenting practices often pinned to other troubles ailing America's youth.

In a stew of intense negative emotions, deprived of the revitalization of intense positive experiences, and now ushered into a new era where neither physical nor economic safety seems assured, young people face a mental health landscape that seems dire indeed. As a college professor who researches the psychology of emotion, a public intellectual who writes and speaks about higher education, and the mother of an adolescent, I am desperate to understand the challenges facing America's youth and possible solutions to them.

My urgent attempt to accomplish that understanding is this book. In these pages, I will argue that there is a common solution to both addressing the youth mental health crisis and remaining true to the educational mission of secondary and higher education—and that solution is creating living and learning environments characterized by both compassion and challenge. Our thought leaders battling about whether students need more challenge or more care have it wrong—our young people need both. This work will not be easy, and it will certainly not be accomplished by scolding students about how much they've been coddled or expecting them to be able to face their fears on their own, without support. Rather, one needs to set up the conditions that allow students to feel safe enough to rise to challenges, and then one needs to create opportunities for them to do so.

Emotional states like fear, anxiety, and sadness are complicated amalgams of our biology, our interpretations, characteristics of our circumstances, and the influence of the people who surround us. To thrive, our young people need to learn in settings characterized by safety, belongingness, and support for embodied mental health. Once these settings are in place, to thrive they then need to engage in practices associated with confronting fears, embracing uncertainty, and play. As people in the business of caring for and educating young human beings, we need to establish these settings and scaffold these practices.

I believe that to accomplish this work we will need *voices*, *science*, and *solutions*.

Voices. We need the voices of actual students living and feeling and breathing on our campuses—too often, dusty academics speculate about the lived experiences of the students who occupy our classes and live in our dorms without going to the source and querying them. For this source of evidence, I will turn to a qualitative research study in which my colleagues and I interviewed several dozen undergraduate students across an array of types of institutions and demographics to get a sense of what is working for them in the classroom and what is not, how they view the emotional aspects of their learning, and the factors that they find motivating in their educational journeys. I will refer to these interviews throughout the text as the Student Voices project. Before launching this study, we obtained ethics approval from the Assumption University Institutional Review Board and all participants provided both verbal and written informed consent. I made every effort to keep the quotes and student characteristics as true to their originals as possible. In cases where details could be possibly identifying, I took creative liberties to ensure the students' anonymity.

Science. I supplement these student insights with scientific insights and research studies sourced from psychology, sociology, pedagogy, and neuroscience, sharing information about how the brain works and why anxiety happens, how people manage uncertainty, and how they recover from mental duress. Scientific knowledge is imperfect and ever evolving, and so where relevant I also highlight the gaps in our knowledge and the complexities surrounding the degree to which important decisions should or should not be based on a shifting landscape of knowledge.

Solutions. To be sure I don't present only my perspective on these issues; the content of the book is also informed by interviews with experts from fields including higher education, clinical psychology, sociology, human services, and improv from across the United States, some of whom are people who dedicate their lives to helping adolescents and college students actualize their goals.

Finally, interwoven with the science and interviews of experts and students are reflections from my own lifelong struggle with panic disorder. The journey of writing this book was a very personal one in which I developed insights into my own inner workings as I wrote, a path that I hope you will join me on. The content of this book was shaped not just by my scholarly expertise but also my lived experiences.* I have wrestled frequently in the throes of anxiety, gotten muddy and bruised in the trenches. I know quite well how terrifying it can be to be unable to trust your own body—to react to ordinary situations with extraordinary terror. I think that an unruly body and an apprehension of the future have been with me since the very beginning of my existence and is why as a toddler I was so drawn to the tale of Toby and his fire-breathing, finger-scraping night of fright.

We are ever what we ever were.

THE JOURNEY AHEAD

In the first part of this book, we'll consider the epidemic of mental health issues among young people, the nature of anxiety, and the need for what I will call compassionate challenge to support youth mental health. In

---

* As we like to say in psychology, "research is me-search."

the next three parts, we will examine compassionate challenge from the perspectives that psychologists examine all aspects of the human experience—at the level of bodies and brains ("Bodies," part 2), as thinking, feeling beings with minds ("Beliefs," part 3), and through our actions and behaviors in the world ("Behaviors," part 4). I will argue that before taking on challenges, young people need resources to help balance the budgets of their bodies, that they need safety, and that they need to believe they are autonomous, that they are competent, and that they belong. But to truly conquer their monsters, young people also need challenge. We will see that challenge does not have to mean confrontation or unyielding rigor but rather the practice of equating uncertainty with motivation and purpose rather than anxiety, becoming comfortable with discomfort and vulnerability, and striving to play.

I wrote this book to be accessible to anyone who is in the business of educating young human beings—that includes those young human beings themselves, their parents, their teachers, and the people directing their campuses. That's a big tent, and so this book takes a wide perspective rather than drilling down into much specific advice. I hope to share more targeted advice following publication, in essays and in conversations on various campuses.

When I use the word *youth* throughout the book, I'll be referring to anyone in emerging adulthood, roughly ages fifteen to twenty-four. While the student interviews and many of the examples will be specific to college, there is no bright line separating a seventeen-year-old high school senior and a seventeen-year-old college freshman. As exemplified by my own personal experience shared in the first few chapters of this book, many of the mental health issues college students struggle with begin before they ever step foot on campus. In addition, fewer and fewer contemporary college students fit the old stereotype of a student in their late teens living on campus with parents footing the bill for expenses—the number of returning students, commuters, and working students now quite outnumber "traditional" students. For all these reasons, while the content of the book will lean toward youth and higher ed, the issues, examples, interviews, and at times advice will also be quite relevant to high school teachers, administrators, parents, and older students.

Finally, this book is about how we can make changes to educational settings in the U.S. to better support youth mental health. Unpacking that statement into parts, this book, first of all, concerns itself with how we can craft learning environments for students. Thus, there are several candidate causes for increases in mental health problems that we won't be talking about much, such as social media or increased political polarization.* Geared as it is for educators, this book is also not primarily about how to understand the causes or treatment of *clinical* levels of anxiety, depression, or other mental health struggles. Understanding how psychologists diagnose and treat clinical levels of mental health struggles will help us understand the current crisis, and so these issues are briefly explored in chapter 1. But immediately thereafter I will then make the case that youth is a critical period during which core abilities of emotion regulation, sociality, and motivated goal pursuit are established, and thus our focus as educators should be crafting learning environments that support youth mental *health*—both for students who may be struggling and for those who are not.

Historian Kevin Gannon writes that for us to rise to meet our present moment, with the myriad crises and opportunities facing higher education, what we need is "radical hope . . . an assertion of faith in a better future in an increasingly uncertain and fraught present." Writing this book lent me reassurance and inspired some radical hope for the future. I hope that reading it does the same for you.

---

*If you are interested in this topic, you might enjoy my book *Hivemind*, which considers how social media and smartphones have affected our ultrasocial selves in both positive and negative ways.

PART ONE

CRISIS, COMPASSION, CHALLENGE

CHAPTER ONE

CRISIS AND COMPLEXITIES

F OR MOST OF THE FIRST two years of high school, I didn't speak. Not to teachers, not to peers, not to support staff. Rumors swirled that I was mute, that my silence combined with my penchant for wearing long hippie skirts instead of pants meant that I belonged to a religious cult and thus was not allowed to talk to anyone, that I was a snob who thought I was better than everyone else.

The plain truth was, I was terrified. Of what I'm not entirely sure—in middle school I had, if anything, been too loud, too boisterous, somehow just *too much* for a girl. This zeal had led to a whole lot of social rejection that didn't matter much to me at the time but which I was determined to avoid in this entirely new school system. I found dialing myself down hard to modulate, though. The less I spoke, the less I felt I could speak, my voice snaking ever inward until I was nearly silent, and any occasion that required speech turned my insides to ice and my ears to fire. At the time I didn't have the knowledge to label these reactions. It would take until college for me to look back and realize that this was the beginning of my lifelong struggle with clinical levels of anxiety.

Truly debilitating symptoms didn't begin to haunt me until my sophomore year of college, when I began volunteering for a twenty-four-hour hotline to help parents under stress in caring for their kids.* The purpose of the hotline was to offer stressed parents an outlet. The hope was that

---

*This story and some of these sentences first appeared in an essay I wrote for the *Chronicle of Higher Education*.

when they felt at a breaking point, they could call the number and talk things out with a friendly voice rather than take their anger and stress out on their children. Some shifts were overnight, and so the hotline would forward the line to the private lines of the volunteers. Since the hotline was listed publicly and splashed on fliers around the Boston subway, it wasn't hard for sexual predators (monsters of another kind) to figure out that the hotline was staffed mostly by young college women with young college women voices, who had to listen to at least enough of your story to determine you were a bad agent rather than a parent needing help before we hung up. Their "parental stress" stories would start innocently enough—usually with misbehaving daughters—but progress in nauseating detail until they twisted into shapes that no healthy person would want intruding on their thoughts, their breath on the line coming quicker and quicker.

Away from home for the first time in my life, alone in a dorm room in the dark of night, I could always tell when a particular call was suspicious. The first few syllables of the men's voices, tight with arousal and anticipation, would be enough to unfurl something deep in my belly. But endlessly conscientious, I would clutch the receiver with white knuckles and let him talk until I was sure, until the narrative built into something truly stomach clenching. This was around the same time that my low-simmering social anxiety boiled into full-blown panic attacks.

While in popular speech the phrase is used to mean a lot of different things, a true panic attack is all-encompassing and utterly incapacitating. When one strikes me, every biological system in my body rebels—the respiratory, the digestive, the neurological. Most times, I must confine myself to a bathroom, lying on the floor shaking and gasping for air and repeatedly sick to my stomach, the cool tile against my forehead the only balm. The physical symptoms would be more bearable if they didn't also come with an unnerving sense of being separate from my typical waking self (depersonalization) and unmoored from ordinary reality (derealization), my swirling thoughts a deep, dizzy tangle from which there is no respite.

A friend once asked me why, when I felt a panic attack coming on, I didn't just go for a walk and take some deep breaths. The advice was so incompatible with my bodily experience of a panic attack that I had no idea how to respond.* When in the pages to follow I make the argument that we need to face some of our most feared experiences head-on, I know how hard that is and what a slow and arduous process it will be for many of our young people.

I started having these attacks while helming the overnight shifts on the hotline. Then they began happening before my daytime shift. And sitting in my pajamas eating Lucky Charms in my mother's kitchen. Then during class, when I'd have to flee. The tendrils of anxiety spread throughout my daily life—any sign that an attack might be on the horizon froze me on the spot, my voice caught in my throat.

Professor after professor would respond to my classroom silence by scribbling on my papers, "Would love to hear you share some of these insights in class!" I would pledge to try, but whenever I thought about participating, my mouth would run dry, my pulse would escalate, and I'd feel lightheaded. By the time I could even think about trying to master these symptoms, the conversation would have moved beyond the point I wished to make.

I am now a college professor and a keynote speaker, literally talking in front of large groups for a living. I will discuss this remarkable transition from mute pupil to public speaker, how I regained my voice, in the next chapter when I introduce the concept of compassionate challenge. But first, let's lay some foundation for the rest of the book: how mental illness is diagnosed,** what implications this process has for our consideration of the mental health crisis, what anxiety and depression are and are not, and what conclusions can and cannot be drawn about causes and solutions of the crisis.

---

*After reading these pages he corrected me: "You did know how to respond. You wrote it up in your freaking book." Fair enough.

**There are increasing calls to abandon the term *mental illness*. The well-thought-out reasons range from a desire to decrease stigma, to focus more on human variation than categories, and to move away from a medical model of psychological functioning. As you will see in the pages that follow, I am very much in agreement with these aims. I will thus more often use other terms but will use "mental illness" in the context of discussing psychiatric diagnoses specifically (which at the time of this writing still very much adopts a medical model).

But first I'd like to spend some time considering why I chose an organizing metaphor of monsters for this book's content and the tripartite structure to the remaining chapters. For a monstrous lens will help us unpack the difficulty with which we all—not just our youth—struggle with how best to think and act as a body in an uncertain and often terrifying world.

REVEALING OURSELVES: A MONSTROUS LENS ON BODIES, BELIEFS, AND BEHAVIORS

The word *monster* comes from the same root as the word *demonstrate* and can be understood as "that which appears" or reveals itself. Monsters are omens, signifiers—they carry a message. As is true for all works of imagination and art, close examination of monsters can divulge the themes and patterns of our collective truths. Psychological phenomena are most comprehensively understood by examining them at three levels—our physiological experience as brains and bodies, our mental experience in the forms of thoughts and beliefs, and our actions and behaviors in the world.

Bodies. Monsters are intricately related to our ambivalent experience of living within a biological body, representing all that is fraught about such an arrangement, and all that can go wrong. The zombie rots, its flesh flaking off and its orifices beginning to ooze, a sped-up version of our own inevitable decay. Vampires wrestle with their physical lusts, their desire to penetrate other beings and exchange bodily fluids with them, to dissolve the physical barriers of the body between self and other. Once a month the werewolf's smooth, carefully manicured human body grows fur and fangs, and all socialization and culture are left in a puddle on the floor along with its ripped-through clothes. Sometimes civilized, he is pure animal once more.

Sigmund Freud addressed the concept of horror and the monster in an essay called "The Uncanny." He noted how many monsters in children's stories exact their terror by wounding or stealing major body parts—piercing the tender eye, lopping off and collecting heads—and thought this was not coincidence but rather that our obsession with these stories was related to our fears about our own messy, unpredictable bodies. They revolt on us, as in a panic attack or an inconvenient sexual attraction or cells multiplying out of control, and they are inevitably disassembled by the slow violence of decay. "Freud saw the severed body part as just the beginning of terrifying possibilities," historian Scott Poole writes in his excellent book *Monsters in America*, "the ultimate fear, the heart of the uncanny darkness, spilled over from the feeling of nausea evoked by the sense of something that refuses to respect the categories of the known and knowable." Thus the monstrous relates not just to our equivocal experience of our bodies but is also intimately bound up with learning. The monstrous relates to uncertainty about the future, that which we can and cannot know—and our beliefs about what that uncertainty means. And as we will see throughout the rest of this book, uncertainty is key to understanding anxiety and mental health.

Beliefs. We human beings are not just bodies but are also thinking, feeling beings with minds—and the content of our minds shapes our experience of both our bodies and the larger world. Here in the mind, uncertainty looms large. In terms of that which can be known and that which cannot, Freud thought that the feeling of the uncanny arose from those thoughts and desires that you believed you had successfully repressed but hadn't, the energy of these demons becoming restless to make themselves known to you and to the people around you. He traces the etymology of the German word for the uncanny, which is *unheimlich*, and shows that it is a subversion of the word *heimlich*, meaning "that which is familiar and homelike." Surprising, maybe, but again not a coincidence—he argues that we are discomforted by hiding from ourselves things that are familiar and known, turning our back to them. He points out that much of what we consider unsettling involves repetition, recurrence. Body doubles, déjà vu, becoming lost and retracing your steps, and someone else reading your thoughts and intentions all involve this doubling. The *unheimlich* occurs when something that we tried to hide from ourselves is instead cast into the light, and we recognize it as part and parcel of our own selves, our own terrible selves in the mirror.

In an excellent depiction of just this principle, novelist Patrick Ness penned a vivid monster story for young adults called *A Monster Calls*. In the story, a thirteen-year-old boy named Conor is haunted each night at 12:07 a.m. by a hulking black and green mass of a monster cobbled together by the tree limbs in the dark outside his window. But Conor isn't really frightened of this twisty, dark monster. Perhaps he isn't that afraid because despite his horrifying appearance, the monster seems gentle, more prone to spinning tales and giving advice than threatening violence. But more important, Conor isn't frightened by the creature because he is too fixated on real-life terrors to spare some fright for the monster—for his beloved mother is wasting away due to cancer. Worse, he has occasionally wished that the end would come already, so he could stop waiting and worrying about when and how the loss will happen. In his guilt and his horror at how his own brain has betrayed himself (and worse, betrayed his mother), Conor's mind concocts the branched, dark giant to haunt his nights until he confronts this truth about himself and—even better—realizes that this wish for his mother to die is an errant brain cloud, a natural thing, nothing he is responsible for or that stands in for his true desires.

The story reads a lot like one of Freud's famous case studies, the truths that we cannot face taking outsize monstrous form in our psyches. While the title is *A Monster Calls*, it is really Conor who has instead called the monster, summoned it out of his growing terror about the impending loss of his mother and his own desire to end, once and for all, the uncertainty that it represents. Like Toby from Richard Peck's *Monster Night at Grandma's House*, we find these monsters are swirled together based on our limited brains, our largest fears—and also like Toby, only by facing our uncertainties and rising to the challenge can we return to psychological equilibrium.

Our monsters aren't solely about threats, though. Scott Poole notes that we're collectively attracted to the monstrous, even compelled by them—that, in Freudian terms, they are often more Eros (life and sex drive) than Thanatos (death and violence drive). He points out that this is particularly true of our fanged, blood-thirsty friends: "Popular fascination with the vampire provides the best example of the strange human tendency to want the thing hiding under our beds to be in bed with us." Broad-shouldered Lestat;* Buffy's chiseled rock-star fling, Spike; Wesley Snipes's leather-clad Blade; even dumb old sparkly Edward of *Twilight*—all ripe for longing.

---

* Don't you dare picture Tom Cruise when you read those words.

And specifically, all ripe for *adolescent* longing. Professor of English James Twitchell notes that a fixation with monsters surges during the adolescent years, perhaps tied to fears of the changing body during puberty, an awakening of the body's sexual appetite, and a dawning realization of mortality. He observes that horror tales and urban legends in the teen years also provide a similar service as fairy tales did in younger childhood, in that they convey information about norms and morals more relevant to a broader and more nuanced social world than that which occupied early youth. Don't hook up in the woods alone, don't bully people online, don't repeat "Candyman" five times in the mirror.

Later in this chapter I will discuss at length how psychologists (and the societies they operate in) decide what is "normal" and "abnormal." Here we see how monsters lend a hand in understanding these collective beliefs as well. For monstrosity can be understood as a "means of inquiry" into how particular societies view what is normal and abnormal, who belongs and who is considered different. Art historian Asa Simon Mittman writes that "monsters both establish and challenge the normative categories they menace, and in both cases, draw our attention to these norms." They straddle the lines between normal and abnormal, between life and death, between human and animal, and by doing so they challenge our categories.

There are two responses to these beings who blend and blur, whom professor of women and gender studies Elizabeth Grosz argues possess "intolerable ambiguity"—we can either stamp them out of existence or we can categorize and thus contain them. Despite the assuredly earnest efforts of its creators, the manual psychologists use to diagnose mental illness doesn't just codify behaviors judged unhealthy to help people. It also performs the second of Grosz's responses to category blurring, the attempt to categorize and thus contain. The diagnostic manual constrains that which society judges unsavory or dangerous, sketches the outlines we want everyone to color within, and thus indicates both judgment and control. It enforces compliance, as *normality* is increasingly narrowly defined and we include more and more traits as possible mental illness. As Mittman writes, "Without a center to hold us in, we are each that much closer to spiraling outward to the edge, to becoming a *mearcstapa*, a monstrous walker of the margins." We may all be monsters, all diagnosed with something, all judged deviants.

In addition, by diagnosing the individual as deviant rather than examining the structures and environments that the individual is asked to comply within, the shapers of a society do not have to question these structures and environments. If we label all the nine-year-olds who cannot sit still and do math problems for eight hours a day with a diagnosis of attention deficit disorder, we don't have to question whether we should be asking nine-year-olds to sit still and complete math problems for eight hours a day. If for the twenty-year-old who feels defeated and powerless in a system where they must work themselves to the bone just to survive and pay rent with no hope of ever escaping, we pronounce major depressive disorder and blame their serotonin levels, then we never have to question the structural inequalities inherent in our society.*

Behaviors. We are biological creatures with bodies that think and feel, but we also act. What is the best way to confront a monster, particularly if said monster is actually a complex configuration of our own worst fears about ourselves and our society's decisions about which behaviors and experiences are allowed and not allowed? The first step is likely the one that our monster-book protagonists Toby and Conor took, looking the monster straight in the face. Acknowledging your kinship. The monster dissolves when the *unheimlich* becomes the *heimlich*, when the uncanny is recognized as familiar and even lovable.

Eric Goodman, a therapist with over a quarter century of experience helping patients manage their anxiety, uses the fairy tale "Beauty and the Beast" as an analogy to encourage readers to reframe their anxiety. Rather than a horror or a fanged monster, the "beast" is instead a sometimes-unappealing but well-meaning hero. The former characterization brings the anxiety-filled person a sense of shame or failure, whereas

---

*Importantly, I am not suggesting here that psychiatric diagnoses like ADD or depression are never warranted or require treatment; instead I am arguing that we are likely overdiagnosing (other) people whose struggles are related to being asked to operate in systems that don't support their mental health.

the latter allows them to curiously approach anxiety as a sidekick with helpful messages for their life's journey.

Confronting our monsters also opens a path toward growth. In a bracing and brave series of essays called *Final Girl—and Other Essays on Grief, Trauma, and Mental Illness*, writer Kelly Baker takes a hard look at how her love of the horror genre was both born of and helped her live through trauma, loss, and struggles with her mental health. "I needed to know that I could be the final girl, too," she writes. "I could be the one that looks directly at all the carnage surrounding her and is still able to walk away, mostly in one piece. The final girl survived. I could, too, even if I was left with nightmares that will never go away." For monsters are never completely and forever vanquished—they merely shrink into quiescence, and they leave their scars.

Both monsters and our own struggles with mental health, then, are all about messy, unpredictable bodies, about navigating intolerable ambiguity, about our desire to control and tamp down and tame experience, about our sense of what is normal and what is other, and about how we can best respond to the challenges of life. How do we help young people shed their armor, read their physiological arousal as challenge rather than threat, embrace their vulnerability, and leap into not-knowing in order to learn? It isn't going to be either by shock-and-awe thrusting them into situations they fear or by helping them avoid experiences. Rather, it will be by engaging them and drawing them into learning environments that help them understand their own power. We will help our youth learn and grow through the practice of compassionate challenge.

But we first need to understand the shape of the crisis we face.

EVIDENCE FOR AN EPIDEMIC

Before the onset of the global coronavirus pandemic, before the killing of George Floyd set off a national reckoning with racism in the United States, before accelerating climate change and political polarization, researchers and clinicians were already issuing increasingly dire warnings about escalations of depression, anxiety, and self-harm among children and adolescents. Researchers found sharp increases in mental health symptoms in young people beginning in the 2010s and among those who sought counseling services on college campuses, a steady increase in not just self-reported depression and anxiety but also self-harm and suicidal ideation.

Unsurprisingly, the social ramifications of lockdowns and social distancing, the educational disruption, the widespread personal losses, and the financial challenges of the global COVID-19 pandemic did nothing to improve these statistics. In October of 2021, the American Academy of Pediatrics, the Children's Hospital Association, and the American Academy of Child and Adolescent Psychiatry joined together to declare rates of mental health difficulties among children and adolescents to be nothing short of a national emergency. They wrote that during the first two years of the COVID-19 pandemic, "more than 140,000 children in the United States lost a primary and/or secondary caregiver, with youth of color disproportionately impacted. We are caring for young people with soaring rates of depression, anxiety, trauma, loneliness, and suicidality that will have lasting impacts on them, their families, and their communities." Such loss and stress are likely to have effects that extend well into the futures of these youth.

Throughout this chapter you'll hear from two clinical counseling experts I interviewed. The first expert is Elizabeth (Elly) Romero (pronouns: they/them), a clinical counseling psychologist who specializes in working with ethnic minorities and immigrants, the LGBTQIA+ community, and the Deaf community. The second expert is Ryan Glode (pronouns: he/him), who works primarily with children and adolescents with obsessive-compulsive disorder (OCD). He is also the founder and president of the Rhode Island chapter of the International OCD Foundation, a nonprofit focused on OCD awareness, treatment, and advocacy. Elly's and Ryan's insights confirmed and extended what I read in the scientific literature.

I asked our clinical experts about the effects of the pandemic. Elly Romero couldn't stress enough how much COVID took an already maxed-out industry and poured an avalanche of new need on top of it. The struggles were particularly acute for anyone facing a major transition—eighth graders, seniors in high school, first-year students in college. Increasing awareness of the impact of racism on mental health also meant that many Black, Indigenous, People of Color (BIPOC) clients wished to enter treatment specifically with someone who could relate to their lived experience. Thus, clinicians like Elly (who is Latino) were particularly overwhelmed with new clients. Their community was "screaming for services," and there was only so much of them to go around.

The avalanche of need hasn't wound down as COVID cases have fallen—quite the opposite. It is difficult to provide statistics because so much of this varies not just by state but also by region, and it waxes and wanes, and depends on whether you wish to see a counselor for talk therapy or a psychiatrist (the latter can also prescribe medication). But both statistics and stories indicate a widening gulf between the need for services and the people and offices available to provide it. As with so many other systems, the pandemic put an unbearable weight on the already under-funded, under-staffed, and under-supported system of mental health services, and even privileged people with extensive resources are finding it difficult to access help. Educational developer Lee Skallerup Bessette considers all the public health campaigns to encourage people to seek mental health services and poses a poignant question in the title of her essay: "You Can Ask for Mental-Health Help, But Can You Find Any?" One analysis by a mental health policy institute reports that two-thirds of primary care clinicians reported difficulty in connecting their clients with psychiatric services. Alarmingly, the predicted shortage of physicians of all types is predicted to hit psychiatry particularly hard, as data from the American Association of Medical Colleges estimates that a full 60 percent of psychiatrists are over the age of fifty-five and thus likely to retire in the upcoming decade or two. Clearly, there is an epidemic of need for services. We need to act quickly and decisively to intervene, as anyone desiring help should receive it. But as I dug a bit deeper into the question of whether the epidemic of need was tied to true changes in severe levels of suffering, I encountered several complexities.

For one, the claim that we humans are in the throes of an anxiety epidemic is one that recurs throughout history. One can trace beginning ideas about anxiety to classical antiquity, where scholars like Cicero and Seneca write about both their observations and proposed treatments for people gripped by unreasonable fears in the presence of safety. In 1881, the physician and psychiatrist George Miller Beard wrote a book called

American Nervousness: Its Causes and Consequences in which he claimed that Americans were suffering from something he called "neurasthenia," a generalized fear of everything. He attributed rising rates of neurasthenia to an overabundance of dramatic social changes and the stress and over-scheduling of modern life. In a long poem published in 1947, the poet W. H. Auden diagnosed his generation as living through "the age of anxiety." Each generation seems to feel that they have a unique relationship with anxiety, one tumbling into another and into the always uncertain future, longing for a mythical time in the past when life was more secure, bodies behaved themselves, and you could trust the path before you.

Another difficulty in determining whether the epidemic is due to real changes in mental health symptoms arises because our tools of diagnosis and assessment for clinical symptoms are constantly changing. If we are testing with different devices and measures at different times, how can we be sure that we are testing the same thing? When one attempts to control for changes over time and other confounding variables, the picture looks murkier than a clear crisis. For instance, a group of researchers in 2019 conducted a statistical process that allows one to collapse across studies with different methods to find an overall take-home message. It evaluated forty-two studies from around the globe that collectively involved over a million participants over two time points, the earliest study published in 1978 and the latest in 2015. They did note an increase in mental distress over time, but it was a pretty small effect, nothing that would warrant the headlines we are seeing.

Another challenge to knowing whether there are truly greater rates of clinically significant mental health problems deserves a little more of our attention, I think, and that is our changing relationship with mental health struggles and how willing we are to talk about them.

COMPLICATING THE QUESTION: DIAGNOSTIC BOXES AND THE SPECTRUM OF EXPERIENCE

We all have enduring curiosities we can trace all the way back to our childhoods. For you, it might be dinosaurs or romance or calculating the trajectories of shooting stars. Sometimes one can even pinpoint the source:

a favorite book or pivotal life experience or liminal moment. My lifelong fixation is the blurry dividing line between healthy mental experiences and behavior and unhealthy ones—how and whether and why we draw that line.

Whether cause or consequence I'll never know, but over a few years in middle and high school I checked out Mary Anderson's young adult novel *Step on a Crack* from the library some twenty or thirty times. The book tells the story of a happy, well-adjusted teenage girl (named Sarah, as it happens) whose life is nonetheless punctuated by odd, sporadic episodes of kleptomania and nightmares where she murders her mother. In the twist ending, it turns out that her parents are genetically her aunt and uncle and that her mother, whom she thinks is an aunt, abandoned her as a young toddler in a fenced-in cemetery. The trauma of abandonment combined with the wounds she suffered trying to scale the cemetery's wrought-iron spikes were buried deep in her psyche. Every time she got a postcard from her "aunt" on her world travels she would be plagued by scary dreams and compelled to steal a reminder of her early life with her natal mother—a scarf, a vial of perfume, a small toy. Throughout the book, Sarah struggles to reconcile how she can be so happy on the one hand and so disturbed on the other, the relationship between traumatic events and their physical and emotional consequences, and whether she should think of herself as "crazy."

This fascination with the causes and consequences of mental health symptoms was also my entrée into teaching, as in graduate school I teamed up with my dear friend Jennifer DiCorcia to teach a series of courses in Tufts University's Experimental College on just these topics. We took a wide, creative scope—analyzing not just psychological science but also short stories, novels, plays, memoirs, and films. We watched *One Flew Over the Cuckoo's Nest* and *The Three Faces of Eve*, read *Sybil* and *I Never Promised You a Rose Garden* and *To Be a Mental Patient*, and delved into quite a bit of contemporary psychiatric science. Some of the major questions we pursued with our students were these: How do we decide what is "normal" and what is "abnormal"? What does "abnormal" even mean? Does demarcating certain experiences as unhealthy or "abnormal" buy us anything, or does it simply stigmatize those already suffering from difficult experiences?

One candidate definition is that abnormality could mean outside the statistical norm, behaviors and experiences that are highly unusual. But many mental illnesses are anything but uncommon. Lifetime prevalence rates for anxiety and depression are such that even if you personally win the lotteries of both genes and life stress and escape from ever suffering from a bout of mental health struggles, you can bet that your spouse or child or best friend won't be so lucky. Also, infrequency isn't helpful for the flip reason—are we going to diagnose feats of creativity, intellect, or generosity as somehow pathological?

Another possible characteristic we could use to delineate mental illness is the presence of suffering, the experience of some sort of mental pain or anguish. But while all the mental illnesses in psychiatry's diagnostic bible have as one of their criteria that the experience or behavior must involve impairment of some sort (the person's occupation, health, or social relationships must be adversely impacted for us to consider it a disorder), some people in the heights of a manic episode or a delusion may not profess to be suffering. Also, many human experiences involve quite a bit of suffering but are not mental illness. Anyone who has ever grieved an untimely death or struggled with poverty or harassment can attest to this fact.

Often students propose "strangeness" as a candidate for identifying psychological abnormality. But while some psychotic symptoms common to disorders like schizophrenia may seem strange from the outside (for example, hallucinations and delusions), a much greater proportion of people suffering from mental health symptoms are grappling with depression or anxiety or cognitive problems, all of which are common, ordinary experiences. And on the flip side, if you get to talking to a lot of people, you find that many of them have had some very unusual experiences—ghosts, aliens, thought insertion, Big Foot, precognition. Every now and then some big survey makes a splash providing evidence that most Americans believe in some peculiar claim or other. Given how common these experiences are, and that for most people they don't introduce any impairment, presumably these experiences are not mental illness but just part of being human.*

---

*Why these experiences are so very common even in the presence of mental health is a fascinating question for another book.

In the beginning of these courses, students work first alone and then to-gether on a worksheet that lists a variety of behaviors that may or may not be "abnormal" in various ways—after a hysterectomy, an elderly woman denies having a left leg that is very much attached to her body, a ten-year-old wants to tattoo his entire body blue—and that intentionally call out the additional complexities and difficulties of labeling a behavior as abnormal. What if there is no suffering, what if there is no impairment, what if the symptoms can be better attributed to a medical issue or the imagination of childhood? The class considers these cases and then comes up with a list of criteria for psychological abnormality . . . and a list of qualifiers that make drawing that line difficult. We then create a working definition of clinical struggle with mental health, which semester after se-mester looks like this: *impaired functioning over a period of time with respect to expected performance suitable for this individual person in their relevant context.*

In sum, to meet criteria for a mental disorder you need to have a marked change from your typical functioning, it needs to be out of bounds with the stressors or demands placed upon you, it needs to last for a sig-nificant amount of time, and it needs to take into account your personal traits, experiences, and previous history. Each of these elements is rela-tively abstract and involves a fair amount of subjective decision-making. Thus, while in clinical psychology and psychiatry we use the same frame and terminology as medicine—symptoms, diagnosis, disorder—these decision points about presence or absence are not based in laboratory tests or objective observations but rather deeply subjective, personalized judgment calls.

These judgment calls aren't completely arbitrary, as clinicians are working from specific criteria and guidance provided to them from the American Psychiatric Association (or the World Health Organization, outside the States), collected in the *Diagnostic and Statistical Manual of Mental Disorders* (*DSM*, currently in its fifth edition). But—and this is a big but—these supposedly objective criteria are *themselves* the result of judgment calls, set by a conference table full of clinicians and researchers debating and jockeying to leverage their personal theories. Lore has it that one prominent scholar working on the early versions of the diagnos-tic manual exclaimed about a proposed criteria for obsessive-compulsive disorder, "We can't use that as a symptom—my wife does that!" Despite its scientific sheen, each edition of the *DSM* is also very much a product of the sociocultural moment that produces it—witness the fact that homosexuality didn't stop being considered a mental disorder until the *DSM*-II was published, in 1973.

Furthermore, it isn't just your clinician who is weighing in on your diagnosis. They also must consider the guidelines from your health insurance company about which disorders "count" as needing treatment and thus whether they will get paid. These same companies are restricting the amount of time the clinician can dedicate before making their decision, as the company will only reimburse for increasingly short windows of time with their clients. Even more worrisome, the pharmaceutical industry takes a strong interest in the setting and regulating of these criteria. It's a fast decision, influenced by financially motivated external parties, about whether your brief, limited account of your internal experience meets somewhat arbitrary thresholds of criteria for somewhat arbitrary collections of symptoms.

In addition, unlike some medical pathologies—blood in your urine, abnormal cells in your cervix—mental health symptoms are typically not considered *present* versus *absent* but instead *high* versus *low*. That is, most human traits, abilities, and behaviors exist on a continuum where the majority cluster around the average, but where you can find fewer numbers of extremes at either end. Experiences like anxiety and depression exist on the same continuum, the same normal curve, as all human experience and behaviors.* Like height or extraversion or musical ability, some people are highly anxious, some people are preternaturally calm, and most of us fall in the middle somewhere. So, where is the cutoff point in labeling those on the upper curve mentally "ill" and the rest of us "normal"? Also, who gets to decide?

In a careful and thoughtfully researched book called *Losing Our Minds: What Mental Illness Really Is—And What It Isn't*, the psychologist Lucy Foulkes takes a hard look at even those symptoms that we might think

---

*Though technically some, like mental health following trauma, are skewed such that there are many more people toward the low end and then a long tapering curve on the high end—but it is still a spectrum rather than distinct categories.

of as more unusual and striking, perhaps evidence of serious pathology rather than an outcome of ordinary experience—such as paranoia, the feeling that people are acting in ways that are "out to get you." Even in these more striking examples of unusual experiences, she doesn't find exceptions to the spectrum-of-experience rule. Describing the results of one research study that mapped paranoid symptoms among a large sample, she writes, "It was just one big, gradually changing group, with no sudden shift, no cliff edge, just a gradually smaller number of people experiencing an increasing severity of paranoia." This same principle holds true for worrying, for feelings of worthlessness, for tendency to act compulsively, for frequently losing your temper.

Psychiatric diagnoses are essentially the field determining where on that tail end to insert a cut point, thereby labeling all experiences to one side "normal" and all experiences to the other side "abnormal." These cut points are then treated as gospel, and the practice of applying all those medical terms discussed earlier (diagnosis, symptoms, etiology, disorder, treatment) gives them a sacrosanct sheen, dresses them up in an authoritative white lab coat. These cut points also then allow everyone on the left to feel assured of their psychological normality and health, and for those on the right to bear the stigma of mental "disease," judged abnormal, judged deficient—even though two people on either side of the cut point may have nearly identical experiences, separated just by a symptom or two.

What's more, with each edition of the diagnostic manual the number of behaviors deemed "pathological" creeps steadily upward and stalks around increasingly common, everyday experiences. A famous cartoon by artist Randy Glasbergen depicts a doctor with a stethoscope speaking to an alarmed patient sitting on the exam table. He says to his patient: "We can't find anything wrong with you, so we're going to treat you with Symptom Deficit Disorder." Author Jess Zimmerman writes in her book *Women and Other Monsters* that "if the expectations are too narrow, nearly anything can become monstrous. If you are only allowed to be tiny, it is grotesque to be medium. If you are only allowed to be quiet, it is freakish to be loud. The more you are circumscribed, the easier it is to deviate, and the more deviation comes to seem outlandish or even dangerous." As we increasingly set boundary markers around behaviors, labeling some as problematic and others as healthy, we run the risk of pathologizing healthy human variation.

There has been a rapid expansion of the number and types of diagnoses over the editions of the *DSM*, with new proposed diagnoses including caffeine use disorder and internet gaming disorder. This expansion of the number of ways that one can be diagnosed as mentally ill obscures the fact that at the same time, scientific research in genetics, clinical psychology, and neurobiology increasingly suggest that there might instead just be a handful of ways that mental health can go wrong, expressing itself in a variety of ways depending on individual experience and context. This research suggests that the most common symptoms across disorders involve dysregulations in mood, anxiety, impulsivity, and what's called executive function, which are mental abilities that include planning, organization, and control of attention. Treatment, too, doesn't look that different from one disorder to the next. Many symptoms of disorders that look very different on paper respond best to the same combination of medications that target the neurotransmitter serotonin and the use of cognitive behavioral therapy, which asks you to tackle unhelpful patterns of thinking and interpretation in your life.

These challenges to determining the demarcation point where individual variation threatens the well-being of an individual enough to warrant a diagnosis makes it difficult to evaluate whether rates of suffering are truly increasing or whether it is instead our definitions and willingness to acknowledge suffering that are rapidly changing. Dovetailing these changes is a positive development that nonetheless introduces more complexity—people's willingness to disclose that they are suffering in the first place.

COMPLICATING THE QUESTION: DESTIGMATIZATION OF MENTAL HEALTH STRUGGLES

Back in 2012, I was traveling home from an academic conference with a lab mate and close friend. He was a graduate student and I was a postdoctoral fellow in the same laboratory, working for the same supervisor. We were sitting in the airport waiting for our flight to take off when, for whatever reason, the stomach flutters and shortness of breath that mark a beginning of a panic attack began their relentless march across my interior. This was a time during which my panic attacks had taken a nasty turn where I sometimes lost consciousness completely. I felt compelled to warn my colleague that this was a possibility. I briefly sketched out the issue for him—but then I also entreated him not to say anything about my struggles to our mutual supervisor. I feared she would think less of me.

It is difficult for me, a mere ten years later, to even enter my own past mind well enough to understand this moment—how I could feel so ashamed of what I obviously felt was a personal weakness that I wanted it to be hidden from my supervisor. My supervisor is a clinical psychologist, an emotion regulation researcher, a friend as well as a mentor, and her personality is such that she would be one of the last people you could imagine judging anyone for anything, least of all *something she actively studies*. Moreover, here I am in this book telling you, a perfect stranger, about the intimate physical and emotional details involved in my experience of anxiety. While I'd like to think some personal growth on my part accounts for some of the differences between then and now, I suspect that changes in social norms are the greater driving force in this shift.

While we surely have a long road of progress ahead of us, in wealthy Western cultures there have been dramatic changes in willingness to disclose and discuss mental health problems. This is a fantastic development for so many reasons. As celebrities and thought leaders increasingly share their experiences of mental health struggles, other people are more likely to talk about their own problems, to reach out for resources, to seek psychological treatment. In a great many ways, this ought to lead to better health outcomes, to nudge the dial of collective mental health in a positive direction. But what it also means is that the forces of increasing pathologizing of everyday behaviors synergizes with a greater willingness to endorse mental health symptoms. The result is that we have moved the goalposts of what mental illness is and isn't, folding in more ordinary behaviors and experiences under its umbrella.

In a setting where mental health care is unlimited and therapists bountiful, this might not be a terrible thing—what's the damage if more people engage in cognitive-behavioral or mindfulness-based acceptance therapy? I've long thought we should all have therapists checking up on our self-talk and routine behaviors the same way we all should have optometrists checking up on our eyes and dentists checking up on our teeth.* But the sad fact is that we are not living in such a world, and behavioral mental health offices being filled up with patients suffering from the human condition is going to box out those who are truly suffering at the tail end of the spectrum. It also might create the perception of a mental health crisis, when what has truly changed is the destigmatization of experiences of anxiety and depression, not the base rates of such experiences.

When I asked them, both of my clinical expert interviewees confirmed that while they, of course, see decreasing mental health stigma as a wonderful thing, it does sometimes lead to an overpathologizing of ordinary human suffering. It can create the feeling that something is terribly wrong when, really, one is just experiencing the slings and arrows of everyday life. Ryan worries that this pathologizing of daily stressors—labeling all anxiety as a problem to be fixed, for instance—teaches young people that they aren't resilient, that they don't have the means to cope. He says he frequently has young people come in for his services and when they begin chatting together about their lives and their concerns, they seem to be functioning quite well—doing well in school, maintaining active social relationships, giving back to the community. He points this observation out to his clients, and they invariably respond, "Yeah, but I'm anxious all the time." He asks what they are anxious about and hears back all the things he is anxious about as well. Establishing a satisfying career, finding true love, being liked by one's peers, climate change, global pandemic. "They haven't been taught by their society that it's okay to feel discomfort," Ryan said, "that we're not happy all the time. We're never going to be." If we are all reaching for an impossible goal, we're always going to be dissatisfied.

Sigmund Freud claimed that the purpose of his psychoanalysis was to turn "hysterical misery" into "common unhappiness" and seemed pretty pessimistic about the likelihood of ever successfully treating the latter. Ryan's approach is to help his clients understand that they know themselves better than anyone and to set aside what parents or their guidance

---

* "Should" here because, sadly, in the United States basic health care is still a marker of privilege.

counselor might think is their "problem" or what society might convey to them about being *shinyhappypeople* all the time. He asks his clients: How can I support you through your life journey, which will inevitably involve some pain and suffering?

Hearing that your experience of mental distress is the result of a diagnosis rather than something inherent to your character can be a huge relief for many people. But it can also mean that you begin to believe that your experiences are something not situational but rather endemic, not changeable but rather inevitable. It has often struck me that many of the college students I teach talk about their anxiety as something that is unchangeable and trait-like rather than a state of being that happens to them sometimes. Pediatric clinical psychologist Lisa Damour confirms this feeling in her book *Under Pressure*: "It is not at all unusual for a girl to say to me, 'I have anxiety,' as if she were describing a grave and permanent congenital defect." Ryan, too, hears this from his clients, and he agrees that it is important to help young people realize that anxiety is a part of everyone and that it is something that their brain does, not something that is inescapable. He worries when he sees clients "fuse" their identity with their symptoms—"I am my anxiety, therefore I can't do this"—where "this" might be get this shot, go into that classroom, or tackle that assignment. As a clinician, he uses acceptance and commitment therapy to help his clients identify the difference between what their mind is telling them to do and what their goals and values point them to do, and how to bridge that gap. Rather than telling oneself, "I am my anxiety," he suggests instead saying, "Oh, my anxiety is telling me to do X, but I can challenge X." Approaching life with the latter interpretation opens his clients up to face their fears.

Elly agrees with Ryan about the uptick in clients being uncomfortable with everyday discomforts, but also points out that much like our original working definition of mental illness, you need to consider the individual's personal context. For many of their clients, there are clear crises unfolding that involve very real threats to the communities to which they belong, and worse, overlapping crises. For instance, they work with Deaf clients relying on lipreading for accessibility. During the coronavirus pandemic, these students were confronted with teachers in masks that obscured their lips. Elly also has Black Latino clients who in the summer following

George Floyd's murder wanted to support their community by attending Black Lives Matter protests—but who feared a possible Immigration and Customs Enforcement (ICE) raid should they attend. For these clients, heightened distress is very much tied to real changes in the world that are outside their control.

Elly's point about context is so important—in general and also because it is an early instance of a theme that recurs throughout this book. Namely, that it is the lack of security and the absence of support that are driving up distress for their clients. Rather than treating these clients for some perceived deficiency in mental health, providing medication and therapy aimed at addressing their symptoms, the more powerful—and more ethical—move would be to address the ways that their contexts are failing them.

If all human experience is on a spectrum, if putting people in diagnostic boxes encourages the stigmatization of mental illness, if more openness surrounding mental distress means we're, at times, inappropriately diagnosing people who are simply experiencing the human condition, and if these diagnoses have little relation to the underlying psychosocial-biological nature of them, then is there anything to be gained by using them? What does all this mean for us in the context of this particular book?

Well, it's messy. Messy in several different and important ways. One, it is difficult to assess whether there are truly elevated rates of clinical levels of anxiety and depression among young people when diagnosing such levels is such a disaster in the first place. Second, rapid destigmatization of mental illness also means that changing rates are going to be increasingly suspect, as more people with severe experiences will be comfortable coming forward and more people also might be conflating reasonable responses to stressful situations for mental health problems. Third, a focus on treating more general difficulties in psychobiological and neurological systems like negative emotionality and impulse control may be more beneficial than a focus on specific labels.

But just because mental health diagnoses are hopelessly messy does not mean they are useless. A helpful analogy might be blood pressure. Blood pressure clearly exists on a continuum from low to high, and extremes at either end can be dangerous—but there is no natural cut point between normal blood pressure and high blood pressure, and that cutoff probably varies quite a bit person to person, due to factors like sex and weight and to the idiosyncrasies of individual bodies. But it is still clinically useful to track a person's blood pressure, to give them a heads up if it is increasing over time, to prescribe first lifestyle changes and then medication if things keep escalating.

These changes in diagnostic thresholds and destigmatization are likely contributing to the worsening mental health statistics among young people and the associated overwhelming tax on the mental health care system. I believe they are intellectually important to consider. But I find it unlikely that they are the entire story, that all the leading advocacy groups for youth health would unite in declaring a national emergency based on changing perceptions and norms alone. And again, even if the base rates have not changed, the need for services clearly has.

So, what do we know about causes of the mental health crisis?

A TANGLE OF POSSIBLE CAUSES

Reader, I must confess something here, early on. I know you may have picked up this book primarily because you want to understand the causes of this crisis. You want to delineate what combination of environmental stressors, underlying biology, broad societal developments, structural inequalities, and/or changes in how we diagnose, talk about, or treat struggles with mental health have combined to lead us to this particular moment. This moment in which our young people seem to be suffering more greatly, struggling more significantly to achieve an emotional equilibrium and to meet the challenges that face them with strength and grace.

When I began writing this book, I believed that this section might occupy a much larger portion of the pages than it now does. I think we all want to understand the causes, in part because that is how our human mind is engineered. Our drive to read novels, to listen to true crime podcasts, to engage in the social grooming that is gossip, and even our destructive attraction to conspiracy theories all reveal our need for closure, for understanding, for being led on a journey that ends with a clear conclusion. It also feels like if we could elucidate simple cause and effect, then the solution will become apparent. Smartphones? Give our teenagers a flip phone. Too much stress from Advanced Placement classes? Shove them into a mindfulness class.

But in researching, reading, and interviewing young people and experts alike, I found nothing but a tangled mess of likely candidate causes, each of which interact and influence each other, and each of which is also bound up in other major shifts in our culture (and on our planet). I don't think there is ever going to be a tidy answer. We cannot ask these questions in a vacuum, see them as independent possibilities—this, yes; that, no. For brains, bodies, and societies all operate not on the level of individual forces driving behavior but in interacting, complex *systems*. The fabrics of our lives are not made up of single strands but interwoven ones, interdependent and operating within properties of the whole, the collective.

Elly agrees. They said that considering all their experiences with students and therapy clients, you must stop looking at each little puzzle piece and instead look at the entire picture. They think that examining puzzle pieces is where administrators and school systems and parents get stuck. You want to be the one to hold up the missing puzzle piece, because then there is an easy solution—snap here, replace here, all fixed. We must resist this impulse, focus instead on the entire landscape. The interwoven fabric of experience that yields the present moment is likely a combination of technological change, social policy, heightened pressures, structural inequalities, cultural changes to parenting practices, and decreased stigma surrounding symptoms of mental illness. As writer and higher education specialist John Warner writes, "It is important to recognize that the problem is not a matter of fixing what ails individual students, but instead reforming the systems that cause harm in the first place." While we clearly need direct interventions for individuals suffering from acute problems, the work of addressing the epidemic will require working within systems to create architecture that encourages mental health.

At this point you may be feeling a little dissatisfied with my answer to the question of whether we are truly facing a mental health crisis in our youth. Are we? Or have we instead shifted the goalposts and lost our tolerance for ordinary human unhappiness? Or have we reduced mental health stigma to a degree that people no longer fear coming forward for help, and so what we're seeing are the true rates of mental health struggles, hidden for so long? Or finally, is the mental health crisis real but an external, societal crisis rather than an internal, individual one? I apologize for any dissatisfaction, but next I'll argue that it doesn't actually matter where the truth lies. For adolescence and young adulthood is a critical period of social and emotional development that will have lifelong consequences for the young people we love and who (even if you don't love any young people) will form our society in the years to come. No matter the nature and extent of the crisis, we need to step forward and help.

ADOLESCENCE AND EMERGING ADULTHOOD ARE CRITICAL

The span of development from childhood to adolescence to emerging adulthood is a critical period in physical and neurological development during which a remarkable biological transition takes place.* The child becomes the adult. Pubertal hormones bend previously straight lines into curves; stubble erupts on formerly smooth cheeks. Culturally, too, we structure adolescence to be a time of new transitions and responsibilities. At this age you may voice your opinion about who should lead our country, at this other age you may now enjoy the power of fermented grapes to dull the sharp edges of life, at still this other age you can operate a several-ton machine made of metal on crowded interstate highways. Biological and societal forces interact, of course. As you mature into a biological creature more capable of delaying impulses, of thinking rationally, you are ceded more responsibility and more control over your decisions.

Some ways in which biology and psychology interact during this period are more subtle, however. For instance, pubertal hormones may not change just the physical landscape of a child's body but also affect brain function in such a way that they become more highly attuned to emotional cues and social input. Most parents of adolescents can observe this process from the outside—previously confident, outgoing children suddenly act like a spotlight is shining on their every action, as though every minute decision and expression might be held up for peer scrutiny. My own daughter at

---

* Roughly, ages ten to twenty-four.

seven leapt onstage in front of several hundred people to sing karaoke "We Will Rock You" at a family wedding (that she didn't know most of the words didn't give her a moment's pause) and a mere three years later hissed at me in the grocery store to not "laugh so weird," because she didn't want to draw a single moment of a single person's attention our way.

Like language learning in the toddler years, the adolescent brain is precisely tuned to take advantage of this social input. The teen years may be something of a "sensitive" or a "critical" period in which environmental input may have its maximal effects—and may also have limited effects if this important input comes too early or too late.

We aren't the only animals whose genetic development is coded such that the brain tunes in to the social environment right when essential input is needed. Songbirds too have a critical period for song learning, where hormones that influence brain function come online in such a way that they are highly attuned to sounds from the environment, and the birds learn their trilling musical notes, right on time. Like feathered friends learning their own specific sweet tune, our adolescents suddenly tune their neural radars to the social environment to master important social, affective, and cognitive capabilities like emotion regulation, the development of friendship, and intimacy.

Like all critical periods, the adolescent critical period represents both promise and peril. If it occurs during a time when the adolescent is embedded in a supportive net of community (family, neighborhood, school, peer group), all can go well. On the peril side of the equation, if they cannot find like-minded friends to explore intimacy with, if their lives lack trustworthy adults who model healthy coping behaviors, if the signals from their surroundings are that they are not safe and they cannot trust the future, the adolescent may instead learn maladaptive behaviors or ways of coping. It is as though the little songbird tunes in to the external environment right on time, but its family has fled, and the wee bird hears nothing but wind and the cries of other species. How will it learn the right notes to sing?

Most of the major mental disorders diagnosed by psychiatry have their average age of onset in late adolescence, right around when many Western youth are finishing high school and starting college. We are more tolerant of extreme mood swings, impulses, or beliefs in childhood and early adolescence. In late adolescence, we expect young people to begin to take on the responsibilities of adulthood and to better control their impulses and behavior, and so this pattern of onset in late adolescence may occur in part because symptoms were present earlier on but only become obvious in their newly adult world. But the predominant reason that late adolescence is such a common time for first emergence of mental health difficulties is likely because of this same critical period. Triggers for spells of mental health struggles throughout the lifespan include hormonal fluctuations (postpartum and menopause are other vulnerable times of life for those who experience these phases), abrupt changes to your social environment, and new life stressors both positive (e.g., starting a new school) and negative (e.g., parental divorce). Adolescence, by nature and by design, is a long series in just these triggers.

Consider: puberty hits and one's body starts morphing and changing in what are often alarming and unpredictable ways. At the same time, one's bloodstream is flooded with hormones that can have strong and often unpredictable effects on mood and cognition. This process can be unsettling for all young people, but for trans youth it can be particularly fraught, as the body is changing in ways that amplify existing distress.

In a luminous and haunting short story "Liddy, First to Fly," writer Kim Fu uses a metaphor of wings to illustrate how confusing puberty can be, when your body is changing in such dramatic and unusual ways, wrapped simultaneously in excitement, secrecy, and shame. Instead of breasts or pubic hair, the titular character Liddy grows dark, iridescent wings out of her ankles. One of Liddy's close friends reflects:

> There was a way in which Liddy's wings didn't strike us as extraordinary. The realm of pretend had only just closed its doors to us, and light still leaked through around the edges. Everything was baffling and secretive then, especially our own bodies, sprouting all kinds of outgrowths that were meant to be hidden, desperately ignored and not discussed, hairs and lumps that could be weaponized against us. On some level, it seemed like this would just be part of Liddy's eventual adulthood, tucking her wings beneath sensible slacks and off to the office, just as our mothers scooped and flattened and plucked themselves raw.

From the safety of adulthood, we may have a hard time remembering how some of these bodily changes at puberty were as unusual and frightening as sprouting wings. At the same time as a teen's exterior and interior body have suddenly betrayed their sameness, become new and even at times feel monstrous, Western educational systems ask the teen also to make several transitions. They leave the sameness of primary and elementary school to the raucous world of middle school, then high school. While all these bodily and educational changes are happening, the adolescent often begins navigating burgeoning romantic and sexual relationships for the first time.

For adolescents headed to college, one morning in August right when the bodily eruptions and shifts have stabilized a bit and the teen has found their social grounding, we cleave them from their cherished peers and roster of extracurricular activities and predictable rhythms and send them off to college to start all over again.

It is a lot!

The pubertal tuning toward the social environment can easily *over-*tune, resulting in social anxiety. "In fact," the psychologist Lucy Foulkes writes, "social anxiety disorder has been referred to as 'the prototypical adolescent disorder' because it represents so clearly what can happen when a fundamental process of adolescence, the 'social reorientation,' goes awry." All adolescents tune their mental radars to the social environment in order to master fundamental learning. Probably, for most, there is a period where the baleful light of social attention is painful. But also, for most, as the adolescent matures, this tuning moderates into a healthy, adult level of attention to social information—that is, social awareness without feeling immobilized by the potential judgment of one's peers. However, for some this moderation may never happen, and the result is social anxiety.

This conception of adolescence as a key critical period has led some researchers to call for greater research on and interventions targeted at adolescence, as when data suggesting critical periods in infancy led to programs like Head Start (a program geared toward lower income families that supports children's social, cognitive, and emotional health). With several other authors, pediatrician Ron Dahl argues that much like building good bone density in young adulthood can prevent osteoporosis in late life, "strategic and developmentally informed investments in adolescents could contribute to a positive impact on the adolescents themselves, their future lives as leaders in adult society, and the next generation to whom they will be parents." It isn't just their parents and educators who should care about investing in healthy development during these crucial years. It is anyone who will share a planet with these future adults.

We have this marvelous period where we could make a lasting difference in the mental health of these burgeoning adults that we love so desperately—we can shape the trajectory of their lives, which paths they take. But like rivers, the flow of their lives during these years also shapes the riverbeds, the tendencies and habits they will use over and over as their lives progress and their neural machinery become more set, less fluid.

We need to act.

But before we do, we need to understand one last foundational set of concepts—namely, the nature of the monsters our youth are facing. What do we know about the anxiety and depression that can help us understand the characteristics of this particular crisis?

WHAT IS ANXIETY? AN IMAGINARY, FUTURE-ORIENTED STATE

Fear is rooted directly in the present moment and is among our most basic emotions. Accidentally drop a metal pan in the kitchen and you can observe fear in your pets—their eyes widen, ears draw back, shoulders contract . . . and then the skittering of claws on the floor as they flee the situation. Fear gets us away from clear and present threat, it operates quite quickly, and it fades quickly once safety is reestablished. A purring creature once again intertwines your legs as you chop and stir.

Fear is having a bit of a moment. In her 2019 book *The Monarchy of Fear: A Philosopher Looks at Our Political Crisis*, philosopher Martha Nussbaum takes a hard look at the emotional landscape in our country and crowns the emotion with a kingship. Anxiety about climate change and its ramifications for the future of humanity is at an all-time high, so much so that the term *eco-anxiety* has been coined to characterize this specific set of fears. As paleoclimatologist Summer Praetorius writes, "The awareness of being on the knife's edge . . . is like learning to live with vertigo, partitioning off a deep sense that we are no longer on stable ground while simultaneously trying to get on with the day, show up to work, laugh with our kids." And consider—climate is just one of a bevy of potential threats making the ground beneath our feet feel unstable.

Anxiety is an affective state that uses the neural and physiological mechanics of the fear response—the same brain pathways, the same fight-or-flight system—but for *imaginary* threats. It is proactive rather than reactive. Anxiety is rooted in the perception that there might be future threats down the road, and that (importantly) you won't have the resources to marshal a proper response.

This ability to both anticipate future threats and prepare a response before the threat manifests is in some ways a marvelous, powerful aspect of our psychobiology. We can imagine future scenarios and start strategizing for ways we might solve or avoid them. Being anxious about your statistics exam motivates you to begin studying well in advance; anxiety about retirement prompts you to save more money for the future; you wear a mask in a crowded subway because you are nervous about infectious disease.

But for anxiety to be productive rather than debilitating, you have to do a very subtle calculus correctly: not only accurately judge the likelihood of certain scenarios (which is hard) but also correctly determine how terrible the feared outcome would actually be and whether you would or wouldn't have the resources to cope with it (which is also hard). Human beings are notoriously bad at estimating the future, and so it is all too easy to overestimate the threat, the value and coping response, or both.

In the absence of a full panic attack, the anxiety response is also muted compared to the fear response, like little revs of a big engine. But you can imagine that if you gently rev an engine over and over and over, across long periods of time, you are going to run out of gas, and moreover that engine is going to wear down. This wearing down can take the form of stress and burnout. As we'll see in the next section, it can also take the form of depression.

WHAT IS DEPRESSION? A SAPPING OF VITALITY

Author of the award-winning book *The Noonday Demon: An Atlas of Depression*, Andrew Solomon famously wrote that the opposite of depression isn't happiness, it's *vitality*. When we think of depression, we think of sadness. Stock images of depressed people usually depict crushed faces, single tears, crouched postures. These are the facial and body expressions we associate with great loss or terrible news; in depression, these signals communicate the experience of grief with no discernible environmental trigger.

People with depression do commonly have negative moods and feelings of sadness. But perhaps even more integral to the experience of depression is a lack of positive emotions, a muting of joy, and a drying up of one's well of energy. Activities that used to thrum and buzz with purpose and enjoyment suddenly seem dull and uninteresting—enervating rather than innervating. A previously taut libido slackens. Hope, too, fizzles, the future seeming gloomy and unpromising, your estimation of your abilities naught.

The relationship between anxiety and depression is a complex one. Both psychiatry and psychological research have traditionally treated them as distinct pathologies. But more sophisticated analyses of people's experiences, especially those over the course of time, have called this distinction into question. For one, almost no one with clinical levels of depression lacks anxiety, and almost no one with clinical levels of anxiety lacks depressive symptoms. While one set of symptoms can certainly dominate over the other, they rarely appear in isolation. Moreover, as I have already discussed, there is a high degree of overlap among all the mental disorders psychologists regularly diagnose, and no more so than anxiety and depression. Researchers conducting genetic and neurobiological examinations of people with strong depression and people with strong anxiety have trouble identifying separate mechanisms. The candidate genes that put you at risk for depression equally put you at risk for heightened anxiety and vice versa; with some exceptions, similar brain circuits seem to govern both sets of symptoms.

Moreover, if you measure people only at one point in time without following them along life's journey to see how their symptoms emerge, progress, remit, and recur, you can't detect how these experiences sequence, whether there is a pattern to them. When you instead take this longitudinal perspective, there is evidence that many people follow a common trajectory where they first begin experiencing anxiety symptoms in one or more of its many forms, and then over time depressive symptoms emerge. This makes sense if you put avoidance in between the anxiety and the depression. You first get more and more anxious in more and more situations, and this leads you to withdraw from experiences you previously enjoyed or were interested in, and you begin in your withdrawal to feel less and less effective, less and less able to act on the world and have it respond meaningfully.

For instance, you obtain a business degree and land a first job at a great sales firm. You are terrified about talking on the phone, though: What if your voice fogs up? What if the client hates you? What if your brain freezes, and you forget your entire pitch? Your stomach churns, your skin grows clammy, your breath comes short. You avoid, you feel better. You are reinforced by this relief, and it is even harder to pick up the phone. But eventually all this avoidance means that you regularly miss your sales target, that your boss calls you out on it in a meeting, you must leave the position, and you feel like you are a failure, that you'll never amount to anything, that you are a salesperson who can't make sales . . . You sink into depression.

Importantly, this transition between "pure anxiety" and the emergence of mixed depressive symptoms has been found to occur most often in adolescence, with anxiety appearing in childhood and through the puberty years and then depressive symptoms rearing their ugly head as you head into later high school and the college years. Data also seem to support the idea that anxiety acts as a causal risk factor for depression rather than the two sharing risk factors or depression coming first. And if you ask people about their perceptions of their own life experiences, they confirm that it felt like their anxiety emerged first and led to depression.

Negative anxiety response styles theory attempts to explain this transition from anxiety to depression through the stories that we tell ourselves about how to deal with anxiety. Specifically, *negative anxiety response styles* refer to the tendency to have ruminative or hopeless thinking about one's anxiety symptoms and/or one's ability to cope with them. Remember

Ryan and his clients who claimed that they *were* their anxiety. Dwelling on the terribleness of the physical experience, rehashing past experiences, reflecting on one's inability to control or prevent the onset or course of the experience, thinking about what it all says about you as a person, and worrying about the consequences of anxious behaviors all count in the negative anxiety response styles category. According to this theory, high levels of negative anxiety response styles predict high possibility that anxiety will transition into depression. It is possible to be high in anxiety and low in negative anxiety response styles—for instance, you are fearful about having another panic attack but don't dwell on it or feel it will affect your life outside the boundaries of the attack. People low in negative anxiety response styles might be less likely to experience depression.

Echoing some of the considerations of the previous few pages, clinical psychologist David Barlow considers research on what he calls disorders of emotion—which include anxiety, mood, trauma, and dissociation-related disorders—and finds that they all have in common neuroticism, which can be defined as the tendency to experience frequent and intense negative emotions. Critically, neuroticism tends to lead to avoidant coping, which then leads to stronger effects on one's ability to function well in life. Oftentimes the avoidance is an attempt to exert control or certainty—*if I avoid, I won't experience*—but it is a false gold, for true self-efficacy declines in the face of avoidance.

In sum, anxiety is a future-oriented imaginary state where we anticipate that future threats await and we'll not have the weapons to battle them. This anxiety leads to avoidance of challenge and new experiences, which creates a life context where our actions don't have impact, where they don't matter, which may then lead to the sapped vital forces that we know as depression.* Truly a horrific, vicious cycle that we wouldn't wish on our worst enemy, never mind the vulnerable, budding human beings we call our children and our future.

---

*Importantly, this is just one model of how some people may experience the transition from anxiety to depression. Both anxiety and depression are highly heterogeneous phenomena that likely are caused by multiple interactions of biology and experience, and many people's experiences will be quite different than this trajectory.

CONCLUSION

It is hard to conceive of a goal more important for a society than to support the health and well-being of its youth. Whatever the role of changing norms and stigmatization, our youth are pleading for help navigating the struggles of their lives. The success or failure with which they meet these challenges cascades forward into our shared future. Since our current youth are our future adults, how they meet the challenges before them may determine the outcome of the many crises that are unfolding (and will continue to unfold) in our collective time on this planet.

I am not a clinical psychologist; I am an academic one. Rather than focus on how to treat active struggles with mental health, after this brief consideration of the dividing lines between psychopathology and the much more prosaic human unhappiness, we are going to instead focus our attention on the conditions that support mental *health*. It is nearly impossible to carve out and delineate the individual trajectories that lead to unhappiness. It is much easier to create environments at home and school that encourage youth to learn in an atmosphere that supports their mental health. As Tolstoy famously wrote, every unhappy family is unhappy in its own way, but all happy families are alike. The recipe for mental health is not terribly surprising or terribly complex—as we will see, it involves safety, belongingness, physical vitality, tolerance of uncertainty and discomfort, a sense of purpose, and play. We will throughout consider how we, as shepherds to the education of our youth, can best structure their learning environments to support these components of health and happiness.

But before we get there, let's spend a little time considering what we know about treatment of anxiety and depression and how this supports my contention that compassion alone won't help us solve our present problems—we also need challenge.

CHAPTER TWO

OUR YOUTH NEED COMPASSIONATE CHALLENGE

I PROMISED THAT I would tell you the story of how I regained my lost voice—how I transitioned from panicked pupil to professional speaker. While full recovery continues to be a lifelong journey, a critical juncture in my path to better mental health was my adoption of a women's studies minor in college. The first few years of college, I was one of those students who sat quietly with her nose in a book before the class began and then a silent observer once it did. While my instructors would write me notes or emails encouraging me to share my thoughts during class, they would nonetheless give me an A at the end of the semester.

In contrast, my women's studies instructors took participation quite seriously. Unlike most of my other classes, the course syllabi regularly awarded something like a third of the grade to class participation, and the instructors announced at the beginning of the semester that no one would get an A without contributing in class. Such pronouncements pit my anxiety against my nerdy pride, and pride won. The first few times I raised my hand and contributed something, I couldn't hear myself speak at all, so loud was the roaring in my ears. I teared up. I probably turned scarlet. But I participated, and then I participated again. Each time was a little easier. I regained my lost voice.

My experience maps perfectly on what psychologists know is the most effective treatment for anxiety: controlled exposure in a safe setting. Like all scientific fields, psychology is ever evolving and some of its seemingly well-established findings have been questioned in recent years. But one of the few certainties in our field, one thing we psychologists know for sure, is that the most effective treatment for many forms of anxiety is exposure to the feared stimulus in a safe setting.

The safe setting is a key aspect of the process. The client needs to know that they will not suffer true harm; the therapist is present and guides them through the process, and as I will discuss, part of the process is learning how to intentionally calm one's own body. But once those pieces are in play, exposure can relieve the underlying fear. Suffer from a specific phobia of snakes? In the context of a therapeutic relationship and with extensive training in relaxation, you can work your way up from viewing photographs to filmed videos of reptilian friends slithering through the grass to handling a snake yourself.

Recall that anxiety relies on a double perception—that future threats are imminent, and that you don't have the resources to cope with them. Exposure therapy targets each of these assumptions, challenging them first in the comfort of the therapist's office and then out in the wild. First, that the situation is not as threatening as you anticipated *or* the feared outcome is much more unlikely than anticipated, and second, that you *do* have the resources to cope with both the threat itself and any possible anxious response you might have.

Also remember that avoidance may be the road linking severe anxiety and eventual depression, as the person feels less and less effective at enacting change in their personal worlds. Structuring young people's home lives and/or policies and practices in their classrooms to allow for or even encourage avoidance of situations necessary for critical learning and development could be detrimental to their mental health. If young people are only ever asked to engage in practices they are already skilled at and comfortable with, they will never learn new skills or master discomfort. They need to be challenged. But at the same time, challenge in the absence of a warm, supportive environment will likely only make fearful students more fearful. They need compassion.

All this may sound reasonable but rather vague and aphoristic. What might compassionate challenge for young people look like in practice? To begin that discussion, we're going to travel to my childhood home.

MANHUNT: COMPASSIONATE CHALLENGE IN ACTION

While beginning to write this book, I read a couple of excellent books on young people's mental health from licensed clinical psychologists—smart, educated people with a wealth of experience who sit face-to-face with young people, talking about both their hopes and their despair. I have already shared and will be sharing many more of these professionals' key insights throughout this book. But their perspectives, while valuable and informative, seem to largely focus on a narrow sliver of young people. Namely, wealthy, protected youth with incredible school systems and parents with the resources and free time to dedicate real effort to the academic and social progress of their children. Their lessons about reducing the monumental pressure of Advanced Placement classes and orchestra chairs and winter-break ski schools are valuable, but probably generalizable only to young people in similar situations.

Would that we lived in a world where all youth had access to such resources. We do not. I wanted to launch this discussion of compassionate challenge by talking to someone who had experience working with youth for whom challenges are less which elite extracurricular to choose and more where the next meal was coming from or which adults could be trusted not to hurt them.

I didn't have to think long.

My father worked his whole life at McAuley Nazareth Home for Boys, a Catholic residential home in Massachusetts for youth removed from their families of origin, usually for reasons of abuse or neglect. Serving a range of ages from young kids to later adolescence and run by caring adults, the home provides a quiet, reflective space for these boys whose introductions to life were tumultuous, if not actively traumatizing. The residence is set on a bucolic landscape, surrounded by tall pines and quiet reservoirs and has an in-ground pool where many of the boys first learn to swim.

Nazareth is a through line in my life, my childhood full of threads woven together with the lives of these young men. Clamming with them on Cape Cod in the summers, walking in a crab squat looking for bubbles in the sand that might indicate an industrious clam underneath. Often sharing a Thanksgiving table and light chatter about music and movies with a boy who didn't have a home that was safe to return to for the holiday. Answering collect calls from alumni in prison for whom life took an unfortunate turn, yet they kept in touch with my dad—these calls still come regularly, years into his retirement. Now in middle age, I sit on the board of directors, where after a career of what I hope are reasonably sized accomplishments, my biggest claim to fame is being Bill Cavanagh's daughter.

One crisp but sunny October day during the early stages of the COVID-19 pandemic, my father and I sat six feet apart on his front porch and talked about youth mental health. A hawk circled overhead, which my father kept a close eye on in case its parabolas brought it close to my mother's chickens. Over our rapidly chilling wine, my father and I discussed the structural impediments facing the Nazareth youth and what he saw as critical determinants to positive versus negative trajectories out of their initial and ongoing stressors.

He first echoed much of the research on the determinants of happiness and success, more broadly speaking. Thinking over the hundreds and hundreds of youths he worked with during his career, the single-most important determinant of whether they overcame their difficult early starts and achieved well-being and a happy life was whether they formed a meaningful connection with another human being. It was sometimes a staff member, sometimes a coach, sometimes one of the clergy, and some-times a peer—but it needed to happen. From my father's perspective, the pivotal aspect of that connection was not just acceptance but also a sense of being valued: that one had something to contribute, something that was important to the world or even just to this one other human being.

This sense of connection forms an important basis, a confidence touch-stone for young people—acceptance, value, social engagement. My father's thoughts fit well into the compassion side of compassionate challenge, the home base from which a person can then push their boundaries and capabilities a bit. I asked my dad about whether he saw challenge as also important for resilience.

He thought for a moment.

"Well," he said, "we had a game we used to play at Nazareth back in the eighties. We called it Manhunt."

"Oh, I remember Manhunt," I said.

Do I. The game combines some of the most brutal elements of Capture the Flag and Dodge Ball. In the version my dad played with his six siblings growing up in a sprawling yard surrounded by woods in Scituate, Massachusetts, there were teams, but rather than competing for a flag, you were competing just to stay in the game, and you could tag people out by thwapping them with tennis balls. There were different strategies that could win you the game. My dad shared that one aunt was a solo hider who was rarely found, a mouse, whereas another was a rabbit constantly on the move, and an uncle was a deer always bounding through the shrubs.

To play at Nazareth, my father and his staff developed intricate maps of the dark, piney woods and reservoirs surrounding the residential home. "Most youth placed with us were from overcrowded urban settings where trusting others was mostly a function of first assessing their power and anger and how it could affect you," my father said. They were also coming to the residential home out of trauma. Manhunt allowed them to relax and enjoy nature, explore, hike, and be physically active. More than this, it also tapped in to and shored up mentalizing skills of creating strategy, estimating and predicting other people's goals and tactics, staying within boundaries of the rules of the game, learning patience, and working with teammates. All while having fun.

The staff paid attention to those youth who exercised the greatest gains in listening to staff and to teammates, how well they supported their teammates who struggled with running or hiding, and how well they adapted to changes—and rewarded them with leadership positions. My father observed that the boys would relax into the game, become one with the woods, and their tight faces would break into smiles. For some, it was a first inkling that they might exert their power and control over the world in prosocial ways. Until then, such license had been granted only to those who abused them or to those peers willing to act out in externalizing behaviors.

I actually played Manhunt as a kid too—around the neighborhood with my little brother and the gaggle of kids on our street, and one Thanksgiving at Naz, with my dad and cousins and aunts and uncles. I can remember being disturbed by it. The tall swaying pines, the sudden emergence of scurry and flight, the threat of being struck still with a walloped tennis ball. That Thanksgiving I was assigned to tag along with a much older cousin, because I was too small to be wandering the woods on my own. Intent on the game, he shushed my worries. I recall trying to move slowly and silently, holding my breath whenever possible, when out of the blue I was hit hard on the shoulder. I yelped. Instinctively reverse-tracking the trajectory of the missile, I was startled to see my aunt Dee impossibly high up in a tree. Surely the height and drama of her ascent was influenced by how small I was at the time, but I was struck, too, by the contrast between the fierce hardness of the strike and her usually gentle demeanor. During Manhunt, it seemed, even people you trusted could be recast as enemies.

Playing with my neighborhood friends was also sometimes emotionally perilous. My favorite hiding spot was a little groove underneath a fragrant cedar tree on the border behind our yard and the next house over. I would curl into a ball on the dirt and wait to be found, rubbing the little fronds of the tree greenery together, because the pleasant smell settled my pounding heart.

These early Manhunt experiences bring up a tension between arousal and learning that will recur throughout this book. I can't tell in my own personal history whether my sweaty-palmed memories of Manhunt were detrimental—drew out my anxieties, made me uncertain—or whether they served as an exposure therapy of sorts, allowing me to feel uncertain, to feel unsafe, but then to see that no fears were realized. Ultimately, everything was fine. After all, my aunt Dee climbed down out of the tree and queried about my studies and creative efforts over pumpkin pie with her usual manner: treating me gently but also like a fellow adult worthy of conversation. Similarly, when my neighborhood gang tired of the game, we moved on to something more to my liking—usually, staging a play I had written about some ghosts dealing with a lot of romantic angst.

Would I have been better off skipping these experiences, or worse?

At Nazareth, state regulations would surely have eventually shut down Manhunt—to reiterate, the practice is forty years in Nazareth's past—but the game's days waned before that could happen. My dad moved into an administrative position behind a desk and didn't feel comfortable letting the game continue without his careful hand and skilled attention to its emotional dynamics. Even despite its early demise, a disgruntled staff member reported my father for poor judgment in what he saw as his too-loose management of the boys' recreational endeavors. He cited Manhunt as an example. It seems difficult to imagine it these days—state-regulated care for traumatized youth who were allowed to run free in the woods, hide in trees, strike each other with carefully aimed tennis balls, and be chased down and essentially attacked. Hunted. Prey and predator. You can easily imagine the whole thing going terribly wrong.

Later on, my mom told me a story of my father taking some Naz boys ice skating and fishing on a pond that he judged safe by testing it first with his six-foot-four, couple-hundred-pound frame. A police officer concerned about the ice's safety stopped by and asked them all to leave the pond. They did—and then after the officer had left, my dad circled back with the boys, and they finished their skating and ice fishing. This may have been a lapse in judgment. If a boy had fallen through the ice, my father surely would have been judged, and probably rightly so.* But I can also slip myself into the skin of these youth, the elation of being free upon the ice in the encroaching winter darkness, of mastery over tricky ankles and slippery surfaces, balancing on single blades, and even the giddiness of safely defying the men in uniform they likely feared were not their friends or protectors.

The days of Manhunt at Nazareth are long over (and probably also the questionable ice fishing), which is probably a good thing for physical safety. But deftly handled, one can imagine the power of these experiences for nurturing autonomy, agency, and a deep sense of play in boys whose early lives had anything but. I hope the hours that used to be spent leaping over boulders, laying strategy, and feeling lungs burn with the pure strenuousness of flight through fields and over ice have been replaced by time on the basketball court or football field. I wonder whether these controlled sports really yield the same mental and emotional benefits as more free-form, uncertain forms of play.

But my real fear is that those hours are now instead spent indoors, peering passively at screens—where no one will fall through the ice or

---

*He told my mom he had a long stick with him just in case.

out of a tree and where two boys won't get into a fistfight over who got tagged out first. Safe. But where not much is learned about the world and how to act in it, the physical strengths and limits of the body, and how to navigate what novelist Philip Roth calls "this terribly significant business of 'other people.'"

Turns out it isn't just monsters and my father's expertise that under-score the need for activity and challenge over passivity and avoidance in our battle for mental health, though. The argument is also supported by literally decades of scientific research on how to effectively manage the effects of fear and anxiety in our bodies, beliefs, and behaviors.

THE POWER OF EXPOSURE: INHIBITORY LEARNING

While I certainly will not be arguing that instructors untrained in clinical psychology should be doing exposure therapy with their students, I do assert that understanding the biology and psychology of how exposure therapy works can help us understand how the broader concept of com-passionate challenge works. Exposure therapy is such an effective tool for treating anxiety for a few reasons.

One is the straightforward biological principle that it relies upon. Namely, our peripheral nervous system has two systems that work in tandem, like a seesaw—the sympathetic ("fight or flight") and the para-sympathetic ("rest and digest"). With a few minor exceptions, as activity in one elevates, the other diminishes, and vice versa. What this means for the purposes of exposure therapy is that it is biologically impossible to be simultaneously panicked and calm. So, therapy for anxiety starts with thorough training in relaxation techniques like deep breathing and body scans—you teach your client how to voluntarily enter a state of physical calm and how to get increasingly good at doing so on command. Then you slowly introduce gradations of their feared stimulus. If they're afraid of flying, you might start with them visualizing a plane, then work your way up to pictures, then videos, then to sitting in an airport together. At each state, the client recurrently relaxes their body. In many traditional forms of exposure therapy, you don't move up the ladder until they can stay calm in the presence of their feared stimulus or situation over a period.

Slowly, their nervous system learns to stay calm even in the presence of this terrifying object or situation.

Something many laypeople don't understand about anxiety is that very often, the feared situation or stimulus (e.g., the spider, the plane, the public speaking) is not the true cause of panic. What the anxious individual really fears is the possibility of entering a panic state—that is the true terror, the real monster. In my Introductory Psychology class we watch a video of a woman working on exposure therapy with her therapist, and her feared stimulus is clowns. The students are somewhat amused and perplexed by her dramatic reactions to clown stimuli—even just pictures of clowns in a book. But part of what makes it a great clip is that it also shows her working through the (il)logic of the situation with her therapist. As they are about to enter a room where a live clown will be making balloon animals and joking with audience members, the therapist challenges her and asks, "Do you think the clown means you any harm?" And the client answers, "Of course not." And then he asks her, "Might you have a very strong physical reaction to the clown?" The answer is yes, and that reaction is her true fear.

Exposure therapy is also essential, because one other thing we know for sure about anxiety is that the absolute worst thing one can do if one wants to ameliorate anxiety is to avoid one's fears. For avoidance of one's fears leads to an ever-tightening spiral of dread. In her book *Under Pressure: Confronting the Epidemic of Stress and Anxiety in Girls*, renowned clinical psychologist and researcher Lisa Damour writes that "tension and turmoil, we find, are strange creatures. . . . When we shrink from pressure and fear, they just take on new, harrowing proportions." Moreover, avoidance of something you fear reinforces that fear twofold. First, you do something more rewarding instead of something you were dreading, which reinforces that avoidance. Second, your contemplating exposure and then avoiding it also results in a quick blush of nervousness and then a sudden reinforcing removal of that negative feeling. Both the replacement activity and the removal of the anxiety make it more likely that you'll avoid similar circumstances when they next arise.

When you avoid situations that involve something you fear, you also deprive yourself of the possibility of ever extinguishing that fear, because you'll never have the experience of being in that situation safely. You may even begin to assume that you were correct to avoid it, because the avoidance kept you safe. Avoidance is so rewarding that it can lead predisposed individuals to withdraw from a widening circle of activities, sometimes even culminating in agoraphobia, or the removal of oneself nearly entirely from functioning society.

Early research on exposure therapy suggested that the important aspect of the experience was reduction in fear as one grew accustomed to the feeling of being in the feared situation. Panic associated with a phobic stimulus like a spider was thought to be learned somewhat like how Pavlov's dogs learned that the sound of a bell meant food was coming, except you're the dog and you have learned that a spider means a panic attack is coming. During exposure therapy, you first learn some relaxation techniques, and then, safe with the therapist and with these new tools in place, a therapist might release a spider, which you watch crawl along a path. When no bite or no uncontrollable panic emerges, the previous neural pathways linking spider with fear are extinguished and you can feel relief. In this model of how exposure therapy works, the important part is replacing the feeling of fear, allowing it to diminish, and thus extinguishing this old, learned link.

But more recent research challenges this habituation interpretation and suggests that rather than your nervous system unlearning this association between spiders and fear (a process known as extinction), in fact, exposure therapy works best when you are in fact laying new pathways, new associations, between encountering spiders and safety. Both of these competing associations still exist in your brain's circuits—we know this because a reminder or new trauma can bring the past association roaring back with teeth—but you are over time developing and strengthening this competing association about safety.

The new focus on safety learning and violating your expectations about a stimulus leading to panic means that the purpose of exposure to one's feared stimulus is not "Stay in this situation until fear reduces" but "What new thing do you need to learn?" You need to identify and disconfirm the belief about danger *and* develop a new belief about safety. I will cover safety in much greater length in part 2, when we consider bodies and brains.

What this new research on safety learning tells us is that even the challenge aspects of compassionate challenge are all about compassion, about establishing trust and safety. Again, anxiety is not a monster to be vanquished but rather one to be tamed. Like the mother and son protagonists in the popular 2014 film *Babadook* who banish their storybook monster to the basement to live on scraps they feed him, we need to learn to live with our monsters rather than attempt to conquer them completely.

LIFE IS EXPOSURE THERAPY

In setting up my interviews with the clinical counseling psychologists I introduced in the last chapter, I assured Ryan and Elly that I wasn't going to be arguing that secondary and higher ed instructors don the hat of a clinician and practice exposure therapy with their students. Ryan actually went out of his way to disagree with me, arguing that not only can we but we *should*—and really, we already are, by assigning class presentations and exams and other assessments in the first place. "And the reason I say that," he said, "is because we all do exposure therapy every day. All of us." In Ryan's view, life is a series of exposure therapies, moments when we stretch out our tender necks and experience something dreaded, and the subsequent moments when we realize "That wasn't nearly as bad as I thought," and are more relaxed and confident the next time we encounter that same experience.

During part of his clinical experiences, Ryan was trained in trauma-informed care in an inpatient setting. He points out that trauma-informed care is all about grounding—you must down-regulate your intense negative emotions before you can engage in meaningful behaviors related to change and growth. (I will discuss trauma-informed approaches to teaching in chapter 4.) But Ryan argues that if you go too far in accommodating demands on the person, then you are modeling that they aren't capable of accomplishing their life's activities when they're anxious, which he feels is both untrue and moreover does them a disservice. Most people get anxious from time to time, but we still show up.

For young people who haven't had much life experience yet, even mild stressors can take on outsize proportions in their mind's eye. Ryan points out that most of adolescent anxiety and avoidance comes up in school-related situations: panicking during a class presentation, worrying about changing into gym clothes in the locker room, and experiencing social forms of anxiety. Some of these experiences may be related to trauma or to more severe mental health struggles and require assistance, accommodation, and a careful plan with clinical experts. But in his practice, Ryan often encounters other students whom he feels have been failed by the system, when the system was just trying to help. They were experiencing much lower levels of anxiety but were nonetheless given accommodations. Clients come to him and tell him that their accommodations allow them to present alone to the teacher or record it and send it in—so there is never an option of helping these students learn to manage their anxiety and acquire the skill. But as the client's clinician, he often discusses exposure therapy with them and their parents (depending on age) as an alternative to accommodations.

"You're going to present to me every day one-on-one," he tells these young clients, "and then we're going to add three people in, then five people, then we're going to have it where you can't see the people but they can see you. And then you can see people, and then we go across contexts, and in different locations." Next, he coordinates with guidance counselors and teachers so that these students can practice in actual classrooms. At the end, his client can present without accommodations. At the end, their anxiety steps back into the wings.

Hannah, a Student Voices participant who was a sophomore psychology major at a historically Black university, told us about an instructor who helped her manage her anxiety surrounding presenting to her peers in the classroom.* When we asked about her worst learning experiences, she told us about a time when she was a first-year student and had to present in a research methods class. She found herself becoming so anxious that she turned her back entirely to the classroom, trembling and stumbling over her words. Finding herself facing her slides with a classroom of peers' eyes burning into her back, she abruptly stopped presenting.

---

*This is our first voice from the Student Voices project, which you can find more details about in the preface.

Rather than letting her continue unassisted or excusing her from the presentation, her instructor gently coaxed her through the process, encouraging her to take some deep breaths and focus on the meaning of what she was trying to convey to her peers rather than the slides or her anxiety. Step by step, Hannah finished the presentation. Hannah remains grateful to this instructor and feels that her assistance has shaped her experiences presenting in every class since. Before that presentation, she would take every opportunity to evade attention and not participate—and not just in class but socially as well. Another first-year experience she recalled was walking into a basketball game after everyone was seated before her and feeling like every single person swung their gaze to her. She whipped out her phone and fled into its soothing embrace, her heart pounding in her ears. After the presentation experience, she found herself more comfortable in these social settings as well as academic ones—a powerful testament to the effectiveness of exposure.

Hannah herself points out the contextual factors here. In most settings, Hannah sees only positive emotions as contributing to her learning and feels that anxiety and uncertainty interfere with her ability to learn rather than help it. But this truism didn't hold for this research methods class, where a highly anxiety-provoking situation led to *greater* learning—and not just within the confines of this one class but beyond it too. "Yesterday in a class, I volunteered to present my project first," she told us. "That would never have been me during freshman year. So I would say that, yeah, anxiety has impacted the way that I learn. It makes me *more* engaged." Critical to her experience, though, was that she was challenged in the setting of a safe, supportive classroom environment.

Certainly, Ryan is not across the board opposed to accommodations. For neurodivergent students and students with disabilities, they are crucial tools in establishing equitable learning environments. But Ryan is concerned about wide-scale accommodations for anxiety, especially milder forms of anxiety, as it works against everything mental health professionals know about how anxiety operates. He also sees effective exposure therapy as the more empathetic approach, and more individualized. "Accommodation is doing something for someone or altering the way that they will do it," Ryan said. "Exposure is breaking it down into concrete steps, starting where they're willing to start and building their way back up." It is exquisitely tuned in to the individual, their context and goals, and where they feel safe beginning.

Increasing numbers of students in elementary and secondary education suffer from what has been dubbed as "school refusal," which is just what it sounds like. Students refuse to get on the bus, to get in the car, or to get out of the car. They opt out. Parents, befuddled, don't know what to do. Do you wrestle them? Threaten a month off *Minecraft*? Ryan has worked with many clients and their parents on school refusal, and it looks a lot like his description of working on class presentations. Day 1, we just sit outside and watch the bus go by or get out to the car for an on-time departure. A few days in, we take a ride—and then ride back home. Slowly, step by step, and the student gets to school, sits outside the school, sits outside the classroom, then enters the classroom. He tells story after story about working with his clients—students afraid of math homework, of taking an exam, of gym class. He steps through the process of exposure with them, patient and caring, showing them how strong they really are, the many things of which they are capable. It is beautiful. A gift.

Ryan himself struggled deeply with formal academics in his early years, especially math. He felt he was stupid, that he would never succeed. But he was privileged enough to be in a good school system with many supports, and slowly through numerous interventions he reached success. "Every single point of intervention that shaped my learning and made me resilient and able to say, 'No, I'm smart, I'm capable, I can do this,'" he said, "was direct, one-on-one interaction with someone who took the time to step back and figure out what was going on and help me through it. It wasn't the teachers who said, 'Well, okay, then you don't have to do it.'" And there were those too. They just weren't of much help to Ryan in his journey to intellectual mastery.

As an openly gay student who attended a conservative-leaning Catholic college, Ryan is intimately familiar with the idea that some students are entering the classroom having experienced levels of stress different from others. He would be subjected to verbal attacks on campus and then have to take an exam—he likened it to having been in a car accident on the way to class, the way his nerves would jangle and he'd be faced with the challenge of quieting his body and mind in order to focus on the assessment. But he sees that as more of a problem with the culture and the system than of the classroom. The exams weren't the problem, the homophobia was. He wouldn't exempt himself from taking that exam or try to scrub away exams all together.

Accommodating the student's anxiety permanently also communicates that the anxiety is a core feature of the person, that it isn't malleable or subject to change. This is worrisome because research from clinical psychology has shown that beyond its role in learning, having a growth mindset (the idea that abilities are malleable and capable of changing over time) versus a fixed mindset (the idea that abilities are traits, inherent and unchangeable) about anxiety leads to better mental health outcomes. It is again the difference between thinking, "Oh, that's my anxiety kicking up," and "I am my anxiety."

These mindsets don't have their effects magically but through their impact on coping behaviors. In a blog post summarizing this research, clinical psychologist Hans Schroder writes, "For instance, those who believe that anxiety can change are less likely to use unhelpful coping strategies, such as alcohol, self-injury or emotional avoidance when faced with difficult life events. Instead, they're more likely to sit with uncomfortable feelings and challenge their thinking in order to feel better." If we can use compassionate learning environments to nudge growth mindset about anxiety, then students might be more open to working through discomfort.

For all these reasons, Ryan believes that when it comes to anxiety specifically, accessibility offices and counseling offices on college campuses should change their focus from accommodations and talk therapy to guided exposure therapy and cognitive-behavioral therapy. It isn't the responsibility of the professors and high school instructors, who are not trained in these techniques, but rather the expertise and responsibility of the college's support services. Too much of counseling in college, Ryan feels, offers band-aid solutions to mental distress, a simple welcoming place to vent about worries. Everyone should have such spaces, but you don't need clinical training to listen to venting, and ultimately such activities take some stress off without changing anything about the underlying problems.

THE ROLE OF VALUES AND NORMS

Clinical psychologist Elly Romero agrees with Ryan—but with an important caveat to both Ryan's arguments and my experience regaining my lost voice. Namely, they think it is critical that the goal of the exposure is consistent with the values and capabilities of the student, not externally determined, consistent with someone else's sense of social norms. As a college student who aspired to be an academic, I wanted to be able to share my thoughts with the whole class, to express myself in group settings. Not all students have interest in striving for a goal of public speaking, and some may be quite content taking in the class silently.

In addition to their clinical work, Elly teaches psychology courses at the college level, and they are always careful to structure their classes so that there are multiple forms of participation available—the chat function on Zoom, small group discussions, prerecorded presentations. They think this is particularly important for neurodivergent students who not only may not have a goal of participating in front of large groups and may also find it much more aversive than neurotypical students.

Elly sees here another clear link between clinical work and teaching. Namely, that both endeavors involve identifying what are internal, autonomously chosen values and what are "shoulds" absorbed (or forcibly thrust on a person) from society. "When we bring our own values to the table," they said, "it makes the environment and the experience so much more motivating and engaging than when those values or shoulds are coming from the outside." There are also many opportunities for compromise between external values and internal ones. Elly often gives their clients the example of fitness. Elly cares not at all about sports or exercise but knows that the societal norm of being physically active is probably a healthy one aimed at a longer lifespan and better quality of life, and so they internally reframe fitness around the value of experiencing adventure outdoors, which is something that is an internal value for them.

Elly also flips roles upside down and asks instructors to do some exposure therapy themselves, sitting with their own discomfort around student behaviors like silence or students with autism soothing themselves by repeatedly clicking their pens or needing to tap. If these behaviors help the student stay in the classroom and learn, shouldn't the instructor be the one to do that work?

There are other important reasons to question the default values and norms baked into our classrooms. In his powerful book *Ratchetdemic: Reimagining Academic Success*, Columbia University professor and program director of science education Christopher Emdin asks us to take a hard look at how the social norms of our classrooms may reaffirm white cultural biases and then punish students for failing to fall into line with them. These practices can adversely affect many students but impact Black students most of all. He asks us to consider whether in elementary and secondary classrooms we are offering good grades not for creativity, effort, and learning but instead for being quiet, still, docile, and obedient. Emdin argues that to be truly intellectually stimulating environments, classrooms should celebrate diverse ways of knowing the world and also prioritize authenticity. "To be an effective educator who creates academically rigorous instruction," he writes, "one's teaching must be centered around the infusion of life and joy. Academic rigor is about being loud, proud, mobile, unpretentious, and challenged to take on whatever obstacles come one's way even if they offer some challenge." Infused with enough joy to be willing to take on intimidating obstacles sounds a lot like compassionate challenge to me.

CONCLUSION

To respond to an epidemic of youth anxiety, we who care for these youth need to arm ourselves with an understanding of how a danger detection system that evolved to keep us safe from harm can go awry and send off warning signals in the absence of threat. We also need an understanding of how clinical psychology intervenes to reset the system to health. This examination suggests that avoidance of feared stimulus is one of the worst things we can do if we want to calm these systems down. We need to help our young people rise and face their fears. In the pages that follow, I will further develop and explore what constitutes learning environments of compassion in secondary and higher education, and then explore practices we can engage in that challenge our students.

But as we do, recall the full title of Toby's tale—*Monster Night at Grandma's House*. Toby is summoning his courage and facing his fears at his Nana's home, a place of safety, belongingness, and play. Where there is a porch swing that flies up high above big hydrangea bushes, where for dinner each night there is corn from the garden dripping with butter, and where he is loved. It would be a much different story if Toby were taken out of this safe setting and plunked in a place where he couldn't be sure that the bugs tapping at his screen weren't actually fingers trying to pry it open, or where the creak on the stairs could be someone who really did want to cause him harm, or where instead of snuggling him on the porch swing, Nana listed a litany of his faults.

We need to challenge our youth in settings of compassion.

PART TWO

BODIES

CHAPTER THREE

INFUSED WITH EROS—EMBODIED MENTAL HEALTH

O NE BREEZY SUMMER AFTERNOON in the world's mid-2000s and my mid-twenties, I lay on a paisley couch in a cottage among the pine groves of Cape Cod. Several of my closest women friends were sprinkled around the combination living-dining-kitchen space of the small dwelling. We were at our biyearly retreat weekend where we spend time together, catch up on each other's lives, play, and set goals. It was this last activity we were working on at the moment, though there was also some play interspersed—as memory serves, I was lying on my back because a henna tattoo was drying on my midsection, and my cousin Elizabeth was spoon-feeding me a gin and tonic so that I didn't break my buzz while the tattoo dried.* "You know we're going to have to do this for our parents one day," she quipped, making me laugh so hard that I contorted and snorted, juniper burning through my nasal passages.

Our friend Julie politely coughed, bringing us back to the list of goals she was sharing with us.

"I would like to be able to run three miles without stopping," she said.

I pushed myself up on my elbows and squinted at her incredulously. "Why on earth would you want to do such a thing?" I asked. "I mean, if you weren't being chased?"

---

* To reiterate, this anecdote is from my twenties—I no longer relate to concepts like "breaking my buzz."

It might be surprising to you that I was surprised, but this conversation occurred before iPhones, before everyone had apps like Runkeeper in their favorites folder and Instagrams full of pictures of their latest mud run or Spartan challenge (and before, at least in my mind, that being-chased joke became so overplayed). There were runners, sure, but it wasn't quite the everyday person thing it is today. Or at least, such was my perception.

Not only would I eat these words many times over in the decade to come, but this ironic moment also foreshadowed a major turning point in my relationship with anxiety. It has led me to believe that mental health is fundamentally tied to Eros, an overall wellspring of health and energy that Freud used to describe our life instinct or drive. In this chapter we are going to consider how many of the active ingredients for youth mental health operate at the level of the body. Quite a lot of research supports the idea that encouraging good nutrition, sleep, exercise, and time in nature can do as much to shore up mental health as any meditation app or visit to the therapist's office.

But first, a brief primer on how your brain works.

BODIES, BRAINS, AND BUDGETS

My favorite two-star Goodreads review of my first book on teaching concluded: "Practical take-aways are great, case studies and examples are great, knowing how the brains of my students are constructed is just TMI." This pithy evaluation made me laugh but also perplexed me. Presumably students are using their brains to learn? And knowing a bit about how brains accomplish learning could be helpful for educators making decisions about how to structure their classes? If you disagree with me and agree with my reviewer, you might want to skip this next section because I am going to talk quite a bit about how young people's brains work, how they operate in conjunction with their bodies, and how this understanding can help schools, educators, and campuses support their mental health.

The popular version of how the brain works, from what I can tell, goes a little like the following. You have one part of your brain that is lizard-like and animalistic, and this part is responsible for your emotions (including our friend fear), your biases, and your stress response. You have another part of your brain, more recently evolved, that is careful, rational, and able to delay gratification, and whose functions are largely attributed to your frontal cortex. Things happen in the world—sights, sounds, hugs, punches, promotions, breakups—which you detect with your sense organs (eyes, ears, skin). Both your emotional lizard brain and your careful, evolved rational brain weigh in (often opposing each other), one wins, and you act.

This is not how your brain works. None of it.

For one, there is no meaningful separation of emotional areas from rational areas at the level of the brain. Even those areas that might be found to specialize more in one versus the other are in constant and continuous interaction, aimed at responding to challenges and supporting the organism's survival. For another, your entire brain reflects the evolutionary pressures influencing the human species, and other animals (including lizards) evolved based on their own pressures—the attractive idea that the brain added layers like floors of a house has been proven false, and you'd have to go pretty far back in our evolutionary history to find a common ancestor with lizards. As one viral article put it,* "Your Brain Is Not an Onion with a Tiny Reptile Inside." For yet another reason, while both your sensory perception (what you see, hear) and your action selection (what you do) are certainly *influenced* by the objective reality unfolding around you, the larger part of both sense and action happens entirely within your skull—and oftentimes before the information from the world even has a chance to make it into your brain. Your brain is a predictive machine.

In her succinct, fascinating book 7½ *Lessons About the Brain*, North eastern University neuroscientist and prolific science writer Lisa Feldman Barrett illustrates our predictive brains well with a story told to her by a gentleman who had served in the Rhodesian army in the 1970s. He was leading a small group of soldiers in a training exercise in the woods when he was startled by a line of guerrilla fighters carrying heavy weaponry and stalking through the woods. He immediately flipped into action, loading his own machine gun and preparing to pull the trigger when a fellow soldier stopped him with a touch on his shoulder.

---

* As viral as academic articles get, which is of course not very.

It was not a line of enemy fighters crossing their path at all, but a young boy leading some cows.

Feldman Barrett wasn't at all surprised by this story, for it fits right in line with the predictive nature of our brains. The soldier heard some rustling and saw some movement. His environmental context and memories of being in a similar setting predicted the line of guerrilla fighters, and so that's what his brain experienced first—and what his body began to respond to before his fellow soldier intervened. The external input, the objective reality of the boy and his cows, was slower to process than the story being told to him by his brain based on his emotional state, his past experiences, and the context of the forest during wartime and his role as a soldier. Critically, though, with this new experience, his brain would likely make a different set of predictions the next time something that looked like an enemy might instead be a friend. This updating of predictions based on experience, Feldman Barrett points out, is what scientists like to call learning.

While we're here, let's stay with Feldman Barrett for one more of her seven (and a half) lessons about how the brain works, because it will be critical when we begin to consider how to shore up mental health. It also works well with the prediction story because they're tied together. She argues (and this isn't terribly contentious; it's supported by quite a lot of evidence) that the principal purpose of our brains is to manage the budget of our bodies. She uses the metaphor of budgets to represent the complex interactions of all the biological systems in our body—the metabolic, the immune, the cardiovascular, the microbiome. Our bodies are incredibly complicated systems of interacting elements that all influence each other, but just as an artist can represent an array of convoluted and subtle influences in a single image, our brain can represent these internal states as an overall general affect or mood. How positive or negative, how sleepy versus activated.

A few years ago, I trained for a half marathon with my friend Julie.* One day, we were running ten miles at 5:30 a.m. because that was the

---

* Yes, this is the same friend I ridiculed for wanting to run three miles at the chapter's opening.

only mutual time we could find in our work- and parenting-full lives. She provided the headlamps. I can't quite recall whether it was a great run or a terrible one, but it was one or the other, because I remember having a whole conversation about why this run was so different from the one we ran just a few days previous. We lamented that it was probably ultimately a nut that could be cracked by science, but it would require knowing almost an infinite number of variables—our sleep quality, the exact balance of nutrients we imbibed the week before, whether we were fighting off a cold, whether our relationships were running smoothly at the moment, our degree of work stress, where we were in our menstrual cycles, the barometric pressure, and on and on and on. We wished that our smartwatches could just read all these variables and spit out, "great/shitty day for a run"!

This is the essence of the body budget. It is a representation of where your body is at any given moment. More than this, Feldman Barrett argues that we're constantly engaging in behaviors that result in deposits and withdrawals from this budget. Deposits look like sleep, nutrition, fitness, time with friends and family, sunlight, positive emotions, a sense of purpose. Withdrawals look like stress, illness, loneliness, effort, lack of sleep, despair about world events. The currency of the budget is all the internal workings of our bodies and brains—hormones, neurotransmitters, glucose, insulin, and so forth. Sometimes calculated short withdrawals followed by deposits can translate into greater system fitness in the same way that stressing your heart with a run followed by rest and a good meal can strengthen your heart. This is not just a metaphorical example but a literal one, since your cardiovascular system is one of the elements feeding into the whole budget.

These two brain lessons of Feldman Barrett's are tied together (the one about predictions and the one about budgets)—because anyone who has ever balanced a financial budget knows well that one of the best ways to effectively manage a budget is to make good predictions. You save the most money by either avoiding surprise withdrawals or making significant deposits in advance of them. Correspondingly, one reason our brains operate predictively is because this is the most effective way for them to manage our budgets. The biological principle undergirding this balancing act is called *allostasis*, and Mother Nature has threaded this principle throughout so much of existence because it is so effective. The best way to maintain allostasis is to build a brain that effortlessly predicts and begins preparing to meet demands before they ever present themselves.

What is important here is that allostasis is not only how your brain manages the budget of your body and maintains physical health—it is also how it manages and supports mental health, for a stark division between brains and bodies doesn't make a lot of sense. In a book we'll consider at more length in the next chapter, clinician Bessel van der Kolk writes, "It is amazing how many psychological problems involve difficulties with sleep, appetite, touch, digestion, and arousal." But in this new conceptualization of how brains work and what they're for, it actually *isn't* that amazing. Your brain is part of your body, and so of course your bodily experiences affect your mental experiences. There is not a bright dividing line between physical health and mental health.

There is also not such a bright dividing line between your brain's and your body's ability to manage its internal budget, your experiences within your body, and how *other people* and the systems you are embedded in help you manage the demands and rhythms of your life.

THE BODY IS EMBEDDED IN A FABRIC OF EXPERIENCE

My favorite theory of resiliency during stress belongs to psychologist Wai Kai Hou, director of the Centre for Psychosocial Health at the Education University of Hong Kong. He calls it the "drive to thrive" theory. Combined with a conceptualization of our brains and bodies as budget, it powerfully explains quite a few mysteries about who fares well and who struggles following stress. To develop his theory, Hou studied refugees and people living through extreme conflicts. He makes the argument that resilience lies not in the individual and their personality and coping mechanisms but rather in the routines of their lives, their "interwoven psychosocial and communal activities, procedures, and practices," and the degree to which these activities, procedures, and practices are or are not disrupted by stress and trauma.

To illustrate the power of these interwoven routines, Hou borrows principles from material science—specifically, and intriguingly, the study of fabrics. He argues that our mental health is integrally tied to a complex, interlinked series of threads that are made up of our social supports, our social standing, our finances, the demands on our time, and, yes, threads that overlap with our body budget—our physical health and energy levels. The interwoven nature of these threads is such that pulling a single thread doesn't have a large effect, especially on fabrics built with many interlaced threads. But the nature of fabrics also means that if you pull enough threads, eventually—and sometimes quite suddenly—you'll transition from everything seeming fine to total catastrophe. The fabric will tear, and everything will come to pieces.

Hou argues that one of the central ways that we maintain these fabrics is through routines. Some of these routines he characterizes as primary (sleep, hygiene, eating) and some as secondary (leisure, employment, goal work, sociality). These routines combine and provide support for easy, automatic functioning. Brains are predictive organs, remember, and another method of minimizing budget expenditures is to make things routine, automatic. Hou thus argues that one of the best ways to flourish is to have interdependent personal, social, and material resources (body budget deposits) that are interwoven with each other and sustained by routine life practices. It also means that the primary way to build resilience is not to focus on the individual and their personality or coping strategies but rather to build resourceful, sustainable, routine-based, supportive environments around them: a safety net, one might say. Or learning environments of compassion, one might also say.

I love this theory for its simplicity, for the compelling data that support it (we'll get into some of this data later when we talk about the context of trauma), and for how many little life mysteries it explains. Here's just one: Even though I'm one of the biggest animal lovers around, it has always struck me how much more disturbing a pet death can be than, say, the death of a relative you loved very much but saw infrequently. It seems untoward. But I think the fabric theory explains why. No matter how beloved, some distant relatives are people we might share the occasional email with and enjoy seeing at holidays. They aren't woven into our daily lives. Their sudden absence doesn't affect the moment to moment of your life rhythms, the fabrics right under your feet. If your family dog passes, on the other hand, you have no greeting in the morning. No morning walk. No afternoon wrestle. No fur to cry into when your aunt passes. Many fewer moments of laughter. A whole conversation topic subtracted from your daily chatter with your spouse. A huge interwoven thread has just been yanked from your tapestry, and the effects are overwhelming.*

What do these brains, budgets, bets, and fabrics collectively mean for mental health? Quite a lot, actually. Human beings need to shore up mental health by making more deposits than withdrawals, and we need our societies to develop systems and structures that support these efforts for all citizens. We all need to work within our contexts to find the best-fitting body budget deposits and then build our life routines around them: sleeping well, exercising, spending quality time with friends and family, engaging in creative pursuits, spending intimate time with our romantic partners, and/or giving back to the world are just a few possible such behaviors.** Additionally, we need to do what we can to design a life (and a world) where these behaviors are routine, automatic, and where engaging in them takes little effort. By extension, these arguments mean that to support the mental health of the youth in our lives, we parents, educators, and other supportive adults need to help them do the same.

In an analysis of how this theory could be applied to specific stressors, Hou and some colleagues considered the challenge of the COVID-19 pandemic. Many people suffered horrifying traumas during the pandemic— sudden loss of loved ones, undergoing emergency and intensive care unit (ICU) treatment for the disease oneself, being deprived of saying good-bye to loved ones or supporting them through their medical travails. Others suffered major stressors like economic hardship following job loss. But even those of us who were privileged enough not to suffer these more extreme stressors endured major disruptions to both the primary (sleep,

---

*Of course, this fabric account also explains why the loss of a *human being* who was part of your daily routines is the most devastating loss of all—but that wasn't a mystery that needed explaining.
** "Best fitting" here is key—not everyone has a body that makes exercise possible and/or rewarding, not everyone has a romantic partner and many are not interested in having one, etc. Deposit activities will vary for individuals.

hygiene, food) and secondary (socializing, family rituals, cultural touch-stones) routines that make up our well-being and resiliency. I have often seen the claim that we've all been traumatized by the pandemic. But for those of us who were lucky enough to avoid major losses, I think the better fitting explanation for the commonly expressed tension, stress, depression, and mental dizziness is that our fabrics were all majorly disrupted—like a giant beast vigorously used our fabrics for a trampoline. In their article, Hou and colleagues recommended that to shore up mental health during the stressors of the pandemic, people should focus on regularizing as many of their life routines as possible.

To some extent, the social regulation of each other's body budgets is part of the human condition—the very purpose of friends and families may be that they're people who help us regulate our body budget. But it also suggests that parents need to create opportunities for their children to learn to regulate their own body budgets rather than hand-holding them through such regulation through adulthood. It means that parents with the means to do so need to model good body regulation themselves—"Do as I do, not do as I say"—rather than burning through all their own body resources. Finally, it means that our society needs to provide resources for all parents to be able to make this choice, rather than requiring them to spend all their body resources just to survive and provide basic needs to their children.

We also need to appreciate the deep stress that the transition to college represents. As I discussed a bit when considering adolescence as a critical period, transitioning to college means young people bounce from one set of social fabrics to an entirely new situation where they must establish new grooves, relationships, and behavioral patterns. This is an extraordinary tax on young people's body budgets and mental health, and we need to be sure to support them through it. First generation college students may need special support for this transition, since their parents won't have the life experiences to be knowledgeable guides to some college-specific chal-lenges. In chapter 6, when we consider the critical role of belongingness for motivation, I'll discuss some powerful work by sociologist Jennifer Morton on the challenges faced by first-generation and minoritized stu-dents in particular, removed abruptly from the embedded fabrics of their social and cultural networks at home.

What these body budgets and predictions and fabrics also suggest to me is that mental health is embodied. The first step to mental health is supporting physical health, safety, and well-being, and I will focus on these elements of mental health for the rest of this chapter. Two major scientific resources we will be drawing on are a recent report from fifty research teams evaluating the current state of knowledge regarding youth mental health, and a special collection of articles about these research efforts published in *Nature* journals. These resources summarize what the researchers call "active ingredients" for youth mental health. Active ingredients are those aspects of an intervention that are responsible for improvement, that drive success. We'll return to this report throughout the book, but in this chapter we'll focus primarily on those active ingredients that relate to the body—for example, basic needs, sleep, and physical activity.

First up, our most basic needs.

ACTIVE INGREDIENTS FOR EMBODIED MENTAL HEALTH: BASIC NEEDS

In 2016, professor of sociology and medicine at Temple University Sara Goldrick-Rab started a bit of a revolution. Having long researched college affordability, she left her post at University of Wisconsin-Madison to join Temple and also to found the Hope Center for College, Community, and Justice in Philadelphia. She *also* published the now renowned book *Paying the Price: College Costs, Financial Aid, and the Betrayal of the American Dream*. The culmination of six years of research, the book analyzes how the combined forces of skyrocketing college costs, declining public support of universities, increasing reliance on student loans, and decreases in net family income coalesced into the student-loan debt crisis. The result is not just too much debt, though—her research indicates that because of steep financial pressures, large numbers of college students are also food and housing insecure.

Through the Hope Center, Goldrick-Rab has launched a movement to support the basic needs of college students, dubbed #RealCollege. Basic needs include food, housing, health care, hygiene, transportation, child care and elder care (where applicable), and so on. Access to the technology required to support these other needs and to do the academic work required of them are also core basic needs to succeed at college. The Hope Center conducts research, advocates for changes in policy, and disseminates the compassionate message of meeting students' basic needs as a first step in their education. In all this work, Goldrick-Rab and the Hope Center focus especially on institutions that are minority serving or broad access (including community colleges). In one representative research study, the Hope Center found that during the initial COVID-19 crisis, about 7 percent of college students reported having gotten sick with COVID—but for both racial and ethnic minorities on the one hand, and students who had experienced food insecurity, depression, and anxiety on the other, these rates were elevated well above the average.

It is so intuitive (one might even say basic) that a person cannot engage in higher-level processes like learning and choosing to confront their fears if they do not know where their next meal is coming from or whether they'll have a safe place to rest. This is the essence of the classic hierarchy of needs credited to theorist Abraham Maslow. In his frame, physiological needs and need for safety are fundamental, followed by needs for social belongingness and self-esteem, with a state of achievement and transcendence called self-actualization at the highest, most rarified level. Importantly, Maslow's theory may have been strongly influenced by his time working with Indigenous people of the Blackfoot Nation, though their version prioritized community to a much higher degree. The importance of community and a sense of belongingness for establishing learning environments of compassionate challenge is a theme we'll take up in more depth in chapter 6.

One basic need supported by the Hope Center is physical safety. At residential colleges, campus sexual assault presents one of the most salient threats to safety. In an extraordinarily researched and written book, *Sexual Citizens: A Landmark Study of Sex, Power, and Assault on Campus*, sociologists Jennifer Hirsch and Shamus Khan share extensive interviews of students on their campus about their sexual goals, experiences, and assaults. They take an approach that Wai Kai Hou would appreciate, examining the interwoven fabrics of campuses to determine which structural components support sexual health and which instead make sexual assault more likely.

Reflecting on their analysis of the student interviews, Hirsch and Khan note that an important factor in whether an unpleasant sexual experience is ended quickly or escalates to assault is whether you are in control over the space you are in—and note that wealthier students have access to better, bigger spaces and resources like Uber to get out of dangerous situations. While it is an issue without an easy solution, they also observe that the entire design of residential colleges makes sexual assaults more likely. "The almost tidal flow of students in and out of each other's bedrooms is a defining element of residential higher education," they write. "Dorm life is a fundamental sexual assaults opportunity structure." Surprising no one, alcohol plays a huge role in the perpetration of assault. But dismayingly, it also plays a large role in healthier sexual interactions, with youth reporting that they intentionally use alcohol to facilitate sexual encounters and reduce their own nervousness about these interactions.

Hirsch and Khan believe (as do I) that to build campuses where all students can thrive and there are far fewer sexual assaults, we need to simultaneously address issues of power and inequality, substance use, and mental health. Here, I let them speak:

> But just as explanations that are purely psychological (sociopathic perpetrators) are incomplete, so, too, are ones that are entirely cultural (toxic masculinity). *We are all responsible.* Most of us have never committed assault. But all of us have allowed social conditions to persist in which many young people come of age without a language to talk about their sexual desires, overcome with shame, unaccustomed to considering how their relative social power may silence a peer, highly attentive to their personal wants but deaf to those of others, or socialized to feel unable to tell someone "no" or to give a clear and unambiguous "yes."

Like so many other complex issues that face us, changing the landscape of sexual assault means targeting the interacting systems that work to support it. I encourage anyone interested in these issues to read Hirsch and Khan's book and call for colleges and universities to take up their charge.

Basic needs like food, housing, and physical safety are the bare minimum for supporting embodied mental health. As promised, we will soon return to how beginning to run was a major turning point in my battle with panic, and we'll consider how exercise is another powerful active ingredient for youth mental health. But first, an important preamble.

ACTIVE INGREDIENTS FOR EMBODIED MENTAL HEALTH: CREATING AN INCLUSIVE BUILT WORLD

We cannot talk about the embodiment of mental health without addressing how disability can adversely affect mental health twice over: first, through varied inherent challenges such as chronic pain and disruption to routines, and second, through society's discriminatory response to disability.

In *Uncanny* magazine's special series on disability, speculative fiction writer Zin E. Rocklyn describes her fraught bodily experiences and these twofold challenges in a haunting essay titled "My Genre Makes a Monster of Me." She grapples with both the pain in her physical body (from scoliosis) and the horror of operating as a pained body in a society that treats dark-skinned Black women like herself as less deserving of sympathy and admiration than other beings. Confronted with these twinned injustices growing up led her to a love of horror, of monsters in all their isolation and their pain. But even there she finds no true representation, no mirror to see herself in. "We are the forgotten monsters," she writes, "the invisible help, the unheard, yet influential magic who deserve to be front and center, who deserve to be seen for all that we are: beautifully flawed and like all humans." She powerfully vows to create these narratives herself, stories of strong Black women richly portrayed, deserving of love, and vital to the story. Her debut work doing just that, a luminous and horrific tale called *Flowers for the Sea*, was nominated in 2022 for a Nebula Award for best science fiction or fantasy novella.

Artist, design researcher, and writer Sara Hendren considers how the entire world is crafted around an assumption of one normative body type in the compelling book *What Can a Body Do? How We Meet the Built World*. She reveals that the concept of "normal" as average or the center of the bell curve of human variation is a relatively recent conception, invented along with statistics and, more sinisterly, the eugenics movement. Earlier conceptions of human variation compared all presumably flawed human bodies against godlike ideals that were known to be unattainable. She writes that "disability is a common part of human life—an ordinary experience, infinite in variety, replete with creativity and heartbreak, from sources internal and external, and carrying social stakes everywhere." She challenges us to consider how differences in ability meet the titular built world, rather than believe that disability resides within the individual. Ability and disability reside less in the physical body and more in the structures and supports that either do or do not meet them.

In an essay for the journal *Hybrid Pedagogy*, novelist, instructor, and Paralympic athlete Arley Cruthers reflects on teaching in a body that constantly presents physical challenges. She writes that her visible movement disability seemed to encourage students to share their own troubled experiences being a body, visiting her in office hours and discussing their struggles with weight gains and losses, with injuries, with assaults. As surgeries and relentless treatment transformed her disability from visible, in the exterior, to invisible (in the form of chronic pain), this deeper relationship with her students dissolved. She went in search of it again. "Creating a pedagogy of care required unlearning many of the lessons I'd absorbed about disability," she writes. "It required thinking not just about my own body, but the systems that police our bodies, that exclude, marginalize and enact violence on some bodies." By instituting a pedagogy of care in her classrooms, one explicitly focused on learning about her students as individuals, she reforged these deep connections.

This lesson Cruthers learned is consistent with the research in the remarkable *Everybody: A Book About Freedom* by Olivia Laing. In the work, Laing considers the ambivalent experience of living in a body capable of both pleasure and pain in a society that restricts and regulates certain bodies and certain bodily activities—but where bodies can also be a source of movements for social change, for freedom. "We're all stuck in our bodies," she writes, "meaning stuck inside a grid of conflicting ideas about what those bodies mean, what they're capable of and what they're allowed or forbidden to do." While the topics in Laing's book range widely over decades, considering artists and social activities and writers, she anchors the book by continually returning to the life of psychoanalyst and medical doctor Wilhelm Reich.

An intellectual companion to Sigmund Freud and a person whose life's work inspired many illustrious figures from James Baldwin to Susan Sontag to Kate Bush, Reich argued for the liberating power of a sexual revolution and also thought deeply about the damages that trauma and chronic stresses like poverty and housing insecurity could wreak on mental health. He thought that sexual and emotional repression were damaging too, and talked about a steady tension in repressed people, expressed in their voice, carriage, and smiles, that he perceived as a kind of rigid armor. It released during orgasm and body therapies like massage or primal screaming, resulting in a physical sensation of rippling release that he called streaming.

Both Reich and Laing warn that taking off this armor is frightening, likely due in part to uncertainty. "Pleasure is frightening," Laing writes, "and so too is freedom. It involves a kind of openness and unboundedness that's deeply threatening both to the individual and to the society they inhabit. Freedom invokes a counter-wish to clamp down, to tense up, to forbid, even to destroy." This latter impulse can be expressed by the individual attempting to shut down vulnerability and bodily responses, leading to Reich's sense of character armor.

How can we help students and instructors put aside their character armor and engage in the acts of learning and of connection, so vital to education? We will reflect on this topic in greater depth in the fourth section of this book, "Behaviors."

In the meantime, in all the active ingredients to follow, we need to appreciate yet again the power of context and how these active ingredients will look very different from person to person. Some active ingredients may not be relevant to some youth at all. Some might be inaccessible to them, and as Elly Romero called to our attention, others may simply not relate to their values. Consider the following active ingredients a menu from which to choose those most relevant and most full of promise for the particular individual.

ACTIVE INGREDIENTS FOR EMBODIED MENTAL HEALTH: PHYSICAL ACTIVITY

My own transition from running skeptic to habitual jogger was probably made possible only because of a particularly nerve-wracking period of my life. I had tried running multiple times in my life, usually dragged out by a friend—a roommate in college, my boyfriend-turned-husband who ran on cross-country teams, my friend Julie who had cleverly used the argument that I could run with my dog and it would be good for my furry friend. It always felt terrible, and I never took to it.

But I happened to download a Couch-to-5k app on my phone and decided for one last try, right at a time in my life when stresses were many, uncertainty was high, and I was conflicted about some drama going on in my personal life. I found that in this context, the rhythm of my feet hitting the ground was soothing. Time out running was also time with no one clutching at my apron strings or my email threads—there was just me, and the air. The pounding of my feet and pounding of my heart. Stimulating music. As the app moved me from short bursts to longer stretches of running, I started purposefully immersing myself in thinking about thorny issues, because doing so made my feet fly faster. I got in touch with angry feelings that I didn't usually let myself feel. "And, moreover . . . ! And, what about . . . ? And, how could you . . . ?" At the end of the run I would feel purged, cleansed.

Research on a concept called anxiety sensitivity suggests that running also had beneficial effects for me because it inured me to elevations in heart rate, in breathing, in a certain degree of muscle and stomach clenching. One psychological attribute that seems to differentiate people prone to anxiety from their calmer counterparts is the degree to which they are sensitive to the signals of their interior. These signals include bodily changes like heart rate, stomach movements, and variations in breathing. Collectively, these signals are known as interoceptive cues. People high in anxiety sensitivity tend to both detect these signals with greater ease and be more likely to interpret them as harbingers of a panic attack. For instance, small digestive tumults that might not even register to a placid person are detected by the anxious person and then interpreted as a potential warning.

Running is hard work, and feeling these signals in safe circumstances likely helped me tolerate them when those same signals arose in social circumstances. In fact, some forms of therapy for anxiety explicitly expose people to these signals in safe settings as another form of exposure therapy. Such practices might involve soliciting dizziness by asking the patient to spin in circles, creating hyperventilation by having them breathe in rapid huffs, or elevating heart rate by asking them to . . . run on a treadmill. This link between exercise and reductions in anxiety sensitivity has been studied in the laboratory and found to be effective.

And then, I got addicted. If it had been a few days since a good run, my early morning brain would pound out the pavement in my dreams, much like sleeping late on weekends leads to endless dreams of rich, dark coffee. My body learned to need running, to crave it, and my unconscious mind got a little ticked off when I didn't deliver. But in addition to this physical reliance, I also grew cognitively and emotionally invested. For running is also where I do my best creative work. When I'm experiencing a period of lower stress and my brain doesn't have problems to work out, it works on connecting ideas and communicating them instead. Lectures, essays, book chapters assemble themselves in my ambulating mind—more often than not, they then further unspool in my hot shower afterward and then I have to scramble to write them all down before they wither and fade.

Let's pause here for a moment, as this will become important in chapter 5. My mind uses this running time to circle and connect and ruminate. During times of stress, it circles and ruminates on the sources of that stress, the causes of that anxiety. During times of low stress, it circles and ruminates on creative work related to my goals. We will return to this interesting relationship between anxiety and motivation in just a few chapters.

Most remarkably, my panic attacks quietly stepped offstage, into the shadows. They became tremendously infrequent occurrences, mere glimmers of their previous selves. One would still grip me here and there when multiple triggers piled up. But mostly I relaxed into life. As a psychologist I know that I can't take a step back and consider my infinitely complicated life, the exact combination of aging and growing wisdom and shifting hormones and relationship security and neurodevelopment, and claim that I know for sure that learning to run was the turning point. But it sure feels like it.

Movement and exercise contribute to mental health in many different ways. In *The Joy of Movement*, psychologist and science writer (and exercise coach!) Kelly McGonigal takes a deep dive into the science of what exercise and physical movement provides for humanity. "Movement offers us pleasure, identity, belonging, and hope," she writes. "It puts us in places that are good for us, whether that's outdoors in nature, in an environment that challenges us, or with a supportive community. It allows us to redefine ourselves and reimagine what is possible." As we did already, McGonigal notes that physical fitness is not possible for all people, and there are multiple paths to some of these outcomes. We can build community and competence through volunteerism, through career activities, through art. But her years of research on the physical, psychological, and social impacts of fitness have led her to believe there are few activities that give us so much at once.

For many abled people for whom physical activity is a possibility, this link between being physically and mentally fit is so intuitive it almost feels silly to write about. We feel it in our bones—or more appropriately, in our hearts and in our muscles. When we feel like we are physically more than a match for our days, it is easier to feel mentally a match for our days. Being physically fit shores up the budgets of our bodies, allows for more energy, easier recovery from illness and injury, better sleep, and improved confidence.

A review and statistical meta-analysis of more than a thousand research papers on youth physical activity and mental health revealed that interventions aimed at increasing physical activity may assist in reducing symptoms of depression in particular, though large variations in methodological quality limited the conclusions. The authors speculated that such interventions probably worked through a combination of factors that were psychological (for instance, distraction from worries and feeling more in control), neurocognitive (for instance, enhanced activity in reward circuits), and biological (for instance, improved sleep and cardiovascular function). Both they and some of the young people they interviewed cautioned that such interventions would need to be tailored to the individual in terms of activities one enjoys, degree of interest in physical fitness, and level of activity at the start of the intervention—and again, will not be accessible to everyone. Beyond physical limitations, the symptoms of depression often make kicking up an exercise regimen the furthest thing from possible. Please don't advise a currently depressed person that they should consider exercising because you read in a book somewhere that it could help. They've heard, trust me.

But physical fitness is just one method, one often-important ingredient, to building lives resilient to beastly attacks of depression and anxiety— which is good news for those of us who have harried lives or uncooperative bodies or have other restrictions that mean we can't invest time and money in physical fitness.

ACTIVE INGREDIENTS FOR EMBODIED MENTAL HEALTH: WHY YOU SHOULD GO TO SLEEP RIGHT NOW

When I was growing up, my mother's stock response for any time I professed the slightest stress or emotion or rebellion was a shrugging, "Oh, you're just overtired." It drove me, in clinical terms, absolutely bonkers. It seemed to diminish and flatten any real objections I had to the demands of life, to how our household was run, to whatever newest indignity my two brothers had inflicted upon me into nothing more than the prickly discomfort of someone who hadn't gotten enough rest. But of course, she was right more often than not. A good night's sleep solved most of my woes.

For sleep knits up the raveled sleeve of care. According to the Dalai Lama, sleep is the best medication. As an old Irish proverb has it, the best cures in a doctor's book are a good laugh and a good sleep. While the exact mechanisms of how sleep restores us still elude science, it is intuitively without a doubt that it does, and it is a restoration that we cannot live without—mammals who do not sleep die.

One of my best friends who was a personal trainer always asked her clients first if they were sleeping well, and if they said no, she would send them off to fix their sleep habits before she'd consult with them about launching a new fitness regimen. *Under Pressure* author and adolescent well-being expert Lisa Damour shares something similar about her work with teen girls: "When a girl who is bone-tired says that she feels fragile, breathing techniques aren't the answer." First, fix the sleep. Then address whatever problems remain. We all know that a lack of sleep doesn't just make your eyes itch and your head swim; every barb feels sharper, every task more daunting, every worry more worrisome. The problem is, in a country notorious for sleep deprivation in general, our high school and college students may be sleeping least of all.

Sleeping well during the adolescent and college years is a difficult feat. First, you have a shift in your body's internal rhythms, something called the sleep phase delay—it isn't only that your teen suddenly wants to stay up late chatting with her friends and spend mornings buried under the duvet and a few cats. For sure, there are social and academic pressures to live through the full school day, then complete a roster of extracurriculars after school, then homework . . . all the while checking in with social networks. But there is *also* a hormonal, neurodevelopmental shift in how the adolescent body functions, where her circadian rhythms change to make her more of a night owl. This biological and environmental shift chafes against our school systems, which crank the start time for school progressively earlier as a child ages—precisely the opposite thing that it should be doing, as any parent of a kindergartener who pops awake at 5 a.m. and a teenager whom you must drag out of bed at 1 p.m. to go apple picking can attest.

So this phase delay is a battle. Then we have the overscheduling of the privileged set, the dizzying rush from class to lacrosse to chorale and then back to the dorm for hours of cramming and paper writing and discussion boards. And the overscheduling of the less privileged set, the dizzying rush from one freelance job to another to home to care for younger siblings and then to stay up late for the same hours of cramming and paper writing and discussion boards.

Then we have the massive amounts of caffeine . . .

Then we have the phones . . .

So good, uninterrupted sleep is hard to come by when you are fifteen to twenty-four years old.

All this is vitally important to our consideration of mental health, because sleep and mood are inextricably linked. A systematic review of the literature revealed that across studies, there is a clear and likely bidi-rectional relationship between sleep quality, sleep amount, and depressive symptoms in college students. In one of the largest studies of college students' sleep and mental health, comprising nearly eight thousand students over six diverse campuses, researchers found that nearly two-thirds of their sample met criteria for "poor sleep," ranging from low duration to problems falling asleep to disruptions throughout sleep. Anxiety and depression were differentially related to poor sleep, with anxiety problems associated with sleep disturbances and medication use, and depression associated with greater levels of trouble functioning throughout the day due to sleepiness.

But poor sleep may also be a double whammy of sorts in our consid-erations here, because poor sleep not only may predispose one to mood and anxiety problems; it may also directly interfere with one's cognition, with all the abilities students need in order to succeed in their studies. One of the most compelling theories for why we sleep in the first place is that it supports processes involved in the consolidation of new memories and skills.

A recent research study equipped their college-aged participants with Fitbit-style activity monitors capable of assessing overall rest and time spent in various sleep stages. The researchers recruited participants from the same undergraduate course in chemistry, which allowed them to assess the associations between the way the students were sleeping and how they scored on specific exams and assignments, as well as how they did over the entire semester. Amazingly, sleep variables predicted *a full quarter* of the variance in their grades at the end of the semester. That is, when predicting variations in how well the students did in the course as a whole, knowing how much the students slept improved the researchers' estimate by about 25 percent.

A narrative review of the literature on circadian rhythms and sleep-wake disturbances in young people indicates several strategies that might be helpful in better regulating sleep and the biological rhythms: managing light exposure such that one is exposed to bright light in the morning and not much light in the pre-bed hours, engaging in regular physical activity during waking hours, and maintaining a regular sleep-wake schedule.

These strategies were also found to be helpful in reducing depressive symptoms and may be particularly beneficial for those whose depression is marked by sleep difficulties. The authors also interviewed several young people suffering from depression and noted that barriers to implementing these strategies include balancing the pressures of school, work, and social time. They also note that policy changes could be helpful, including one of my personal favorites: delaying school start times for adolescents to better match their internal phase delays.

In sum, good sleep habits may be one of the most effective targets of intervention for not just youth mental health but also youth academic performance.

ACTIVE INGREDIENTS FOR EMBODIED MENTAL HEALTH: WILD MINDS, FOREST BATHING, AND THE SCOPE OF ATTENTION

In a few chapters I will discuss how anxiety and motivation are both psychological states that attempt to control the future by increasing energy and narrowing attention on a problem to be solved. In these moments, body and brain become more aroused, distractions fall away, and you pursue your goal, whether it is avoiding threat or approaching reward. It is important for any organism, human beings very much included, to be able to rouse the body to action in moments that hold peril or promise. But these states are physically, emotionally, and mentally taxing. In other words, they burn through our body budgets. Before engaging in motivationally intense tasks or periods of time, we need to shore up our body budgets with all the ingredients of embodied mental health that we have considered thus far—nutrition, sleep, socializing, and physical activity. But we may also need time in mental states that are the opposite of focus and engaged pursuit. We need time to relax our brains, to let them wander.

Barbara Fredrickson is an eminent psychologist whom many credit with being one of the founders of positive psychology. Psychology as a field really took off in the aftermath of the world wars, in response to the large-scale suffering and loss endemic to that time. Psychology had thus been focused on the goal of bettering human lives, but with a distinctly negative lens—fixing what has gone wrong rather than increasing well-being. Treating mental illness instead of encouraging mental health. Finding problems rather than amplifying potential. Beginning in the 1990s, Fredrickson and others began nudging the conversation in the other direction, toward positivity, through innovative research, conferences, and grant funding.

Some of Fredrickson's earliest work focused on the issue of attention. She demonstrated that negative emotional states largely heighten attention on the details of a scene or a stimulus, resulting in a narrowing of the scope of attention. Which makes a lot of sense, because if you have a problem to solve, you need sharp focus to figure out the details of the problem and how to fix them. She also demonstrated that positive emotional states largely *broaden* attention, opening the scope of focus to take in details from the periphery. Using these data, she formulated her broaden-and-build hypothesis, which argued that evolutionarily, this broadening of attention when feeling positive makes sense. In times when you are not under threat, when you're feeling good, then you can pick up your head and start looking around you. You can make connections, build relationships, and come up with new goals. Subsequent research confirmed her findings, demonstrating that positive mood inductions had positive cognitive effects, including boosting creativity.

Soon after this theory and associated research really got off the ground, an important caveat to these principles was demonstrated, and you might already be guessing what that is. Cleverly, this caveat was revealed through tapping in to the motivational power of both sex and dessert. Psychologists Philip Gable and Eddie Harmon-Jones and several others hypothesized that what was really important for the narrowing versus broadening of attention effects was not really negativity versus positivity but instead something they dubbed *motivational intensity*. Was the given situation "pre-goal," one that required you to mobilize yourself in order for action—as a snake in the grass might, but as a big ole hot fudge sundae or attractive human being might also? Or was the given situation "post-goal," one that nudged you to relax, take stock, and muse about what new adventures the future might hold, as contentment, joy, or satisfaction might? These researchers took Fredrickson's paradigm but added some positive pre-goal images like tasty desserts and attractive people. Both anxiety and goal pursuit of various sorts involve the need for narrowed attention.

By their very nature, these broadening, post-goal positive emotions arise when you are content, when you are feeling good, when you have achieved your goals and can kick up your heels and relax a bit. Surely, we're all working on being post-goal all the time. But are there activities that can nudge these sorts of mental states in the meantime? Before we become all self-actualized?

One candidate activity is pretty simple: time in nature. Reviews of the literature suggest that time in nature is associated with a multitude of adaptive effects, both in terms of reducing negative emotions and stress (on the one hand) and amplifying positive emotions and well-being (on the other). That is, both less of the bad and more of the good. The research literature suggests that such effects go beyond just self-reported feeling too, affecting physiological stress reactivity and brain function. As "culinary adventurer" Langdon Cook writes in his book *The Mushroom Hunters*, "You can't think about fugitives and bears and bogeymen if you want to pick mushrooms. The woods are dark and deep, but mostly the darkness is in our heads." Time in nature forces this shift in attention from external threats and internal worries, instead broadening to the landscape, opening wide to the possibility of small treasures poking their heads out of the moss. In the early 1980s, the Japanese minister of Agriculture, Forestry, and Fisheries gave name to the practice of routinely visiting the forest to take in the atmosphere there. He called it *Shinrin-yoku*, or "forest bathing."

Being in natural landscapes can also invoke a sense of awe, a state of being that has both cognitive and emotional elements and that is associated with well-being. The cognitive elements of awe involve a sense of change in one's perspective, usually in settings that challenge one's existing knowledge or understanding of the world. You might feel awe the first time you behold a giant redwood tree or the depths of the Grand Canyon. You might also feel awe when confronted with incredible feats of athleticism or generosity, when the capabilities of the human body or spirit render you temporarily unmoored. Fascinatingly, early conceptions of awe were bound up with terror, often in reaction to visitations from ethereal spirits. Monsters, too, can evoke awe.

Positive psychologist and awe expert Michelle (Lani) Shiota reflects on how human beings are likely one of the few species capable of truly complex mental models of how the world works—we can think abstractly, untethered by objective reality, and imagine whole worlds of possibility. When these models are challenged, when we are faced with a blank space or a gap in understanding we are humbled to fill, we feel awe. "Awe seems to produce a little earthquake in the mind," she writes, "a moment of cognitive malleability offering a chance to expand and reconstruct one's mental model of the world." A little earthquake in the mind—what a beautiful image. While not uniformly positive, awe most often introduces positive emotions and may indicate a moment of possibility, when we're open to change. It might be a worthwhile (if ambitious) goal in the classroom.

I understand the appeal of forest bathing. But my personal inclination bends toward the sea. The salt, the sand, the roaring waves and soothing tides. The vastness of both breadth and depth. The tiny sea creatures who scurry when you tip rocks and the massive mammals that undulate in the deep. Everything about the ocean soothes me, enchants me, restores me. Nearly every time I visit it, whether sharp, cold New England beaches or placid, warm tropical ones, I kick myself for letting it be so long between trips. It is restorative on what feels like a cellular level.

Find wherever your natural space is, and bathe in it. Encourage your young people to do the same. Even better, intentionally craft in-person courses and classes to leave the four cinderblock walls of your institution and get outside with your students.

TEACHING EMBODIED MENTAL HEALTH: SCAFFOLDING BODY REGULATION

Writing in the *New York Times*, dogsledder and author of *Welcome to the Goddamn Ice Cube* Blair Braverman considers whether motivating her dogs to run one hundred miles in the Arctic offered lessons for enduring the challenging 2020–2021 winter of social distancing after months of stress and lockdowns. One major motivational lesson she shares is so in line with the content of this chapter that when I read it, I gasped. Namely, one of the principal tasks of a human being leading a team of sled dogs is to regulate their body budgets for them.

Dogs (mostly) don't understand language. You can't tell them how many miles are left to go and how to save physical resources, how to pace themselves. Only you know how difficult the path ahead is, and how much farther they must go. You must construct their environments to show the dogs now is time to rest, now is time to eat, now is time to stop and play. More than just regulating their budgets, though, this also builds trust into the relationship. The dogs know to trust that you'll feed them when they start to get hungry, that you'll pull the sled aside when they start to get tired. And it is this trust that allows them to reach their full potential: "And it's this security, this trust," Braverman writes, "that lets her pour herself into the journey, give the trail everything she has without worrying about what comes next. You can't make a sled dog run 100 miles. But if she knows you've got her back, she'll run because she wants to, because she burns to, and she'll bring you along for the ride." These same principles apply to the biological creatures we love who walk on two limbs rather than four—our youth. As parents, educators, and campus leaders we can help young people regulate their budgets through programming, scaffolding, and other offerings. We also can remember that, although in education we are primarily focused on learning, young people are using their bodies to learn.

While ultimately they will need to learn to regulate their own bodily systems, those of us in the business of educating young humans can scaffold this regulation for them through modeling, through carefully designing the school systems and learning environments around them to encourage healthy regulation of sleep, eating, and activity, and by designing classroom activities that respect that students are bodies as well as minds.

CONCLUSION

Minds arise from the interaction of brains, the bodies these brains reside in, and the social fabrics these bodies are embedded within. To support youth learning and mental health, we need to craft learning environments of compassionate challenge. Our first step is to support their safety and basic needs, to scaffold and nudge regulation of their biological rhythms like sleep and physical activity, to embrace youth with disability and to honor their particular strengths and challenges, to slow down and spend time in settings that encourage us to broaden our attention, and to design learning experiences that respect our embodied natures.

These are ideals. We know that the world is not ideal. What happens when a significant thread of a youth's tapestry is snatched so hard that everything unravels? In the next chapter we'll consider how to support young people enduring toxic stress and trauma.

CHAPTER FOUR

UNRULY BODIES IN AN UNPREDICTABLE WORLD

I T WAS THE CURTAINS, pendulous with blood, that triggered my loss of consciousness.

That the blood was fake and that I was physically safe didn't matter to the sensitive nerve running from my brain stem through my neck, down to my heart, and then out to my abdomen. The tenth of the twelve cranial nerves, the vagus nerve plays a usually pleasant role in calming the body down when it is time to relax, lowering both heart rate and blood pressure. The vagus nerve is often studied in the context of well-being and mental health, and you can find unfounded claims on the internet about how to stimulate it to make yourself happier.

But triggered suddenly, these drops in blood pressure and heart rate can be too precipitous and result in a loss of consciousness. In fact, one theory of the vagus nerve is that it contains not only more recent pathways and functions related to the calming effects of the parasympathetic nervous system, but it also contains evolutionarily older pathways and functions linked to organisms playing dead in the face of mortal danger. The latter function may explain why a substantial minority of human beings pass out when they encounter needles or blood—large enough numbers to qualify for an entire subtype of phobias (blood-injection-injury phobia) in psychiatry's diagnostic bible, the *DSM-5*. The fancy name for this sudden loss of consciousness, I would learn in my doctor's office the following Monday morning, is *vasovagal syncope*. But most people just call it fainting.

I was at my friend Jenn's bachelorette party. We had started the day at the spa, where we got full body massages and where the masseuse chided me to be sure to drink lots of water because she had worked out so many knots that I was sure to be dehydrated. Instead of heeding her warning, we next indulged in more than a few cocktails and glasses of champagne at a favorite Harvard Square restaurant and bar. It was close to Halloween and so the upstairs where we tucked away for a private dinner was decorated with grinning jack-o-lanterns, their flickering leers an additional warning left ignored. Likely because both the special occasion and our willingness to imbibe many adult beverages were obvious, the waitstaff were slow bringing out our meals. We ran late for the final leg of our adventures. Given the proximity to the spookiest of holidays and my friend's and my penchant for seeing horror movies together, when we discussed whether we should go out clubbing, to a show, or to some other event, the bride-to-be instead said she wanted to attend . . . GoreFest 2010.

A burlesque, audience-involvement theatrical performance, GoreFest had a reputation for being funny, scary, and, well, gory. Our friend Phil had attended the show the week before and ominously warned us not to wear shoes we were very attached to. The slow service at dinner meant we arrived after the show had already begun, and the staff was reluctant to let us in even though we had tickets. We played the bachelorette party card and he relented. "You'll have to sit in the front row," he explained, handing us some plastic capes to wrap around us and button at the neck. "Now be quiet as we go in."

The room was small and hot. I wasn't worried about the bawdy or the scary aspects of the show—I love burlesque and I quite like a good fright—but I wasn't thrilled about the potential for gore. Likely due to a lifetime of dealing with an unruly body, I'm easily disgusted. So when the cast starting popping zits and spraying what was probably Cheez Whiz into the audience, I was already not having a good time. During one song, one of the actors roamed the periphery of the audience and pretended to vomit in his hand, then smeared what I hope was oatmeal down my caped chest. I gagged.

I made it through most of the first act, though sweating and somewhat nauseated. But as the first act ended, rather than curtains being drawn to close the scene, the lights started to dim. Wondering why they weren't using the curtains drew my attention upward to the velvet drapes tied above the stage. They weren't just gathered but actually drooped, heavy with some unknown burden. Phil's comment about our shoes came back to me, and I had the sudden realization—those curtains were filled with fake gore, and at the end of the show they were going to pull a draw cord and unleash a tide of blood, soaking us like an audience full of Carries.

When the lights finished going out, so did I.

I woke up in a small room backstage with my friends and crew from the play all staring at me, an ambulance on its way. In addition to saddling me with forever guilt that my dear friend's bachelorette party ended in an ER on account of my weak body,* the event brought me to my doctor, where she explained the functions of the vagus nerve and that some people are more sensitive to its sudden activation than others. She also educated me about common triggers, which include heat, dehydration, and pressure around the neck. Over time and as these fainting episodes piled up, I was able to identify additional, personalized triggers—feeling trapped in a social situation, for one. Being unable to escape the intrusive hands of men, for another—the effects of the overeager oatmeal-smearer would be echoed in the effects of an airplane caresser, an administrator's wandering hands at a conference dinner, and, in a particularly harrowing experience, a long empty hotel hallway stretching darkly between such hands and the safety of my room.

In this chapter we'll consider how living with an uncontrollable body in an often unpredictable and sometimes actively traumatizing world can affect learning. Our young people need both compassion and challenge to learn, but the compassion piece comes first for a reason. This is true for all our students, but particularly for those who live in bodies that are particularly unruly, for reasons of genetic happenstance or because the circumstances and events of their lives have taught them that the world is not a safe space for them. In the previous chapter, I covered the neuroscience of how deeply mental health is grounded in physical health and

---

*Though since it was Halloween weekend, it did allow Jenn and our friend Jasmine to play a rousing game of Fake Blood or Real Blood? in the ER waiting room.

regular, predictable rhythms. In the second of two chapters focused on the body and brain, I will discuss how important it is to establish safety for these more vulnerable students.

We begin at the start of my academic career, in the study of trauma.

WHAT IS TRAUMA?

In graduate school I studied with Lisa Shin, professor of psychology at Tufts University and a leading expert on brain function in posttraumatic stress disorder. Her research involves recruiting people who have experienced trauma to perform attention, memory, or emotion tasks in a brain imaging scanner. She then examines whether there are differences in brain function between people who are faring well and those who are suffering from significant posttraumatic symptoms: panic attacks triggered by reminders of the trauma, nightmares, and/or feeling emotionally numb. Lisa's hope is that by understanding how brain function differs among those who recover well from the trauma versus those who continue to endure psychological difficulties, we can both illuminate pathways to resilience and eventually intervene following trauma, nudging everyone toward greater wellness. Indeed, her work in recent years has moved from studying basic difference in brain function among trauma-exposed people who do and don't suffer from posttraumatic stress disorder (PTSD) to using these brain differences to try to predict who will respond best to which types of treatment. "Not everyone will respond well to every available treatment," she told her educational institution's newspaper in an interview. "Developing a way to predict a patient's response to a given treatment would be beneficial because it would speed up the improvement of symptoms." In my time in Lisa's lab, we worked mostly with veterans with combat-related PTSD, parents of small children who had suffered severe burn injuries and were being treated at a major children's hospital in Boston, and recent amputees.

Beginning with my dissertation, I moved away from the study of trauma and into studying the interaction of emotions and quality of life in a wider range of human experience. But trauma wasn't done with me yet. In the spring of 2011 during my early years as a faculty member, my undergraduate honors student Erin Fitzgerald brought a laptop and a set of emotional stimuli to her study-abroad program in Tokyo. Her intent was to study cross-cultural differences in how Japanese versus American undergraduates succeed in using a technique called cognitive reappraisal to tune down their negative emotions. But that March in 2011 a massive earthquake and tsunami struck Japan, devastating both the country and its nuclear reactors, an event that has been called the world's first "complex megadisaster." Erin, a remarkable human being as well as burgeoning scholar, spent her remaining time in Tokyo scrambling to help the embassy get American citizens from far-flung locations across the country to the airport. Once she was evacuated herself, we retooled our approach and collected data from both American and Japanese citizens working in the embassy—data on their emotion regulation strategies, their symptoms of depression and PTSD, and their stories of living through the initial trauma.

One of the difficulties in understanding PTSD is determining what constitutes a trauma in the first place. In studying this question, we travel the same path we did in our first chapter when we considered how psychologists think about all mental illness. The spectrum that applies to all human experience also applies to the spectrum of stress. Diagnosis of PTSD is like all other diagnoses, a somewhat artificial demarcation between what are adaptive versus maladaptive reactions to an extremely stressful event—there is no bright dividing line between those with PTSD and those without, only judgment calls about how many symptoms in what severities should constitute a "disorder." For the most current version of the *DSM*, there are 636,120 different configurations of symptoms that could qualify you for the diagnosis of PTSD. There are also lots of people who might be suffering but don't quite hit the right combination of these somewhat arbitrary symptom clusters, but that doesn't mean they don't need treatment and care just as much as a person who does meet the criteria. For instance, in my years of conducting diagnostic interviews for PTSD, I frequently interviewed people who were suffering many reexperiencing symptoms (e.g., flashbacks) and hyperarousal symptoms (e.g., panic at triggers) but who failed to meet criteria for the avoidance symptoms (e.g., avoiding thoughts or memories of the trauma) and thus did not receive the label of PTSD.

But PTSD stands alone from all the other diagnoses in the *DSM-5* in that it is the only mental illness that *requires* an external environmental event rather than being solely focused on your internal experience and personal behaviors. You cannot, after all, be traumatized in the absence of having experienced a trauma. But then this opens an additional host of definitional issues. Who gets to decide what constitutes a traumatic versus nontraumatic event? What criteria should we use?

Presumably, trauma is the extreme end of the experience of stress. At the bottom of this stress spectrum is a general arousal or tension that accompanies just being alive and awake and interacting with the world. Then there are those times when the stress kicks up a bit. Midterms and finals (for both students and their instructors), fights with significant others, or when your car is on the fritz at the same time you need a root canal. While unpleasant, these stressful times don't wear down your coping resources, and they are relatively temporary.

Next up is what we might think of as more toxic or chronic forms of stress, when our coping resources are truly being depleted. Nursing a parent through a chronic illness. Or living through a global pandemic. This sort of stress has significant impacts on our relationships, well-being, ability to work. Toxic stress sometimes results in physical manifestations like flare-ups of autoimmune conditions, headaches, nightmares, and—an example from the coronavirus pandemic—unprecedented levels of cracked teeth as people clenched and ground their jaws while asleep. Continuing down the pathway of stress, at the extreme end is trauma, events that are of such intensity that they deserve a category unto themselves—abuse, assault, witnessing someone being killed, living through a natural disaster, or suddenly losing a loved one to a global pandemic.

The experience of trauma is so disruptive that it blows people's usual coping mechanisms out of the water. Clinician and trauma scholar Bessel van der Kolk states that trauma, "by definition, is unbearable and intolerable." The earliest edition of the *DSM* to include PTSD took a firm stance that a traumatic event was something remarkable, described as an event that would be "outside the range of usual human experience and that would be markedly distressing to almost anyone."

Interestingly, the concept of trauma has changed remarkably over the last few decades, a pretty short period of time in the history of a field. Contrast the original *DSM* definition of trauma as being *outside the realm of typical human experience* with the Substance Abuse and Mental Health Services Administration's definition of trauma: "an event, series of events, or set of circumstances that is experienced by an individual as physically or emotionally harmful or threatening and that has lasting adverse effects on the individual's functioning and physical, social, emotional, or spiritual well-being." Using the SAMHSA definition, any set of circumstances perceived as deeply stressful by an individual would constitute a trauma.

Most people suffer psychologically in the immediate aftermath of a traumatic event. But following some weeks or months of disorientation, most people regain or even exceed their previous levels of functioning, whereas for some unlucky folk (probably due to a combination of genetic risk factors and life supports) the aftermath goes on and on, in the configuration of hyperarousal and reexperiencing symptoms we know as PTSD. Nightmares, panic attacks triggered by a car backfiring, an inability to plan for the future. The mind seems unable to move on from this experience. Research on the neurobiology of PTSD probes how the mind becomes stuck on this experience and often focuses on memory. Why is this one memory unable to be woven into the tapestry of other memories, of other events in one's past? Why for some people is it always burning, constantly in the forefront of the mind? Some progress has been made in answering this question. A previous history of trauma makes you more vulnerable to PTSD following subsequent traumas. So do certain patterns of attention and memory. Effective social support is a protective factor. But the answer to this question remains an active and important area of scientific study.

Whether a more stringent definition of trauma or a looser one is used, the unfortunate reality is that a substantial number of our young people have experienced one or more traumatic events, and a significant minority may be suffering from either full PTSD or subthreshold psychological symptoms. Next, we'll consider the effects of trauma on the body, the brain, and young people's capacity for mental health and learning. We will also see what we can do to establish secure classroom environments for them. We'll end the chapter by contemplating some data on resilience following trauma. This last section will bridge us to the next part of this book—the power of beliefs.

BODIES LEARNING TO DISTRUST

As I discussed in the first chapters, fear and anxiety are psychological states that have at their base an ancient neural circuit wired for defense, the activation of which triggers behaviors that will help the organism survive a perceived threat to safety. Trauma is more complex than simply a frightening experience—it often involves massive disruption to all the life rhythms we considered in the previous chapter and can also involve losses that invoke sadness—but it is primarily understood as an event that involves fear. Indeed, one edition of the *DSM* required that the traumatic event evoke intense "fear, helplessness, or horror." In addition to activating behaviors related to flight, the defensive circuit involved in reactions to survival threats also protects the organism by initiating behavioral inhibition. Behavioral inhibition is a fancy term for shutting down (inhibiting) those behaviors required for exploration, play, and social connection—all components of effective learning.

A comprehensive overview of all the impacts on trauma on developing brains and minds is beyond the scope of this book, but let's consult a few reviews and then move on to consider how we might provide the first step toward establishing settings of compassion—making classrooms secure places for students to explore new ideas and develop new skills.

In a remarkable book spanning an entire career, Bessel van der Kolk considers the long-term effects of trauma on the human body and brain. His conclusions are right in the title: *The Body Keeps the Score*. He argues that when someone has been traumatized, the trauma results in a constant orientation toward possible additional threats in both the present and the future, and this vigilance detracts from one's ability to attend to the work of living. "For us humans, it means that as long as the mind is defending itself against invisible assaults," he writes, "our closest bonds are threatened, along with our ability to imagine, plan, play, learn, and pay attention to other people's needs." Fear arrests all other processes and directs attention to the possible threat. This threat orientation occurs at a physical level, the nervous system oriented toward protection rather than exploration. As we'll see in the next chapter, the brain also contains systems oriented toward seeking and exploration that are critical for learning, and it is just these systems that are inhibited under threat.

Trauma, thus, could do the most damage during the early years of a human being's life, when all the social, emotional, and neurodevelopmental tasks of learning require exploration, social connection, and play. Research on trauma in childhood has focused on the concept of adverse childhood experiences (ACEs), which refer not just to incidents of physical, sexual, and emotional abuse but also deeply stressful experiences like acrimonious divorces, poverty, racism, neighborhood violence, and having a parent who is grappling with their own mental health struggles or substance abuse. Greater levels of ACEs have been linked with elevated risk for poor physical and emotional outcomes, including cancer, chronic diseases, and mental health difficulties. A recent assessment of ACEs in a nationally representative sample in the United States identified economic hardship as the most common parent-endorsed ACE, affecting nearly a quarter of the sample. These rates of economic hardships are alarming because low income and poverty are linked with a host of other risk factors and disrupted protective factors.

Dena Simmons is an educational leader and founder of LiberatED, a social-emotional learning collective focused on racial equity. Dena has written extensively about the effects of ACEs on the well-being and education of Black youth in particular. She points out that the effects of trauma are different across individuals. In an essay for the Association for Supervision and Curriculum Development, Dena writes that in third grade she vomited every night from the anxiety of living in an unsafe neighborhood, but she translated this anxiety into overachievement, into a determination to find a way out of her uncertain childhood by controlling what she could. The roads away from trauma can take many paths.

This book focuses on encouraging mental health in learning environments rather than on how to clinically treat students who may have been harmed by their early experiences, whether those experiences be abuse, neglect, or the trauma of living with racism. How can we establish this sense of safety in our classrooms? How can we best serve our traumatized students?

BODIES LEARNING TO TRUST

In the tussles over the degree of protection and care we should provide for our students, no issue has been more ridiculed than safe spaces and trigger warnings. The famed parody website *The Onion* ran a razor-sharp piece on the concept, in which the supposed mother of a supposed daughter who lamented the previous lack of a college safe space reflects, "If this safe space had been here then, my Alexis would have been able to surround herself immediately with people who would have reiterated and reinforced all the views she had when we first sent her to college—but sadly, it wasn't, and she was left to deal with that new, unwanted idea on her own." Safe spaces tend to be parodied as rooms with soft walls and music, puppies and crayons, provided to students who may feel threatened by views or opinions that are different from their own.

While it is a big world and I'm sure one might be able to find instances of such bubble-wrapped rooms, the literal concept of a safe space is something very different. It is meant to be a space where you can relax from the onslaught of the outside world, to put down your masks and personas, and where you can presume that your ideas will be received with goodwill. In other words, a space like the one we all ideally have in our own living rooms. (Consider: for residential college students, our campuses *are* their living rooms.)

As I will discuss at much greater length in a few chapters, play likely evolved so that organisms can practice being physically and emotionally off-balance to prepare for real-life scenarios when they might be quite dangerously off-balance. But young dogs don't playfully wrestle if they lack food, and young birds don't dip and dive for the pure pleasure of doing so if there are predators about. The possibility of play dawns when the situation is safe and there are resources and time to spare—play is something that is immediately dropped from an organism's behavioral repertoire under "harsh" conditions.

Emerging research on safety learning, which I began discussing in chapter 2, further suggests that to set the stage for new learning, we need to help our young people learn new associations about safety in settings where they were previously anxious. For instance, a student who has a panic attack during a class presentation may begin to fear not just presentations but also that particular class, and then any class, and then any material having to do with school. This form of learning is called overgeneralized fear, and it can cascade into paralysis.

There is a difference between learning that a threat is not as scary as originally conceived (for example, imagine being startled by a rustling noise on a dark walk to your friend's house and then realizing it was just a pet cat) and cues that signal true safety (for example, the warm light of your friend's porch light promising companionship and warmth). Both learning the *absence of threat* and the *presence of safety* hold the power to diminish anxiety. The former might reduce anxious responding and avoidance, but the latter might also encourage positive emotions, exploration, and social connection.

Writer John Warner argues provocatively in his regular column for *Inside Higher Ed* that actually, all the fervorous disagreement about safe spaces may boil down to terminology. Using some tweets and op-eds as examples, he demonstrates that the anti-safe-space people (whom I would categorize as pro-challenge) are arguing that safety is synonymous with comfort, that safe spaces mean that students are never challenged or discomforted in their pursuit of knowledge and truth. On the other hand, the pro-safe-space people (whom I would categorize as pro-compassion) see safety as akin to security. In this frame, safe classrooms are analogous to the seatbelts and harnesses that keep you from deathly harm on a rollercoaster so that you can have fun in your challenged arousal. To prepare for getting uncomfortable in tackling difficult material and controversial topics, students need to have some rails in place to let them know that these efforts will not result in harm. Warner quotes professor Cornel West:

I want to be able to engage in the grand calling of a Socratic teacher, which is not to persuade and convince students, but to unsettle and unnerve and maybe even unhouse a few students, so that they experience that wonderful vertigo and dizziness in recognizing at least for a moment that their world view rests on pudding, but then see that they have something to fall back on. It's the shaping and forming of critical sensibility. That, for me, is what the high calling of pedagogy really is.

A crucial part of this argument is that West's students "then see that they have something to fall back on" during this moment of being unhoused and challenged. It is this security that allows students to feel free to be unhoused.

Trust, after all, is the essential part of a trust fall.

We need to help students feel that the classroom is a safe space for exploration. While not all our students will be trauma exposed, we can return to the study of trauma to understand how to establish learning environments of secure exploration— and consult with an expert on the topic.

TRAUMA-AWARE PEDAGOGY

Karen Costa is a faculty development facilitator specializing in online pedagogy and trauma awareness and contributor to the edited book *Trauma-Informed Pedagogies: A Guide for Responding to Crisis and Inequality in Higher Education*. Karen has been active in the world of higher education pedagogy for some time, managing a growing consulting business for faculty members seeking help managing the demands of an academic career and bettering their teaching. When the COVID-19 crisis hit and higher ed abruptly pivoted online and the death toll began its steady climb, Karen's particular expertise at the intersection of online teaching and trauma-aware pedagogy became strikingly relevant.

Luckily, she agreed to an interview. Karen and I began our discussion with definitional issues of trauma. Karen speculated that if you queried one hundred mental health professionals for a definition of trauma, you'd likely get a hundred different answers. There is no blood test for trauma or even a reliable checklist of characteristics. To a large extent, whether an event is traumatic or not is rooted in its impact on the individual experiencing the event. What matters are its effects on the person, not its precise shape in the eye of an outsider.

Karen has most often taught in a community college setting. More of these students than not come from under-resourced backgrounds, and the number of those disclosing experiences that would meet anyone's definition of trauma is haunting. I recall a keynote talk I gave at a conference of accounting teachers at community colleges. A shy but enthusiastic participant approached me and asked how to handle the emotional impact of a student experiencing a drive-by shooting on the way to class—because that had happened just the previous week.

Trauma-aware teaching had been an ongoing discussion in K–12 teaching for a while but rarely talked about in higher education until a global pandemic shut the world down, pivoted much of higher education online, and resulted in widespread disruption and personal loss. Karen reflected that students' experiences of trauma and a need for greater emotional security in the higher ed classroom were both present long before the pandemic, but the crisis provided an opportunity to have those important discussions. "It came at a terrible price, but it opened the conversation," she told me. "I don't want to go back to before, when we pretended everything was okay." Her work with faculty often takes the form of talking about how stress and trauma can affect executive functions (cognitive abilities like focusing attention, holding information in working memory, and organizing one's thoughts), and helping faculty shift classroom policies or teaching practices to meet students where they are. She also helps faculty reframe situations where they might read certain student behaviors as a personal attack or an individual failing, and instead guides them to be open to the idea that it may be stress, trauma, or lack of resources that are driving those behaviors. For instance, a student frequently missing class or assignments might be neither "bored" nor "lazy" but instead is balancing a full-time job with caretaking a family member at home with long COVID. The student might be struggling with their mental health. They might be housing insecure and surfing friends' couches, sleep deprived and not quite sure where their next meal is coming from. These are all possible reasons a student might miss class or assignments that have nothing to do with their dedication to succeeding in the class.

What might a trauma-aware classroom look like? According to a report by the Substance Abuse and Mental Health Administration, the six principles of trauma-informed care are (1) safety, (2) trustworthiness and transparency, (3) peer support, (4) collaboration and mutuality, (5) empowerment and choice, and (6) a careful consideration of cultural, historical, and gender issues. Trauma-aware pedagogy implements these care principles in the classroom setting. Like many other important movements in teaching—such as universal design for learning (structuring classrooms such that they are accessible to students with disabilities without them needing to request accommodations) and culturally responsive teaching (prioritizing students' diverse experiences and the ways that they learn)—creating a trauma-aware classroom has a lot in common with excellent teaching in general. Pick up any recent book on pedagogy and you will see these themes highlighted as good practice: psychological safety, choice, transparency. It just so happens that what is good for trauma-exposed students is good for students in general.

Another trauma-informed pedagogy expert, Alex Shevrin Venet, argues that trauma is a *lens*, not a label—that we don't need to focus so much on the definitional issue, on whether a person has experienced a "qualifying" trauma or not. Rather, we can appreciate that some of our students have endured unendurable experiences, that others come to the classroom from lives of great stress, and that shaping our learning environments around supporting these groups also provides support to everyone sitting in the classroom.

In her powerful book *Equity-Centered Trauma-Informed Education*, Venet calls us to understand that when applying a trauma lens to our instruction, we would be suspect to not also include an equity lens. She defines equity in education as threefold: (1) all students can access high-quality education, and this does not vary by their income level, race, or ethnicity; (2) they are able to engage in intellectually rigorous and challenging academic work; and (3) they do all these things in a system that values them as people. Meeting each of these needs means that all students having access to great school systems is just a start, a bare minimum. To be truly equitable, all students within these systems should be encouraged to take AP courses and extracurriculars. Grading should be scrutinized for bias, and no student should encounter racist, sexist, or homophobic treatment at the hands of peers, faculty, or staff. It's a high bar but a crucial one.

What is an example of how a trauma-aware lens fails if one does not also include an equity lens? Many trauma-informed workshops recommend that high school teachers should consult and collaborate with their school's counselors—missing the fact that one in five students live in a school district with no such counselors, and that institutions lacking school counselors are more likely to be in low-income communities and to serve primarily students of color.

Venet identifies trauma as not the event itself but whether one has the *resources to respond* to challenging events—that resilience looks like having the adequate safety and support systems to endure these markedly stressful occurrences without feeling alone. Powerfully, she argues for change at the levels of practice (developing our lens), pedagogy (transforming our classrooms), and policy (shifting the larger systems).

Another leading light in trauma-aware teaching is Mays Imad, professor of genetics, biotechnology, and bioethics at Pima Community College and founding coordinator of their Teaching and Learning Center. Writing in *Inside Higher Ed*, Imad claims that teachers need to create what she calls "learning sanctuaries" where students and instructors work together to create meaning, purpose, and knowledge. "In such a sanctuary," she writes, "the path to learning is cloaked with radical hospitality and paved with hope and moral imagination. And it is our connections, the community of the classroom and our sense of purpose that will illuminate that path." I love the image of learning sanctuaries, settings where one is safe to explore, to be vulnerable, to take risks.

We did not ask our interviewees in the Student Voices project about trauma, and almost none of them volunteered information about such experiences. But one of the most frequent themes that arose from the data, a conviction that arose from their collective voices, was the importance of feeling safe to take risks in the classroom. Curiously, students repeatedly used the word *relief* to describe the experience of encountering classes marked by this welcome and support.

A FEELING OF RELIEF

Analee is a sophomore studying health sciences in a small liberal arts college, and she talked at length about these feelings of safety in the classroom and their effects on her motivation and learning. She used the word *relief* more than any other student. Interestingly, when we asked about what teaching practices were most associated with this feeling of relief, she talked about instructors who made the effort to get to know her as an individual person, who asked questions of their students and who noticed them. She used an example of a Spanish instructor who complimented her about her shoes in class—just that tiny moment of mutual kinship, a realization of personhood, stuck with her several semesters later.

Analee also appreciated instructors who asked follow-up questions about student understanding and who would check in with her if she fell behind. This relief and degree of comfort wasn't just important for her emotions, however, but also influenced how hard she was willing to work—she would be more likely to dig deeply into the readings, prepare for class discussions, and throw herself into assignments when she felt connected to the instructor.

A first-generation Guyanese student, Analee is under pressure at home as well. She knows that her parents have dedicated much and sacrificed more to make her college studies possible, and she feels a determination to work hard and give back to the next generation. Analee also looks up to her older siblings who finished college and another woman relative who is an entrepreneur—she feels that she has big shoes to fill. Combined with these pressures and the fact that she works a significant number of hours to help contribute to tuition and is a commuter student on a primarily residential campus, she especially appreciates when she enters a class and it is a warm setting rather than a chilly one (this concept of warmth versus chilliness in academic climates will be explored in the "Beliefs" section of the book). Which isn't to say that she feels that classes should be casual. "The best professors and classes have two levels," she told us. "One is a level of seriousness and professionalism and the other is a level where the class feels comfortable and enjoyable. If the class is too serious, it's almost like there is too much pressure, like the energy in the room is just off." The best classes were both serious and welcoming.

Analee was far from the only student who described for us the important role that feeling safe in the classroom played and how it contributed to her learning. One of the most common reflections by our participants when they thought about their best learning experiences was the importance of the instructor seeing students as individuals. When these students reflected on how an instructor makes students feel "seen," they frequently mentioned casual conversations at the start of class or during office hours. These "small talk" conversations are not just small but are building blocks to forming authentic relationships, which students report are a great source of motivation and learning. A chemistry major named Todd reflects similarly that before COVID, he would walk into his honors thesis advisor's office almost every day. "I'd just be like, 'Hey,'" he said. "Not even to always ask a question. If I had twenty minutes to kill, I'll go just chat with her. I loved that." Another student, one who commuted to a primarily residential campus, seemed to realize during our conversation that he feels more of a sense of a social life on campus with his professors than his fellow students. Indeed, office hours held by professors (set-aside time for student questions and conversations) emerged as an extremely frequent theme in the interviews, where students cited these marked-off times as important for reducing confusion about class concepts, ameliorating anxiety about upcoming exams or papers, and getting to know one's professors on this more personal level.

One ramification of this one-on-one connection is that it seems to put students at ease in the classroom, which makes them feel more comfortable and willing to participate. Sometimes this feeling of comfort and relief has more to do with other students in the class than the instructor. One of our interviewees reported that if he could bond with the students in the class, or if he knows them already, then it enhances his learning experience. He intentionally works with his friends to select general education courses so that he can build this safe base intentionally himself. He feels a bit marooned in classes where he wasn't able to use this strategy and doesn't know other students. At the same time, he reflects that if an instructor is careful to build a sense of classroom community and an atmosphere of comfort, it can replicate that same experience he seeks. "If the professor tries to make the class more engaging, or if the professor tries to do what they can to get the students involved," he told us, "then that builds the same relationship between the students as it would if I were to pick a class with some of my friends in it." He purposely creates such atmospheres, but sometimes it isn't necessary—the instructor's intentional welcome organically creates it.

How instructors respond to student contributions also plays a signifi- cant role in feeling cared for and safe to take risks. One student describes comfort or relief when the professor does not intimidate the student. Intimidation may be conveyed by how an instructor responds when a student contributes during class. Several students reported that instruc- tor encouragement and gentleness during exchanges led them to want to participate more, such as this student reflecting on his experiences of professors gently redirecting and affirming him even when he has answered a question incorrectly: "Well, I know I'm wrong," he said, "but at least I know that my perspective wasn't completely rubbish or anything. It makes me more motivated to participate again."

All these student thoughts are highly consistent with extensive re- search on the importance of relationships in education. In their book *Relationship-Rich Education: How Human Connections Drive Success in College*, educators Peter Felten and Leo Lambert share the results from similar qualitative interviews with not just students but also faculty and staff at in- stitutions across the country. They conclude that relationships are not only important for student success but may even be *the most important* factor. Similarly, writing in a review of the research literature on the importance of "humanizing" online instruction, Michelle Pacansky-Brock, Michael Smedshammer, and Kim Vincent-Layton argue that "instructor-student relationships lie at the heart of humanizing, serving as the connective tissue between students, engagement, and rigor." Like Analee told us, if the classroom is a secure setting and the relationship between the instruc- tor and their students is strong, students aren't just happier—they work harder and learn more.

We have considered the role of providing a trauma-aware classroom environment that is marked by empowerment, choice, and cultural sensitivity. One tenet of trauma-aware pedagogy and establishing safety in classrooms deserves a bit of a deeper dive, I think, and it is one that brings us back to the opening anecdote of the chapter: what about triggers that can result in emotional distress, panic, or, as in my experience, even a loss of consciousness?

BODIES, TRIGGERED

There are several ongoing wars between the compassion folks and the challenge folks that never end. They just go into remission, everything blessedly quiet until some new skirmish—usually an op-ed, sometimes a research article—causes everyone to take up arms again and enter back into the fray. Whether it is the debate over banning laptops and smartphones from the classroom or not banning them, whether to demand that students on Zoom turn their cameras on or allow them to leave them off, whether online instruction is equal (or inferior, or superior) to traditional, "face-to-face" instruction, these skirmishes are nothing if not reliable. One of the worst of these battles, in my mind, has to do with whether an instructor should employ so-called trigger warnings or content advisories in their classroom.

Trigger warnings are commonly thought to have evolved out of feminist chat rooms in the 1990s, where women discussing their own histories of trauma wished to give others a heads-up to content that could elicit strong reactions from readers with a similar trauma history, though there is also evidence of the practice in college classrooms going back to the 1980s.

The idea in its original form is that if one is sharing something—a story, an image, a reading, a film—that is likely to trigger a posttraumatic reaction (for example, a panic attack) in someone who has endured a related trauma, you should give a heads-up that you are about to share such a stimulus. The warning is meant to allow the traumatized individual to activate their coping mechanisms, whatever those may look like. For some people, it may be deep breathing exercises. For others, it might look like distracting one's attention during the trigger. For even others, it might be leaving the room. Ideally, a trigger warning allows the person to remain engaged in the learning process without suffering unnecessarily severe side effects through it. Students with PTSD report lower GPAs and are more likely to leave their institution. If the classroom were made more inclusive for them, including through trigger warnings, the hope is that we could nudge these rates in a positive direction.

I first encountered the concept of trigger warnings while still a graduate student, teaching one of my first courses in psychology. It was a course on media portrayals of mental illness and as such, we watched several films in full together. One film my co-instructor and I chose was *Thirteen*, which depicts two middle school students who battle substance abuse, self-harm, and depression. Soon after the class session where we viewed the film, one of our students—a thoughtful, quiet, and engaged senior—visited my office. She gently explained that she struggled with resisting self-harm in her daily life and that the somewhat glamorized, sensational depiction of the behavior in the film had intensified her compulsion to hurt herself. It made it harder for her to resist. She went out of her way to explain that she didn't want us to not show the film or ones like it in the future—she just would have appreciated a heads-up that these scenes would be shown in class so that she could be mentally prepared to engage in the coping strategies she had learned in years of therapy. In other words, she asked for a trigger warning. This was the first time I had heard the term. Reflecting back on the fact that this was early graduate school and she was a senior, I realize that only a few years of life separated us. I was grateful for the educational moment.

Historian, educational developer, and author of an upcoming book on pedagogical kindness Cate Denial writes vividly of her personal experience with being triggered. Reading the symptoms of panic she describes in the essay posted on her website is like reading a firsthand account from my own mind—the bodily revolt, the wooliness of dissociation, the hypervigilance. But worsening all this tumult of a prototypical panic are her flashbacks, which she writes "are often terrifying because of the loss of self involved, the realization that a thing feels real and yet isn't, the re-experiencing of pain." A friend of mine showed a rape scene in a psychology class without a trigger warning and a student lost consciousness and vomited, presumably a vasovagal incident much like my own that opened this chapter. While I've never had such an incident in class as a student, I have come to consciousness more than once on the floor covered in my own sick, and I can tell you that it is an experience that would definitely interfere with me learning the class material that day.

Many scholars have objected to trigger warnings based on the argument that I myself marshaled in our first two chapters—that avoidance of anxiety-provoking situations is detrimental to the resolution of the anxious response. Psychologist Richard McNally of Harvard University* writes in the *New York Times* that trigger warnings work against effective therapy for PTSD because they encourage avoidance of reminders of trauma. In a viral article in *The Atlantic* that morphed into a bestselling book, psychologist Jonathan Haidt and attorney Greg Lukianoff warn of increasing demands from college students to be protected from discomforting or offensive material in courses, speakers, and readings. They write that trigger warnings, along with related concepts like microaggressions (very small acts of racism, sexism, or homophobia that despite their modest nature accumulate into harm), "[presume] an extraordinary fragility of the collegiate psyche, and therefore [elevate] the goal of protecting students from psychological harm." Along with encouraging avoidance and thus potentially forestalling the resolution of anxiety, Haidt and Lukianoff fear that such prioritizing of psychological well-being enforces what they call a vindictive protectiveness, a campus culture where everyone lives in fear of offending others.

Much like John Warner wondered if most people would agree on safety if we instead called it security, what has always struck me about the trigger warning debate is that a lot of the rancor boils down to a matter of semantics. So many anti-trigger warning arguments I have read eventually have a paragraph of what we should do instead of trigger warnings—and these alternatives sound exactly like trigger warnings to me. For instance, a recent skirmish in the battle occurred when professors Amna Khalid and

---

*Full disclosure: Rich is my academic grandfather—the doctoral advisor of my doctoral advisor, and a warm and engaging scholar.

Jeffrey Aaron Snyder published an essay in the *Chronicle of Higher Education* titled "The Data Is In—Trigger Warnings Don't Work." They review the research literature on the topic and find no experimental evidence that use of trigger warnings improves mental health or levels of distress, for those with or without trauma histories. But then they go on to say that they are no fans of the "shock and awe" practice of "springing distressing content" on students with no warning. Snyder shares the specific example of viewing Spike Lee's *Do the Right Thing* in class but first letting his students know that the film will depict graphic neighborhood violence and grapple frankly with issues of race and racism. To me, this is a trigger warning and consistent with my own practices in the classroom since that early experience in graduate school.

To further understand the definitional issues at play here, I reached out to sociologist and criminologist Alison Cares, who teaches and researches at the University of Central Florida. She has committed most of her career to ending violence against women, first in community outreach and education at a sexual assault and domestic violence services agency, and then as a researcher. Among her many research projects, she has spent the last few years investigating faculty use of trigger warnings and how they are perceived by students.

Alison agrees with me about the definitional murkiness that surrounds the trigger warning debate. Based on her collaborative work on trigger warnings in the classroom, she feels that what a lot of faculty are doing has more in common with a "content advisory" approach—avoiding that shock and awe effect rather than thinking explicitly about trauma-exposed students in the classroom.

But it is still the trauma-exposed students who might be served best by the heads-up. Alison references a major study in which the conclusion was that not many students experienced distress in the classroom following exposure to graphic material. But when you scrutinize the figures and tables in the paper, they reveal that something like one in five students do experience significant distress. This is certainly good news for most of the class, and consistent with the interpretation that not that many students are distressed—but is still bad news for a substantial minority of students. It may look like a small effect in the aggregate, but for those students whom it affects, it can feel like anything but a small thing. Alison also notes that the major opinion essay by Richard McNally that I discussed earlier claimed that if students required trigger warnings, they might need PTSD treatment. She is mystified by this argument—even if we accept that statement as true, don't students needing PTSD treatment still deserve a college education? "I will say this," Alison told me. "I find it completely ironic that the people who criticize trigger warnings and label students as snowflakes for needing them are often the same people who make their living through the written word or the spoken word." She scoffed. "C'mon. You know that words matter."

I note that in reading the research literature on trigger warnings, the introductions to all these articles follow the same path: Trigger warnings evolved out of feminist chat rooms and were then extended to the classroom. Students requested more and more trigger warnings and demanded the ability to opt out of assignments or lessons that included triggering material. But *also* over and over in these academic articles, these articles cite Jonathan Haidt and Greg Lukianoff's op-ed in *The Atlantic* as evidence for the claim that students have been demanding more and more trigger warnings and the freedom to skip assignments. This op-ed does contain anecdotes of such cases but no scientific data. No statistics, no prevalence rates, no research. The piece does not purport to be anything but a persuasive essay with a set agenda. Alison agrees and notes that data on the actual prevalence of trigger warning use and whether these warnings are accompanied by such accommodations is sorely lacking—and part of the impetus for her own research on the topic.

Most of the time, Alison uses trigger warnings in her own courses on crime, domestic violence, and assault (though she views her trigger warnings more as content advisories), but it is rare that she offers individual accommodations for academic assignments or readings. She told me the story of an exception, with a student we will call Beth. Alison was teaching a course on crime victims with a unit on campus sexual assault. Beth had been sexually assaulted as a first-year student. Now a senior graduating among the top of her class, she had worked extensively with a therapist in the intervening years and was managing the psychological aftermath of the assault quite well.

To open the unit on campus sexual assault, Alison assigned students a memoir to read that included a first-person narration of a rape. Beth made a go of reading it. She started having trouble sleeping. Eating. Concentrating on work. She reengaged with her therapist and worked on strategies to get through the assignment, like chunk-reading it in small bits and engaging in relaxation before reading sessions. But nothing was working, and they were past the add-drop deadline for the course. Alison worked with Beth to modify the assignment so that she wouldn't have to read the first-person narrative account of a rape that bore so many similarities to her own trauma still simmering right below the surface of her mind.

Alison felt comfortable making this accommodation not just because Beth had made every attempt to engage with the material, but also because the learning goal for the reading was entirely irrelevant for Beth. Alison assigns that work so that students can truly appreciate how devastatingly a sexual assault can impact someone. Many of Alison's students very much need to learn this lesson. They come to the study of criminology loaded up on episodes of *CSI* and *Law and Order*, eager to catch serial killers and fight crime. These students benefit from taking a step back and humanizing the people involved. Dramatized, detailed firsthand accounts often work well for these students to achieve this learning goal. But clearly that was a lesson that Beth had already learned, down to her very cells, at the hands of her assailant. She didn't need to relearn it in SOC214 on Monday mornings at eighty-thirty.

Since then, Alison has moved toward building lots of choices into her syllabus so that students can guide their experience in the course. This allows those students who want to avoid first-person accounts of assault, for instance, to choose readings more grounded in statistics and research. It also is consistent with many other good pedagogical approaches aimed at maximizing student autonomy in their educational experiences, many of which we will cover in chapter 6. Alison feels that a differentiation of assignments also allows students to make choices about how they demonstrate their learning to her.

This flexibility in assignments and readings, tailoring the course to learning goals that may differ for individual students, is also consistent with research on universal design for learning and also many diversity, equity, and inclusion initiatives. It is great stuff. But it is also much more work for faculty, who are already overburdened and overworked and underpaid—and those are the ones in secure positions. How much more difficult will this personalization and flexibility be for the contingent faculty who currently make up the bulk of instructors on campuses? "For me," Alison said, "fairness is huge, particularly in righting systemic wrongs and getting as close to fairness as I can." She took a moment, and even over Zoom I could see the fatigue wash over her. "But it tires me out. I'm so tired right now." Alison is far from the only faculty member expressing these sentiments to me in the wake of the early coronavirus pandemic years—and faculty burnout can harm both faculty and the students they serve.

Alison's struggles to prioritize her own physical and mental health with the time and energy demands of pursuing quality, equitable teaching highlight one of the central tensions with the advice in this book—everything that leads to good education and to shoring up the mental health of our young people is individualized, is effortful, and takes an enormous investment of resources. In the conclusion of the book, we'll consider how important it is for these issues to be addressed at the administrative and societal level rather than the individual one. But in the meantime, what do we do about the paradox here? To be a responsive, creative, engaged educator or parent, you can't also be burnt out, frazzled, and tired . . . but being a responsive, creative, engaged educator or parent in our current system creates conditions where that is the inevitable outcome.

Lucky for us, faculty burnout is a third expertise of our trauma-aware pedagogy expert Karen Costa.

BURNOUT

I served as interim director of the Center for Teaching Excellence on my campus during the initial higher-ed pivot to online teaching and learning and the disrupted pandemic year to follow. I directly observed the effects on our faculty of the demands to abruptly learn to teach online for the first time, to shift courses from semester to terms, to then learn how to teach in a hybrid format (half the students on Zoom and half in the classroom, distanced, masked), and to then manage how to accommodate students used to the flexibility of Zoom once we returned to face-to-face instruction. There was an initial surge of energy and determination, and faculty put every ounce of their shoulders against the boulder of the semester. Faculty and staff on college campuses were desperate to teach the best they could and to reach as many students as possible. But there was a brush fire of burnout being lit, and queasy, I watched it spread. During one teaching center event, one of our most caring and dedicated faculty members said to me, "I have given up. I am just phoning it in until the end of the semester." She was the last person on campus I ever thought would utter those words.

I sketched out the problem for Karen quickly, knowing from previous conversations that she was more than aware of these issues, that she was observing the same problems.

Karen: "Yes. Yes! So, I have thoughts on that."

Me: "Okay. Good. Tell me. Solve it."

Karen used to work in enrollment management (the office on many campuses that handles student recruitment and retention in all its forms), so she knows the system. She knows that presidents and provosts and leaders are poring desperately over numbers, numbers, numbers—getting reports daily, hourly, on how many students are coming to campus the following year. "But if we're burning faculty out," she said, "then we're destroying ourselves. We are cutting away at the foundation of what we know is our greatest asset." This argument is supported by all the literature we have reviewed thus far, and much of what we will cover in the pages to follow. Administrators and op-ed writers will claim that cutting back on faculty time and resources is inevitable for budgetary reasons. But Karen points out that other priorities seem to get funded, like half-million-dollar contracts with surveillance proctoring companies here, twelve associate dean salaries there, a new athletic building over there. Better faculty funding, whether it be time relief for existing faculty or more faculty positions to ease the burden on everyone and convert more part-time instructors to supported full-time positions, always seems to be last in line at the budget buffet.

Karen also points out that not everyone will be equally affected by burnout, especially when times get tough. Our degree of social support, our finances, our genes, our personality, our upbringing, our privilege, our geography, our physical and mental health—all these factors play into our ability to process ongoing stressors and demands. She uses the metaphor of a funnel to describe how some people have better support than others. Some of us get a small funnel (few resources) and some of us get a really big funnel (many resources). "The pandemic is just this flood of water," she said. "If you've got a big ole funnel, sure, it's going to overflow, but it is going to just trickle over the edges. If you've got a tiny funnel, it is going to be a deluge." The metaphor here is different—funnels versus fabrics—but Karen's observations are entirely in line with Wai Kai Hou's drive to thrive theory. Those with greater, more elaborate supports are going to fare better than those with thinner, fewer ones.

Before we end this exploration of the effects of stress and trauma on bodies, mental health, and learning, I'd like to consider one more topic, and it is one that is increasingly controversial in my intellectual circles: resiliency.

COMPLICATING THE MATTER: RESILIENCY FOLLOWING TRAUMA IS THE MOST COMMON EXPERIENCE

The word *resilience* has become a bit of a dirty word in certain conversations. For some, it has become associated with the idea that we should shame people for struggling and chide them to pull themselves up by their bootstraps and just get over their trauma already. It has also become associated with the American predilection for stories of adversity overcome—and the preference to swap those stories on social media rather than create systems and supports to make true flourishing and recovering from stress easier.*

I am sympathetic to all these critiques.

---

*A prototypical example might be a supposedly heartwarming story of a line cook with cancer who is out of sick time. The whole restaurant of workers pools their vacation time to allow him to take time off for treatment. Rather than be encouraged by the empathy, shouldn't we be horrified by a system that doesn't allow a worker to treat his cancer without losing his job?

But at the same time, the data are very clear that, even following something as terrible as a traumatic event, individual responses of flexible adaptiveness and recovery are more common than is ongoing suffering. I think it is important to share this message not just for intellectual accuracy, painting the truest portrait of what is occurring in people's lives, but also because narratives can shape reality, and as we will see in the next two chapters, beliefs matter. Words create worlds.

In fact, the commonness of resiliency following trauma foiled my original dissertation plans. As I approached the time for me to propose a topic, my doctoral advisor, Lisa Shin, connected me with a collaborator of hers, Scott Rauch of Massachusetts General Hospital. In addition to understanding what is happening at the level of the brain for trauma-exposed people who both do and don't have PTSD, and which treatments might work best for which people, another lynchpin in our knowledge of the disorder is to understand who is at greater or less risk of PTSD when confronted with a trauma.

The trouble with answering this research question about who is at greater or less risk of PTSD is that it is nearly impossible to predict who will soon suffer a trauma. There have been some innovative designs studying high-risk populations like firefighters or soldiers going into combat, but these samples probably have psychological traits that differ from people who don't seek out such high-adrenaline, dangerous careers. Scott had some ongoing collaborations with Spaulding Rehabilitation Hospital in Boston, and many of the patients there were recovering from surgical amputations. It occurred to him that losing a part of your body was likely a traumatic experience, and if so, studying this population might open a unique window into traumatic processes, allowing us to study people both before and after the trauma. As surgical amputations occur secondary to a variety of experiences—cancer, diabetes, blunt injuries—it isn't an experience that typically relates to people's life choices in the same way that entering the military does. For whatever reason, no one had really explored the question of whether people undergoing surgical amputation found the experience to be traumatic. Scott and Lisa thought this would make a great dissertation for a graduate student—first evaluating whether the experience resulted in significant rates of PTSD among patients, and if it did, conducting a pre- and post-assessment of cognitive, emotional, and neurological functioning among those who did and didn't go on to suffer PTSD after the amputation.

I agreed that it sounded like a great dissertation topic, and so I spent a year or two of my life by the bedsides of patients who had recently lost their toes, their arms, or their legs. After some training in conducting diagnostic clinical interviews to match symptoms with *DSM*-IV diagnoses, I interviewed patients at length about their experiences. We talked about their medical problems, their feelings of depression and anxiety, and their flashbacks and their nightmares.

Except that very few of them were having any of these symptoms. I diagnosed only a single case of PTSD in the surgical patients I interviewed. Distress was low, nightmares were rare, and patients talked at length about gratitude toward their treating physicians and hopes of greater function or reduced need for medical care now that the troublesome body part had been removed. Some even discussed feeling a sense of realignment of life priorities and a deep happiness to be alive. While this muddled my entire dissertation plan, it was also quite a beautiful experience to talk with these patients about their insights into their life journeys. It was also hard to be upset about people faring well after a difficult experience.*

The entire research career of a highly respected scholar underscores the idea that resiliency is the most common response following trauma. Psychologist George Bonanno has studied people following their harrowing life experiences for decades. He translates these decades of scientific investigations for a popular audience in his compelling and immensely readable book *The End of Trauma*. He has studied spouses enduring bereavement, soldiers encountering wartime atrocities, and people working in the World Trade Center on September 11, 2001. He uses sophisticated statistics to map trajectories of symptoms over time, and again and again, across these disparate traumas, he finds the same patterns. Approximately two-thirds of people are faring just fine after a traumatic event, smaller

---

*I should note that a (possibly fatal) flaw of this study is that a substantial number of patients we approached for interviews declined to participate. It could be that only the well agreed to participate.

numbers were having symptoms before the trauma and continue to do so afterward, and another small group suffer initially but then gradually recover. The account that most people expect and which is most often portrayed in the media—someone faring well and then suffering immediately and not recovering—is actually the least common outcome.

The body *does* keep the score, as does the brain that is part of and manages that body. But it does so in continuous, networked, interactive ways. We can never erase our traumatic histories, for they are woven into our experiences and expectations of the world. But psychological trauma is not the blunt force injury of the word's origins, an injury from which one can never recover. Instead, as I discussed in the last chapter, new experiences constantly update the predictions our brains make, and our brains are also exquisitely sensitive to context. There is great hope for recovery from trauma and for establishing long-term resilience.

In the 2009 book *The Empire of Trauma*, two French anthropologists enter into a deep study of what they see as a rapid shift in cultural ideas about trauma and posttraumatic symptoms over a mere several decades. They see the concept as having moved out of the realm of clinical psychiatry and into the realm of everyday speech and meaning making. They believe that this new concept of trauma is not the same idea as it was in the beginning. Trauma is no longer conceived as a harrowing experience outside the realm of typical human experience but rather one way that human beings (at least in Western cultures) make sense of the past. "Both misfortune and violence are understood to be phenomena that leave traces of the past in the present," they write, "and that may even require immediate treatment in order to ensure they do not burden the future." This reconceptualization and broadening of the concept of trauma, they find, is rooted in greater humanitarian impulses and a reckoning with the past with the aim of social justice. They feel that this is largely a laudatory development, one focused on more equitable treatment and greater care for individual human beings.

I agree. At the same time, I believe that we need to be careful about word choice and what our choice of framing says about what we expect for human resiliency, for our inherent strength, and for the challenges we should and shouldn't take on. Drawing on his own work, as well as decades of work by other scholars in clinical psychology, psychiatry, and affective science, Bonanno finds that people who fare well after stress and trauma are marked by what he calls *the flexibility mindset*. This mindset is characterized by three interrelated beliefs: optimism about the future, confidence in one's ability to cope, and a willingness to think about threat as a challenge. "The individual beliefs that contribute to the mindset feed into each other," he writes, "and by doing so they synergistically expand and reinforce the broader conviction that we will be able to adapt ourselves to the challenges at hand and do whatever is necessary to move forward." Expanding the concept of trauma to encompass much more ordinary experiences of stress could increase pessimism about coping rather than optimism, decrease one's estimation of coping potential, and freeze action. Recall that anxiety is based primarily on a dual perception—that there are imminent threats, and that one won't have the ability to cope. It is only by dialing down our perception of threat and dialing up our estimation of our coping ability that we stand a chance of reducing anxiety.

I'm particularly wary when I see the concept of trauma stretched to include truly daily, typical events. For instance, I have seen in my own circles the label *trauma* applied to having to take exams worth a lot of points in a class. Whole pockets of TikTok now exist where people without clinical training diagnose everyday behaviors like emotional avoidance or trouble sleeping as evidence of trauma. In response, many joke TikToks bemoan things like, "Do I have a personality or am I just a series of trauma responses?" It seems like a social-media-era rekindling of a dangerous era in the 1980s and 1990s when a few popular books encouraged people to look to commonplace behaviors like irritability or trouble paying attention as evidence of repressed memories of abuse—a dark time both for those with histories of abuse and for psychologically vulnerable people looking for an explanation for everyday unhappiness.

I ask Karen about these issues. I tell her that I attended a wonderful webinar by someone we both admire in the field. I agreed with so much of what the presenter was sharing, until she got to this slide title: "How Do We Teach the Lonely, the Fearful, the Broken?" I recoiled from the title, both because it seemed to contradict the empowerment that marks so much of the trauma-aware approach and because I could never see my students in that light, no matter what they had endured.

Karen agreed. "Look," she said, "we contain multitudes." All our students, ourselves, and our shared communities bring both strengths and challenges to the classroom. But at the same time, she believes that putting resilience before the trauma and insisting that the person rise to some external definition of challenge has the potential to retraumatize them. She thinks instructors instead need to respect student autonomy and communicate to them, "I think you're amazing. I think you are so smart, and so strong. Let's do this together. I am here to support you." And she thinks it is important that instructors do so in an academic way, not a clinical one. That teachers respect the boundary between instructor and clinician.

Uniting so many of the themes of this chapter and also tying it into last chapter's consideration of our body budgets and our social fabrics, Karen pointed out that true resiliency is not some internal powder keg of coping capacity but rather a natural outgrowth of how much support you have, how extensive your resources are. "We don't build resilience," she said. "We get correct care and support, and resilience blooms all on its own." The only road to effective challenge is compassion.

CONCLUSION

Trauma is real, all too common, and our bodies keep the score. Students come to us having suffered assaults on their bodies and minds. Even in atmospheres of health and safety one's body can rebel. But we can teach our bodies a competing set of lessons about safety and about strength, embracing the power of both inhibitory learning and safety learning. As parents and educators of young people, it is vital that we help establish learning environments that encourage students to feel secure enough to take risks.

We who teach don't need to diagnose our students or know their personal histories to provide a safe climate for learning in our classrooms. We need instead to listen to follow the principles of trauma-aware pedagogy, which encourages us to offer empowerment and choice in a setting of security and grounding. Doing so supports both those with trauma histories and those without.

At the same time, the narratives we choose and the lenses with which we view our students and their capabilities also matter quite a lot. In fact, our beliefs can radically shape our approach to the world. While I was finishing up this book manuscript, a beloved friend suffered a sudden health crisis that landed him unresponsive in intensive care. Following a particularly bad turn, I spent most of a few days crying. In between these days I woke in the middle of the night only to cry some more. One Friday in the middle of this, I worked on this manuscript all day. Feeling nauseated, my bleary blurry eyes tracking these words, I couldn't catch my breath. It felt like a giant monster was standing on my chest.

Around 4 p.m. I got a promising text from the phone tree that was providing me with updates. It was a minor upswing, no out-of-the-woods message. But a single line of text delivered digitally, some ten or fifteen words, entirely changed both the interior of my body and my emotional landscape. My stomach settled. The monster stepped off my chest, and I could breathe again.

What strange and remarkable creatures we human beings are, that a series of words can affect a tiny change with such outsize results on our physical and emotional experience of the world. Beliefs matter. Narratives shape realities.

Let's consider how compassionate challenge works at the level of beliefs, specifically through the lens of motivation.

PART THREE

BELIEFS

CHAPTER FIVE

SEEKING ONESELF—ENERGY AND VALUE

M ANY PEOPLE SPEND their whole lives seeking purpose, something to animate their days with meaning and fulfillment. Philanthropist Neda DeMayo found hers at ten years old. At this tender age she saw a documentary on television about the abuse of wild horses, and with a lump in her throat and feet grounded to the spot, she pledged to her mother that someday she would do something to protect these beautiful beasts. It took her several decades of exploration and learning before she opened an American wild horse sanctuary and wild horse preservation campaign called Return to Freedom, but open it she did. She claims that to fulfill one's dreams, one needs to have "passion, followed by correct action." You need to be energized, and then see this desire through with planned steps toward a goal. I love this phrase for its beauty but also for how perfectly it maps onto how psychologists think about motivation—the primary focus of this "Beliefs" section of the book. To support youth mental health, we need to create learning environments that are motivating, that summon both energy and the determination to succeed.

In the next two chapters, I will break motivation down into two elements: energy and direction. In this first chapter of the "Beliefs" section, we'll consider how motivation yields *energy*, and the sorts of learning environments that will engender this aspect of motivation. How do we help our young people find their passions, their vocation? In the next chapter we'll take a closer look at *direction*—asking the question, how can we intentionally harness that energy and point it at valued goals? How can we enact Neda's "correct action"?

We will see that fostering motivation will rely first on youth believing that their goals have true value and purpose, and that they can expect success (yielding energy), and second on satisfying certain psychological needs (autonomy, competence, and belongingness; yielding direction). Shifting beliefs relevant to these needs (What I am doing has meaning; my actions will have an effect; I have control; I have skills; I belong) empowers one to engage in behaviors that may previously have been too intimidating.

THE SEEKING SYSTEM: MOTIVATION

Motivation is a slippery concept, one of those terms that means different things in different situations. We use this same word for the root cause of someone's behavior ("What was her motivation?"), a trait-like explanation for why two people in seemingly similar situations achieve very different things ("He has so much motivation!"), and a state-like descriptor of how our own energy and focus seem to vary over time ("I just need to get motivated").

But what all these meanings have in common, and what the science of motivation indicates, is that motivation comprises two essential elements mentioned earlier: *energy* and *direction*. Motivation spurs a certain arousal, pointed at a certain path. One of the first appearances of motivation in the written record is from the Roman scholar Marcus Tullius Cicero in 45 BCE, where he discusses *motus animi*, or "the stirring of the soul." Motivation moves us, stirs us, sets us into action.

We also usually talk about motivation as a future-focused state of being. It summons the energy to do what we have yet to do. Even the "What was her motivation?" aspect involves a bit of time travel—we mentally dial back to before the behavior in question occurred and ask what drove that choice, that action, that decision. In this way, motivation has a lot in common with our friend anxiety. Both anxiety and motivation fix the future in mind and try to anticipate what may happen in those murky waters ahead. Both result in a burst of energy, a preparation for action.

What makes up this energy? For both anxiety and motivation, energy is provided by the same interacting systems that comprise the body budget I discussed in chapter 3. The fast-moving energy is provided by activation of our sympathetic nervous system, which speeds up our heart and our breathing, and releases glucose to the muscles for movement. Our bodies getting ready for goal-directed motivated action look a lot like our bodies getting ready to flee—the differences are more of scale than nature. Slower, lasting shifts in energy are the result of more gradual changes in hormonal function.

To underscore how the physiological systems underlying both anxiety and motivation are related, let's consider a set of research findings that was initially puzzling to researchers. You may have heard of the hormone cortisol, which has been pigeonholed by popular science accounts as an evil "stress hormone." And for sure, cortisol plays a strong role in the stress response. But it also governs a lot of other important bodily functions. It peaks in the body soon after waking in the morning and then drops slowly but steadily throughout the day, presumably helping with the whole leaping-out-of-bed-to-greet-the-day process. Given its role in the stress response, early research hypothesized and found a link between higher waking cortisol and risk for mental health problems like depression and anxiety. But this tidy finding was complicated by the fact that *other* studies started piling up that showed a link between *lower* waking cortisol and poor mental health. What could explain these disparate results?

A clue might be found by examining the differences between work-days and weekend days. People in general tend to have higher waking cortisol on workdays than on weekends, likely because rising early and greeting a day of work requires a certain degree of arousal, but also because working days may involve more stress and worry. Indeed, morning cortisol levels seem to correlate positively with stress and worry—but only on working days. Waking cortisol may track both how efficiently your body gets you ready to greet the day *and* the degree to which you are anticipating stressors that same day. You can imagine that the former predicts good emotional functioning, and the latter the opposite. It may also be that over time, people who repeatedly have unusually intense morning cortisol bursts related to anticipated stressors begin to experience a blunting of this same response, and that may also be why some studies find lower waking cortisol associated with depression. It's as though your body gives up trying to prepare for yet *another* stressful day. This hypothesis might explain why we sometimes observe links between poor mental health and high morning cortisol response, and sometimes the opposite.

This whole complex picture also tells us something about motivation, anxiety, and even the phenomena of burnout (where people aren't quite depressed but after a long period of intense motivated activity seem to . . . well, burn out). We use the same physiological systems to get jazzed up for a challenge we are excited for, to drag ourselves out of bed for a job that is stressful, and to anxiously ruminate about the future. But even if we love the work of our days and are excited to greet them, revving these physiological systems over and over, day after day, may deplete our body budget in much the same way as low-simmering anxiety can. We need to be sure we balance motivated work with replenishing our body budget with all the activities discussed in the chapter on embodied mental health—sleep, exercise, time with loved ones, time in nature, and time to daydream. This delicate balance of arousal—enough to become stirred, to be motivated, but not so much that one tips into panic (in the short term) or burns out (in the long term)—is the first of several times in this "Beliefs" section that we'll consider motivation as a tightrope of sorts.

Despite these similarities in future orientation and underlying physiology, there are important differences between motivation and anxiety. Anxiety results in a burst of arousal that is uncontrolled, deeply unpleasant, and leaves the person feeling like they cannot cope. In contrast, motivation results in a burst of arousal that is directed toward present actions that can bring about a desired future. In an interview about her book *Future Tense: Why Anxiety Is Good for You (Even Though It Feels Bad)*, psychologist and professor Tracy Dennis-Tiwary notes these similarities. "Hope, ambition, and drive live in that space between the present and the uncertain future," she says. "So, when we engage with our anxiety, we can also leverage all the possibilities of the future." If we can shift our belief from "*I am facing threat, and unable to cope*" to "*I am facing challenge, but have the resources to* *cope*," we may be able to direct this powerful energy away from anxiety and into motivation.*

While all motivation is a future-focused state of being comprising energy and direction, motivation researchers commonly think a bit differently about motivation sourced from without (rewards and punishments) and from within (enjoyment and desires).

ANTICIPATORY EUPHORIA: INTRINSIC MOTIVATION

For a while in the middle of the twentieth century, psychologists were fixated on studying outward human behavior and how people responded to rewards and punishments. Dubbed behaviorism, the movement was based on findings by famous thinkers and researchers you may have heard of, like Ivan Pavlov and B. F. Skinner with their drooling dogs and cats in boxes.** Rewards and punishments and their impact on behavior was going to be the grand theory that could explain all human motivation and behavior.

But research findings that didn't fit the program started piling up. Famously, tiny monkeys separated from their mothers took food from one set of wire mothers but then cozied up to a wire mother covered in soft cloth, even though she offered no food rewards. Mice would walk across electrified grids (surely, a punishment) to reach novel puzzles to solve (suggesting there was something inherently rewarding about solving puzzles that offered no tangible rewards). Worse, a long series of studies indicated that rewarding people for certain tasks actually made them perform *worse*—they worked less hard for less long if they got a prize for doing so.

Collectively, this research led scholars in the latter half of the twentieth century to suggest that yes, people respond to rewards and punishments in certain settings in certain ways. This traditional, easy-to-understand form of motivation came to be known as *extrinsic* motivation. On the other

---

*Hopefully, by this point, you know that I would argue that the best way to shift these beliefs is not to ask folks to chant mantras to themselves about coping potential but to actually provide people with supportive resources.

**Not the dead cat; that's physics. These cats got treats.

hand, *intrinsic* motivation refers to the human tendency to spontaneously "seek out novelty and challenges, to extend and exercise one's capacity, to explore, and to learn." Sometimes, the motivation seems entirely internal.

From an evolutionary perspective, it makes sense to have an organism that responds to reward and punishment. One should approach locations and situations where one found food and shelter and an appealing mate; and one should avoid locations and situations where one previously found contaminants or predators. But if that's all you ever did, you wouldn't have the chance to discover new sources of food, novel mates, and innovative solutions to old problems. For that you would need to explore, to mess about in your environment and travel a little further from home. To seek. To pursue activities for the sake of pursuing them. Because they're fun, and because you are interested.

Though human intrinsic motivation can be extraordinarily complex, it is underpinned by some pretty ancient systems that animate both exploration and play. We are going to consider play in a few chapters, but for now let's linger on this exploration system, what renowned neuroscientist Jaak Panksepp and psychoanalyst Lucy Biven have called the *seeking system*. This system is not the same one that governs extrinsic motivation and consummatory pleasure, which focus on satisfying biological drives like hunger, sex, and sleep. In contrast, the seeking system encourages organisms to increase drives rather than to satiate them, to pursue and to explore, and it does so by amplifying eagerness (energy) and something Panksepp and Biven call "anticipatory euphoria." To conceptualize this anticipatory euphoria, think of fantasizing about adventures that await you on a vacation to a novel locale, salivating as you page through a new cookbook, the blush of anticipation before meeting with a potential lover—each of these embers of eagerness push us to seek out new situations beneficial for our survival and reproduction, much like the fear system drives us away from situations that pose dangers to our survival.

Note that here, too, anxiety is bundled with motivation—both are related to moving toward and away from situations in the world in order to proactively survive and thrive within it. Panksepp and Biven warn that a chronically underactive, underengaged seeking system can lead to depression. This seeking system has much in common with what other researchers have called a "behavioral activating system" within the body and brain, or more simply, approach motivation.

We perceive the sudden drying up of motivation, of anticipatory euphoria, as sometimes monstrous. In the acclaimed film *Everything Everywhere All at Once*, the villain stalking the multiverse has an origin story grounded in the effects of seeing every possibility in the world at once—for if there is nothing to anticipate, to wonder about, to hope for, what purpose is there to living? She becomes a monster who destroys everything in her path.

In addition, monsters who suck out our vitality are common in fantastical lore. Consider vampires, who literally leach the lifeblood from our bodies, leaving us husks or shells. Or the creature in Stephen King's novella *The Library Policeman*, who survived by feeding off the fears of children. In these stories, our vital energy is sapped, and we are left weak and disconnected from our full selves.

On the flip side, you can feel this eagerness, this anticipatory euphoria, when you feel a burst of energy related to intrinsic motivation. Sarah Waters writes beautifully of this sensation in her novel *The Paying Guests* as her protagonist Frances becomes energized on her walks through London, an activity that she is intrinsically motivated to pursue: "She seemed, as she made them, to become porous, to soak in detail after detail; or else, like a battery to become charged. Yes, that was it, she thought, as she turned a corner: it wasn't a liquid creeping, it was a tingle, something electric, something produced as if by the friction of her shoes against the streets. She was at her truest, it seemed to her, in these tingling moments." That the character experiences these bursts of eager euphoria while exerting her body outdoors should be no surprise to us after the discussion in chapter 3 on embodied mental health.

These bursts of motivation are also often social, occurring kinetically in moments between more than one person. Later in the same book, Sarah Waters writes of a moment in which her two characters realize they are attracted to one another. An energy is exchanged, and their futures align: "They smiled at each other across the table, and some sort of shift occurred between them. There was a quickening, a livening—Frances could think of nothing to compare it to save some culinary process. It was like the white of an egg growing pearly in hot water, a milk sauce thickening in the pan. It was as subtle yet as tangible as that." This moment has an obvious sexual tension, but I find the culinary metaphor so apt for so many social interactions, including larger groups. Anyone who teaches or coaches or speaks to audiences for a living has had the experience of combining the same ingredients and sometimes everything gelling just so—and sometimes, equally mysteriously, falling completely flat. Energy amplification in larger, platonic groups is a well-known phenomenon. Indeed, I spent much of my second book, *Hivemind*, considering how shared vocalizations, movements, emotions, and goals can result in transformative experiences where we access a moving collective experience. This shared energy is not mystical—it is the result of changes in neurobiology, cognition, and hormones. But it is certainly compelling.

ENERGY AND INTRINSIC MOTIVATION IN THE CLASSROOM

An occupational hazard of working in the world of teaching and learning is that I collect stories of people's favorite teachers like a dragon hoards treasure, turning them over in my pile now and then to admire them. What you learn when you do so is that while the style of people's favorite teachers varies widely—some are lighthearted and clever, some passionate and thundering, others quietly eloquent—all these favorite teachers have in common two things.

First, they have the power to arrest the attention of an entire classroom, to gather its energy. Whether they themselves think of this ability as a performance of sorts or not, it has performative elements not unlike theater arts. Here theater director Konstantin Stanislavsky describes the renowned actor Tommaso Salvini entering a theater and possessing the energy of the entire audience: "Salvini approached . . . thought a little while, concentrated himself and, unnoticed by any of us, took the entire audience of the great theatre into his hands. It seemed that he did this with a single gesture—that he stretched his hand without looking into the public, grasped all of us in his palm, and held us there as if we were ants or flies. He closed his fist, and we felt the breath of death; he opened it, and we felt the warmth of bliss. We were in his power." Professor of theater research Erika Fischer-Lichte calls this emotional connection between audience members and performers an autopoetic feedback loop. These loops occur not just on stage but in the classroom too. Skilled teachers are practiced masters of energy and capable of such feats of attention. Human beings are tremendously social creatures, and research on emotional contagion in the classroom suggests that "affective crossover," or the emotions of the instructor crossing over and influencing the emotions of the students, is a large component of effective teaching. When positive in nature (negative emotions like frustration and anger cross over too), this affective crossover predicts student engagement and learning.

Second, favorite teachers also have in common that they infect their students with their passion and enthusiasm for the subject. You cannot be what you cannot see. For not just our emotions are contagious but so, too, are our motivations and our goals. In an interview in *The Atlantic* about his teaching career before becoming a magician, the usually silent Teller (of the famous comedy duo Penn and Teller) cites a renowned theory of education as following the rhythm from romance to precision to generalization. Teller says that romance precedes all else. "The first job of a teacher is to make the student fall in love with the subject," he told the interviewer. "That doesn't have to be done by waving your arms and prancing around the classroom; there's all sorts of ways to go at it, but no matter what, you are a symbol of the subject in the students' minds." Especially in introductory classes, instructors "become" chemistry or psychology or literature in the minds of their students—they embody and represent their entire disciplines. Research backs up this claim, revealing that students very often choose their majors based on early experiences in the subject with particularly charismatic professors.

One Student Voices interviewee fit neatly into this pattern. Adam, a student at a small liberal arts college, talked about the frustrations of being a first-generation college student more focused on his studies than some of his wealthier classmates. He spoke of the challenges of being assigned to work in groups with other students who seemed to be at college just to have fun and party—secure in their futures, perhaps able to take on a family business after graduation. He felt no such security. This may have influenced his choice of major, which was marketing—a profession with a lot of practicality, a definite payoff at the end when compared to a major in, say, theater or philosophy. When he was forced by the college's general education requirements to take a history class, he was irritated at the loss of tuition dollars on what he saw as a useless subject, studying "stuff that happened." But he took the course with a particularly passionate instructor who changed not just how he viewed history but also life itself. He describes the experience in just these terms: "That course changed my life forever," he told us. "I literally look at life differently. He gave me a whole new perspective on life as a whole." He kept adding history classes with this same professor to his schedule until he ended up with a history minor.

Our Student Voices participants did not talk about neurobiology or hormones, but they definitely talked about the concept of energy in their classes, both when it is high and contributes to their motivation and when it is low and detracts from their motivation. Adam himself stated this directly: "In class it's a lot of feeding of energies." If you have a professor who seems like they don't want to be there, the rest of the class will follow suit, and there will be dead energy in the room and the hour drags for everyone. But if the instructor is active, engaged, and even joyful, that energy spreads as well.

Another student told us that her mood and motivation "also depend on the teacher's mood in the morning, I just have to say. Fridays are happier than Mondays." Yet another told us point-blank: "Basically whatever the professor is like it reflects on the students, or vice versa. If they're feeling some type of way, then we're also going to be feeling that way." Curiously, students also seem to feel this synchronous drive to be interested and work harder when they sense that the instructor is mindfully present in the classroom, that the instructor is not distracted. When describing mindfully present instructors, students use terms like "100 percent *there*" or even "there-there." On the opposite end of the spectrum, students use similar phrasing to describe instructors who are mentally checked out during class, using phrases like "not really *there*," "not there-there," "phoning it in," "punching the clock," and "going through the motions." One student describes this explicitly in terms of attention: "It's almost like the vibe they're giving off during class because . . . if they're not feeling like they want to be in the class or they're not interested in the material because they're not really paying attention, then why should I be paying attention?" It is striking to me that students seem to be able to detect the degree of focus or presence of their instructors, which is of course a largely internal phenomenon.

All these aspects of synchronous, reciprocal emotion and motivation are consistent with existing research investigating instructor and student emotional crossover or synchrony. Teachers convey greater enthusiasm through a variety of verbal and nonverbal cues like speaking quickly, using gestures and movement, and making eye contact, collectively known as "immediacy cues," and these cues have been demonstrated to be linked to outcome variables like student learning and interest in the course. Teachers also convey enthusiasm through the simple act of being interested in their students as fellow human beings. The luminary educator and activist bell hooks writes, "As a classroom community, our capacity to generate excitement is deeply affected by our interest in one another, in hearing one another's voices, in recognizing one another's presence." This sentiment, too, was echoed by our participants.

Earlier I discussed "warm" versus "chilly" academic climates in the context of students feeling relief and welcome in a course versus a too-serious standoffishness. Research indicates that students from well-resourced high schools appear to be not greatly affected by how warm versus hands-off their campuses are; not so for students who may not have had the same academic supports and are questioning their belongingness on campus. For students from lower-resourced backgrounds, warm campus climates related to higher perceived self-efficacy and expected GPA than chilly ones.

Some students even discussed reframing the arousal of anxiety and channeling it into motivation. Kai, a junior studying computer engineering at a tribal college in the Northwest, told us that when he found himself feeling anxious about academics, he would ask himself, "How can you view this emotion without it chipping away at your energy reserves?" The solution he found was that "instead of it being an anchor pulling you down deeper into the water, view it like a movie. Like, okay, there is something here to reach for. It can pull you out of the water when you are sinking." He was able to translate his fears into motivation by changing his mindset or beliefs about his bodily activation.

The energy element of motivation involves how behaviors can vary in *initiation* (getting started) and *intensity* (the degree of effort). But motivation also increases *persistence* (how long you keep working at your task or goal). These longer-term motivations are best served by a deep sense of purpose, of meaning, the endeavors that, so the saying goes, get you out of bed in the morning.* How can we help our young people find deep purpose in their lives? Even, a vocation?

Let's start with a case study.

I HAVE PURPOSE: IMAGINARTE

This is the story of how Esteban Loustaunau found his vocation. His vocation, fittingly enough, is helping college students find *their* vocations.

Esteban is a professor of Spanish at Assumption University in Massachusetts, where he is also director of a sophomore vocation program called SOPHIA and founding director of their Center for Purpose and Vocation. A Latin American studies scholar, his first book is *Telling Migrant Stories: Latin American Diaspora in Documentary Film*. His path to his present moment was not a direct one, but it was one that was always infused with a sense of purpose. Esteban and I have been colleagues for over ten years and friends for a shorter time than that, but when he agreed to let me interview him about vocation in higher education, I was delighted to first hear his origin story.

He finished graduate school in the late nineties, and his first job was as an assistant professor of Spanish at Augustana College, a small Lutheran-affiliated liberal arts school in western Illinois. The school is in an area that is called the Quad Cities because the Mississippi River divides four towns, two on each side—Iowa on one, Illinois on the other. About a mile from campus is a large Mexican American neighborhood called Floreciente, which means "flourishing." As both John Deere and Tyson have large facilities nearby, multiple generations of people from the same area in Central Mexico live and work there in farming and meatpacking. The

---

*Presumably with some help from our friend cortisol.

neighborhood has an active community center called Casa Guanajuato, which is named after the state most of these neighbors had come from.

One day Esteban showed up at Casa Guanajuato and simply said, "I'm a professor at Augustana. How can my students and I help?" They immediately put this gentle, eager man to work and found ways for him to involve his students in work that combined community service with their learning goals. One of Esteban and his students' first efforts was to clean up a local park. The park was abandoned because it was right at the city limits of two of the towns, and no one wanted to claim responsibility. Esteban, his students, and the community worked together to clean up the park and then apply for and receive grants to fund playground equipment like swings for the children.

Born of this early success were other initiatives threading Esteban's students and the community together, like an after-school tutoring program in the elementary school. People would say to Esteban, "Oh, you're doing community-service learning!" And in the beginning he would be confused—"I'm doing what?" He was just operating as he did in other avenues of life, seeking and growing purpose in himself and in others wherever he saw need.

And then he met his future wife. They fell in love, they got married, they had twins. And looking at the connected communities around them, they realized they wanted to raise their children close to family, and so they began searching for jobs in New England, where his wife's family resided. Esteban was delighted to find a small liberal arts college with an existing community-service learning program and minor, where the academic infrastructure was already built and he wouldn't have to go begging the dean for five hundred dollars if a new project came about. Though he loved his time at Augustana, he was even sadder to leave the Casa Guanajuato community, where he had become vice president of the center and where the sixth graders wanted him to be grand marshal at the graduation.

But it was time to see if he could create that same magic somewhere else. "Could I find a new place," he said, "a new way to engage students in this work of love, this service of love, to their community?" He did some research and soon after joining Assumption University began a partnership with the New Citizen's Center, which was a local school for new immigrant and refugee children who needed tutoring in academics and English. A typical student might have lived for years in a refugee camp in Syria and not only not know English but also be completely unfamiliar with how an American school works—what the expectations are, how you navigate that environment. His first project was to work with his college students to create a guide for new families to local services, connecting them with information about public transportation, clinics, schools, houses of worship, and libraries.

Esteban was so impressed with the work of his students on this guide. He could tell that they took such great care with the details—it wasn't something they rushed the night before and turned in for a grade. They investigated, they got on the phone with churches and charities to be sure they had the most recent contact information. They were working for the common good, not to satisfy an instructor's need to notch off a grade. One of his students was so moved that she worked after graduation for six months at an orphanage in Peru. Once she returned to the States, she got a job at Lutheran Social Services of New England and worked her way up to be the director of their unaccompanied refugee minors program.

But Esteban isn't just finding his own vocation and helping his college students find theirs—which, after all, is part of the job of a professor. He also helps the clients of the centers he connects his students with find *their* places in the world, their missions too. In one of his favorite service-learning projects, he worked with an organization called Ascentria Care Alliance. He gave cameras to their clients, who were unaccompanied refugee minors, and told them, tell us what it is like to live in Worcester, Massachusetts, but tell us in pictures. Once they lined up their pictures, they got a new challenge—to verbally tell the story the pictures told. Describe it for us. And do your pictures all together tell a story?"

The clients displayed their artwork in exhibits around the Worcester community, which Esteban's college students helped plan and run. Esteban named the exhibit *Imaginarte*, which is a play on the words *imagination* and *art*, but which in Spanish is also a reflexive verb meaning "imagine yourself." The exhibit and the photographs became a way for these clients to imagine themselves into being, to discover how their ideas of themselves were changing, morphing over time as they lived in this new country. One of his favorites was of a young girl who displayed a triptych of photographs—in the first, she is in a hoodie, looking scared, probably still dealing with the trauma of crossing the border. In the second, she is hard at work at a desk doing homework, working on her education. In the third, she is depicted with an American flag, and her explanation is that she hopes to study to be an immigration lawyer. "So," Esteban explained, "in these pictures she is telling us that she is still connected to her past, but instead of dwelling in the trauma, her past informs her future and gives her life meaning and purpose. In the present moment she is working hard, and in the future she hopes to go beyond her own needs to serve the common good." This is how you help young people find a vocation.

AN INCALCULABLE GRACE: THE IMPORTANCE OF MENTORSHIP IN MOTIVATION

The scholarship on purpose, meaning, and vocation tells us that the paths Esteban's students travel to find their vocations are not unique. Mentors and guides are critical to setting off on one's journey, finding the best direction to point one's motivated energy. Just as Esteban serves as a model of aspiration for the students in his classes and in his sophomore vocation program, we must be seekers ourselves in order to encourage seeking in our youth.

Professor of theology and ethical scholar Paul Wadell has written about the intersections of friendship and mentoring, about how mentoring young people involves witnessing their lives in a similar way that we stand as witness to the lives of our friends. Both relationships also involve an intentional rearranging of the spaces in your life to prioritize the well-being of this other person, which of course takes significant time and attention. "To have an adult who genuinely cares for them," he writes, "an adult who has no other agenda than helping them discover and move toward what is best for them, is an incalculable grace." These words recall my father telling us that the one crucial determinant of whether one of the boys in his care reached positive rather than negative outcomes was having at least one bond with an adult in their lives who saw their inherent value.

Steven is a human services major in a community college system and a Student Voices interviewee. He told us of his winding history in and out of drug treatment, including some time in prison. His parents were unhoused and dependent on substances themselves, and his childhood was one marked by short stays in various motel rooms and negative interactions with law enforcement. All Steven's risk factors pointed to the life difficulties he experienced, but he determinedly kept returning to the community college system in between relapses, fixed on a better future. One afternoon in a remedial math class, he became so frustrated with the class material and his struggles with it that he stormed out of the classroom and punched a tree. He was done—never going to school again. No more squinting at textbooks, no more dealing with the alarmed side-glances at his prison tattoos from his fellow students, no more feeling down on himself.

But his math instructor followed him outside. She, in his words, gently talked him back off the ledge of his anger and frustration. He could feel the calm and the determination to succeed spreading through him as she talked. "Look," she said to him, "this is just practice. You haven't even had a chance to prepare yet. This says nothing about your abilities as a student." She was patient. She did not shy away from his anger. She believed in him. He views this as a pivotal moment in his commitment to his education, and it is one that has led him to not only complete his associate's degree and a certification in human services and chemical dependency counseling but also led to his actively working to help others who struggle with dependency to recover.

In the vocational program he directs, Esteban's students have time and space carved out for pursuing questions of vocation and for developing relationships with dedicated mentors. In early classes in the program, he probes the idea of vocation with his students, challenging the notion that vocation is either purely about being called to a religious life or simply a more secular version of finding your career path. At this stage of the program, few students identify with the word or understand how it might apply to their lives. So they start playing the game charades to explore intersections of vocation with family life, with discipline of study, with faith and politics and sexuality. In all these conversations, Esteban practices and emphasizes listening and trust among the groups.

In past classes, Esteban notes that students began really responding when they started talking about anxiety, about their deep fears about their lives, their educations, and the world they are living in. The group becomes a community of people who respect each other's fears, who are comfortable with sharing vulnerabilities. Esteban believes that sophomore year is an important year in the college experience, and for those youth who attend college, it is a critical year in young adulthood in general. He believes that many college-attending students from middle-class or upper-middle-class backgrounds are told from birth that they can achieve anything they want in life if they just apply enough effort. If you work hard, the sky is the limit. But he thinks this sense of endless possibility contributes to anxiety, because students set their sights on aspirations that their parents or society tells them should be their goals—surgeon, astronaut, president—and then they get to high school or college and, perhaps based on their particular skill sets or under-resourced preparation, begin struggling with introductory courses, especially in science or math. They get negative feedback and begin spiraling into anxiety: "I'm a failure. . . . I can never . . . I should drop out of college." Or they decide on a very practical career, one that will yield an income they want and good prospects of staying employed, but they find that they hate the subject matter, that their true heart is somewhere else—in the arts, for instance. Sophomore year is when these tensions begin boiling up. This year is often the one where students must choose their major, and it is also the year that it becomes clear that their first-year GPA may have set the stage for the rest of their college career. There are also pressures from home: "We're going to pull you out of Assumption if you don't get straight A's and B's." They can't breathe.

And then they enter SOPHIA, and Esteban, warm and tall and reassuring, tells them, "Look for your vocation and your calling, and don't worry so much." He brings them on a weekend retreat. At the beginning of the weekend they are all grumpy with him. They argue with him that they can't possibly go—this exam, that practice, this other performance. Too busy, too busy. He pulls the Rome card on them—to go on the year-end capstone trip to Assumption's Rome campus, they must attend the retreat. They are very quiet on the bus and won't make eye contact.

It takes about an hour of ice-breaker activities for the students to look around, to laugh, to loosen their joints. At the retreat, some of the most charismatic faculty in the mentorship program share their life histories. They talk about their path to being a historian, a psychologist, a chemist. How they were called to the work, the obstacles they encountered, the divergences from their initial goals. Esteban sees the weight drop off his students' shoulders as they realize, "I am among humans. I am among humans who are not perfect and who have had a tougher life than I have and who changed their major five times. I don't have to have it all figured out right now."

Encouraged by their reading and discussions, Esteban's mentees form definitions of vocation that are elastic and dynamic, stretching and shifting to accommodate a variety of ways of finding one's purpose. And which are also tied to the needs of the world.

As it turns out, purpose tied to the world's needs can be among the most motivating of all purposes.

I HAVE PURPOSE: SEEKING YOUR HORIZON OF SIGNIFICANCE

Philosopher Charles Taylor claims you become authentic when your identity connects with the needs of the world, whether that be nature, politics, citizenship, family, community, or faith—what he dubbed "horizons of significance." Each of us must do this work of finding our own horizon of significance. Beyond probing our own skills, strengths, and weaknesses, how do we manage to find our particular purpose, our entrée into service to the world?

I was blessed to read an entire book on this topic as it was being written. I belong to a friendly writers' group of three professors. Over the last half decade or so, English professor and author James Lang, journalist and English professor Michael Land, and I have helped each other write everything from essays to book proposals to entire books. We most often meet at a coffee shop to fuel our insights and catch up on each other's lives in between giving each other feedback on our writing. At one point all three of us were starting and finishing book projects around the same time, and it was during this year or so that I was lucky enough to read the

earliest drafts of *The Whole Service Trip* by Mike Land, who also is director of the community-service learning program at the same school that
recruited Esteban. Mike's book spins the tale of a cross-country road trip
visiting and engaging in community service with various folks who have
found their callings, while simultaneously trying to find his own.

In the book, Mike struggles with the issues we all struggle with—Am
I doing enough? Does service need to hurt to be true service, or can it be
something we enjoy? Some people feel called to work with rescue dogs
or volunteer in a library. Does that mean you are dodging true service by
spending your time playing with pups or in the dark and peaceful quiet
of words when there are people without homes who could also use your
help? Mike's big, beating heart can be felt on every page of the book, as
can his love of his fellow humans and his nagging sense that he is never
doing quite enough for the world.

If I may spoil the narrative a bit (you should still read the book when
it comes out), Mike's conclusion is that you cannot judge yourself for
the service you feel called to do. Every human being has different life
experiences and different sets of skills, and these combine to match well
to certain types of service and not others. One of the most stirring stories
in the book is that of Return to Freedom's Neda DeMayo, who told us
about the importance of passion followed by correct action at the launch
of this chapter.

Neda's story doesn't stand alone, for many of the people Mike meets
and interviews share similar origin stories for their lives of purpose. For
instance, he met Amanda Rutherford, who told the story of being an
undergraduate on a wilderness trip when she and a friend encountered a
migrant from Mexico under a tree. He had been in the desert for a significant time, wandering, separated from his group, without food for four
days and without water for two. "I had never had that feeling of seeing
another human being look at you as if they've never needed a human being
more," Amanda told Mike, "because they are so scared and so alone." She
began to cry. She connected the man with water and with help. She now
works for the organization No More Deaths, which among other services
leaves jugs of water along the border for thirsty migrants and advocates
for immigration reform to bring policies in line with major tenets of faith.

In one of my favorite chapters, Mike releases previously injured sea turtles back into the sea with Tony Amos, a septuagenarian oceanographer who founded an organization called ARK (Amos Rehabilitation Keep). "This time I'm reveling in the feel of their shells in my hand," Mike writes, "the brush of their flippers against my hands as they swam first through air, then into the mysterious sea. The thrill of a tangible, if fleeting, connection with something so completely, and wondrously, different." There are many more such stories of people finding their purpose in homeless shelters, in planting urban gardens, in caring for children taken out of their homes for reasons of abuse and neglect. Some of these people left their full-time careers for service work, some like Tony pursued their service in retirement, and some volunteer on the side of their other responsibilities.

In the syllabus of Esteban's course on vocation, he encourages his students to view themselves as seekers. I love that this word so closely maps onto what Jaak Panksepp and other affective neuroscientists have argued is the seeking system. In the syllabus, Esteban highlights as seekers many "teachers, students, activists, storytellers, artists, poets, children, parents, ministers, migrants, refugees, outlaws, and others who are seeking ideas and causes to give meaning and bring purpose to their lives." A seeker, he says, is someone who is curious and deeply committed to spiritual and emotional growth, perseveres, overcomes doubt, asks important questions without settling for easy answers, believes in their vision, and patiently listens to a calling. The seeker is a social position that is not fixed but is constantly changing and evolving over time.

All the folks in Mike's book are defined seekers. All of them are living lives of passion, followed by correct action. The portraits he paints of these people are of vivid, fulfilled human beings, acting in and on the world to make it a better place. They are lives that any adolescent would hope for, and any parent or educator would hope for the youth in their care.

CONCLUSION

In this chapter we have considered how motivation spurs energy, in the form of physiological arousal that can mobilize and sustain focused efforts. We also discussed the tight relationship between anxiety and motivation—

that both involve physiological activation at the thought of uncertain futures, but one that spins us toward paralysis and avoidance and the other toward action and approach. As one Student Voices participant observed, how a person frames this arousal can anchor them in the depths of anxiety or offer a helpful hand to lift them out of the churn. Learning environments characterized by models of excitement in the front of the classroom, caring mentors, connections with horizons of significance, and the development of vocation can mobilize this energy.

But energy is only one half of motivation, remember. The second half is direction. Where will this summoned energy flow? Are you going to use it to anxiously ruminate? To exercise? To work on your coursework? To clean your closet?

Next up: determining ourselves.

CHAPTER SIX

DETERMINING ONESELF—DIRECTION AND EXPECTANCY

NEITHER I NOR my ten-year-old Honda Civic were up to this task, I reflected as the world spun in icy circles around us. I was driving myself and a few close women friends to a winter edition of our biannual retreat weekends, and the slippery roads were too much for my old tires—we hit a slick patch and began twirling.

It being our winter weekend, I had chosen a remote cabin hand-built by the owners on a lake. I pictured us on long cross-country ski outings followed by bundling around a woodstove with warm bowls of soup to vent, brainstorm, and set goals together. But when selecting a cabin, this Massachusetts native saw New Hampshire and figured, "Oh sure, New Hampshire is close enough" without googling directions. Turns out, the cabin was in the area of New Hampshire that peeks above parts of the Canadian border, where no one smart drives without four-wheel drive. Skiing, soups, and fires were on the horizon. But between this moment and those moments were not only the skid-out but another where we got so buried in snow we had to use the mats from inside the car to create traction, another at the bottom of a dismayingly steep hill where someone with a much more appropriate vehicle for the roads nearly sideswiped us, and a broken woodstove in our cabin.

Also on the horizon, though, was what was in store for us at every one of these retreat weekends, which was a potent combination of play, goal setting, togetherness, confronting discomforting topics in discussion,

challenging each other to take on challenges, and acts of physical strenuousness in nature. These activities all nurture core psychological needs—
autonomy (choosing one's path), competence (feeling you have the skills
to succeed), and, most of all, relatedness (what I will call belongingness,
feeling embedded in a social net of shared meaning). Meeting these psychological needs is key to amplifying intrinsic motivation.

DETERMINING YOURSELF: AUTONOMY, COMPETENCE, AND BELONGINGNESS

These three psychological needs are key to self-determination theory,
which is the most compelling and scientifically supported account of
intrinsic motivation. The essence of the theory is right there in its title—
human beings have deep, evolved psychological needs to determine their
own lives, their own selves, and the most important of these needs are
autonomy, competence, and belongingness.

Self-determination theory (affectionately known as SDT) was critical in turning motivation science's attention away from purely extrinsic,
reward-based learning, which characterized the dominance of behaviorism, and instead toward the manifold ways that human beings actively
determine their own choices and behaviors. In the words of its creators,
psychologists Richard Ryan and Edward Deci, "The science of SDT takes
seriously our capacities as persons, including our abilities to be aware of
ourselves, to actively learn and master our worlds, to strive to internalize
cultural norms, to reflectively consider our own attitudes and values, and
to make informed choices concerning them." In highlighting the importance of belongingness, SDT also appreciates the ways that we support
the rich selves of our social partners—and how, in turn, they support ours.

The theory does not dispute all the ways human beings are also motivated by unconscious, automatic processes like responding to rewards
and punishments. It instead argues that we must unite the study of these
automatic, implicit forces with an understanding that human beings are
also self-determined and complex. We are not *either-or*, we are *yes, and*.

While I am breaking down false dichotomies, motivation is also not
a dichotomy between extrinsic (purely controlled, engaged in for the

sake of external rewards or punishment) and intrinsic (purely volitional, engaged in for the sake of internal pleasure and satisfaction). In contrast, like every other psychological process we have considered in this book, motivation exists on a continuum from amotivation (lack of motivation) to external regulation to a series of increasingly intrinsic motivations, steps at which the behavior becomes progressively internalized. Some of these intermediary steps include behaviors that are not externally rewarded but those that one engages in for the sake of social approval, those that become personally important to one's sense of self, and those that are fully integrated with one's idea of oneself as a person.

A close look at the brain circuits related to intrinsic motivation suggests that amplifying interest and "seeking" behavior recruits areas of the brain involved in detecting meaning and value *and* those required for focus and active engagement. On the other hand, intrinsic motivation also diminishes activity in a circuit involved in self-referential mental processing. In other words, value is high, you focus all your energies in one place, and you temporarily disengage from rumination and daydreaming. You engage with the present moment.

Singing the song of compassionate challenge, SDT also argues that while you cannot determine someone else's intrinsic motivation (doing so is, on the face of it, the opposite of self-determination), you *can* establish settings that nudge people along to self-determination by creating environmental conditions that support the fulfillment of these needs. Ryan and Deci write, "People are inherently prone to learn, internalize, and grow and to move in the direction of greater autonomy and integration, provided they have the appropriate nutriments or supports." Our youth need compassion, so that they can rise to the challenge of self-determination.

What are these environmental conditions that increase self-determination? Citing a variety of research studies, meta-analyses, and reviews, Ryan, Deci, and colleagues argue that settings that encourage intrinsic motivation are those that nudge choice and ownership, offer activities that are appropriately challenging, and that provide scaffolding and support. Settings that decrease intrinsic motivation involve punishment, surveillance, excessively controlled deadlines and evaluations, "conditional regard" (my feelings about you depend on your performance), and even controlling tones of voice. Collectively, these latter situational attributes contribute to the "chilly" academic climate discussed in the last chapter.

Underscoring SDT's arguments as applied to education, a meta-analysis of 344 research studies spanning 223,209 students reported on the relationships among aspects of motivation and aspects of outcome variables like GPA, intentions to persist at activities, well-being, goal orientation (whether focused on achieving a certain performance or mastering a skill), and self-evaluation (self-efficacy, self-esteem, and so on). They found that more self-determined, intrinsic forms of motivation generally related to high levels of adaptive outcomes (such as higher GPA, higher well-being), whereas less self-determined forms of motivation related to high levels of maladaptive outcomes (such as lower self-efficacy, higher depression).

Intriguingly, "identified" regulation was *more* associated with many adaptive outcomes than was fully intrinsic motivation, suggesting that for certain academic behaviors like persistence, identifying the activity as important to one's self-concept may be even more important than naturally enjoying the activity. This finding makes a lot of sense when you consider how much academic work, even for those subjects you might enjoy, can be laborious and not intrinsically rewarding.

We'll return to these concepts in a little bit when we consider the dilemma poised by grading, but next let's take a closer look at practical ways we as educators of young humans can create compassionate settings that nudge self-determination. We'll consider autonomy, competence, and belongingness in turn.

I HAVE AUTONOMY: CHOICE, CONTROL, AND GOAL SETTING

One horror movie trope is a transformation such that one loses control over one's own mind, body, or actions in the world, helpless against the transformative agent. This agent is sometimes a demonic entity that takes ownership of the body, as seen in countless portrayals from *The Exorcist* to *Hereditary*. Rather than demons or other possessive entities, hypnosis is the transformative agent in the movie *Get Out*. An eerie repetitive clinking of a teaspoon against a cup sends the protagonist into a dark cavern of his own mind called "the sunken place." Sometimes, it's aliens. And of course, it can also be the result of various zombifying pathogens, when one's previous goals in life are replaced by an endless and quite violent search for brains to snack on.

What all these horror tropes have in common is a loss of autonomy, our capacity to make our own decisions, to guide our lives down a path shaped by our values and important relationships. Here, too, a monstrous lens helps us see our values, as autonomy is a core psychological need.

In many ways, autonomy is the cornerstone of SDT, and more research has been conducted on it than on any other aspect of self-determination. Autonomy has been found to be essential for the quality of people's lives in the settings of family, work, and leisure, and across cultures. In the context of learning, student autonomy takes the form of self-directed learning. Self-directed learning includes experiences in which students choose their own course paths, where within a course they choose the types of assignments to fulfill or the topics to focus on, and where they select internships or practicums. Encouraging autonomy also can take the form of asking students to cocreate class policies, assignments, or segments of the course together with the instructor and their classmates. It might look like peer teaching or peer-to-peer feedback on assignments. When the student is at the wheel of their educational ship, that's autonomy. When acting with autonomy, students are aware of their own learning process, guiding their own choices and regulating their own learning, and feeling vital in the process.

This primacy of autonomy is echoed in several other major theories of motivation. For one, the *control-value theory of achievement emotions* is a motivation theory directly applied to the work of the classroom. Developed by psychologist Reinhard Pekrun and colleagues, the theory highlights the importance of student sense of control (autonomy) and student sense of value and purpose (which we covered in the last chapter) for engagement in academic work. Activities and assignments high in control and value engender what Pekrun calls activating positive emotions—affective experiences like curiosity, determination, and pride. Activities and assignments low in control and value engender deactivating negative emotions—affective experiences like defeat, despair, and shame. It isn't difficult to see that high control and value will inspire the application of increased effort (heightened energy and direction) and that low control and value will evoke avoidance and passivity.

One can encourage a sense of autonomy in a classroom through a variety of methods that provide students with the opportunity to guide their own learning. Choice of assignments and assignment topics, self-directed learning based on portfolios, use of group annotations on the syllabus or readings, and game-based learning are just a few. More globally, parents and educators can promote goal setting.

Human beings are, in general, overly optimistic creatures who expect the future to be much better than the past. We anticipate that our future selves will be fitter, wealthier, and happier than our present states. One major way that we set goals for ourselves is to view this future, idealistic self and compare it to our present selves—the gap between the two, the ache that lives there, is motivating. It gives us a boost of energy.

Goals work. Across multiple domains—fitness, finance, hobbies, education, career, substance use reduction, eating healthy—people who intentionally engage in goal setting outperform and out-achieve their non-goal-setting controls, and do so with a decent size of effect. This is rather remarkable when you consider how varied the behaviors are that lead to these effects. Finding the time and will to regularly get on a treadmill seems very different from refraining from clicking through an Instagram ad, which seems very different from the set of behaviors aimed at impressing your boss in hopes of a promotion. But yet these are similar practices of goal setting work are effective for increasing exercise, reducing bad habits, and pursuing career advancement.

In one example of the power of goal setting in an academic setting, researchers recruited eighty-five students experiencing academic struggles into a study that lasted a semester. Students were randomly assigned at the start of the study to complete one of two programs on a computer that involved responding to writing prompts and reflecting on one's personal experience. One group's activities centered around setting effective goals for their academic work that semester; the other group's activities centered around thinking positively. Following the computerized programs, the students went about their semesters with no differences between the groups—experiencing all the ups and downs of a busy semester and its associated work. At the end of the semester, the experimenters collected information on GPA and course loads from the college's records, and participants reported on experiences of the semester. Remarkably, students in the goal setting intervention condition achieved significantly higher GPAs at the end of the semester than they had at the start of the semester, whereas students in the control condition showed no such increase. Those in the goal setting group were also more likely to maintain a full course load over the semester, and their experience of negative emotions decreased over time. While the researchers did not measure students' feelings about autonomy, explicitly thinking ahead about the semester's challenges and making a plan for actions to meet them spelled a more successful semester for students than merely thinking positively.

Goal setting is powerful and worthwhile. But it can also feel a bit mechanical—indeed, early models treated human beings like little machines that would set a goal, work toward it, test to see if it was achieved, and then operate on a loop, either returning to goal-directed behavior or setting a new goal. Goal setting theory can also smack a bit of late-stage capitalism, of a socially programmed desire to maximize and produce, to be endlessly dissatisfied with your present self. It doesn't help that if you immerse yourself in the goal setting literature—as I recently had to do to write a chapter for a textbook project—you come out blinking on the other side, seeing diets and dollar signs everywhere you look.

But done right and aimed at academics and well-being, goal setting can be a powerful tool for visualizing your own ideal future and the self-determined, autonomous steps on the way to it. To truly be effective in goal setting, though, you must be relatively confident about your chances of succeeding. Which leads us right into our next component of self-determination: competence.

I AM COMPETENT: THE CHALLENGE OF GRADING AND BEING GRADED

Tell me if you've ever had a dream like the following. You show up to take your final exam, but suddenly realize that you have not attended a single class all semester or read a page of the textbook and have none of the knowledge required to pass. Another—you show up somewhere very professional, such as to teach a class or lead a conference seminar but find that you are not wearing a stitch of clothing and everyone will be laughing too hard to appreciate a thing you say. Or you need to perform some urgent physical task—catch a ball, stop your child from running across the street—but find yourself unable to move, your voice frozen in your throat, your arms unresponsive by your sides.* All these horrors or challenges are tied to our need to feel competent, to know that we can have a measurable impact on the world.

In the haunting short story "Real Women Have Bodies," Carmen Maria Machado depicts a world in which women have begun fading from the world, become incorporeal, suddenly unable to interact physically with their lived environments. It is a horror of growing incompetence and irrelevance. The protagonist discovers that once faded, some of these women are volunteering to be stitched into cocktail dresses, presumably so they can be worn by living women still moving freely and interacting with the world. When the protagonist's lover begins fading, the lover does everything from rub orange peels on her skin to drive darts into her own hand to continue to feel, to continue to engage with the world and have an effect.

Competence is feeling effective, believing in your core that you have the skills to meet the challenges that face you. We can already see here a direct connection to anxiety, in that anxiety elevates when you estimate that you have low capacity to meet the challenges that lurk in your future. When perceived competence rises, anxiety diminishes. Competence also relates to other popular psychological concepts like self-efficacy, or the degree of confidence one feels in one's ability to meet demands and exert change on one's environment. Coined by social psychologist Albert Bandura, self-efficacy is a key attribute of motivation and is a protective factor in the face of numerous stressors.

For instance, in her bracing and informative read *The Addiction Inoculation: Raising Healthy Kids in a Culture of Dependence*, author Jessica Lahey considers the evidence that one of the best ways to inoculate youth against

---

*This last set of dreams is also influenced by the fact that your brain handily puts you in a state of functional paralysis during REM sleep so you don't hurt yourself acting out your dreams.

substance abuse is to encourage their self-efficacy. Low self-efficacy is associated with low self-esteem, pessimism, and passivity, all traits that have been tied to elevated risk for substance abuse and dependence in young people. High self-efficacy serves as a protective factor against these maladaptive experiences but also can help youth resist peer pressure. To shore up self-efficacy in youth, Lahey argues that parents and educators must (1) provide models of self-efficacy in their own behavior; (2) believe in youth and act in ways that clearly demonstrate that belief; (3) set individual, family, and school goals of learning instead of merely providing accolades; (4) be optimistic; (5) be honest and not overboard with praise; and (6) provide frequent opportunities for youth to demonstrate their skills and competence. These practices in the home can easily be extended to the classroom—we need to believe in our students and be optimistic about their capacities.

Moreover, creating settings where youth can demonstrate their skills and competence is key to what we secondary and higher educators are already doing in our classrooms. We assign labs and lab reports, readings and discussion boards, homework and papers and quizzes and exams. Students take these moments to demonstrate the degree to which they have or have not mastered a variety of skills—and ideally, receive feedback that moves them closer and closer to proficiency, where they finish the course having mastered the relevant skills.

But of course, this ideal is not always the reality. For one, many students don't finish the course having successfully achieved the skills set out as learning goals at the start of the course. For another, the experience of students in our courses is that they work quite hard on their assignments, risking themselves, opening themselves up for evaluation. And then we grade these efforts. We tell some students, a scarce few, "Perfect! You have grasped this skill." We tell the vast majority, to varied degrees, "Nope, sorry; better luck next time." What effect does this process of grading have on our students' self-efficacy and perceived competence?

One Saturday evening during the dark lockdown year of the early COVID-19 pandemic, my small family of three was planning a movie night. My then-middle-school-age daughter had demonstrated extraordinary resilience during the initial pivot to online school and then the first months of remote and hybrid learning. But she had started struggling in math—not completing assignments, failing to put good effort in, forgetting to pass in take-home quizzes. She had one take-home quiz in particular to complete right before grades ended for the term, and switching that grade from a zero to pretty much any non-zero score would mean a very large difference in her final grade. We made a deal—I'd make cookies while she took the quiz, and then we could all cuddle up and relax with a movie.

She took to her room at the basement level, and I heard Taylor Swift crank up. I smiled. Singing on the top of her lungs helps my daughter concentrate on subjects she doesn't enjoy, and sure enough, her rich alto soon rose through the floorboards. I mixed cookie batter and listened to her sing and do math. After a little while, though, her voice abruptly halted. Taylor clicked off. My daughter climbed the stairs and when she reached the top, I could see that her shoulders were heavy and her eyes teary. The quiz had auto-graded and spit out a fifty-five. You fail.

Never mind *her* feeling defeated—*I* felt defeated.

Dismayingly, grades tend to focus student attention on avoiding negative outcomes rather than approaching positive ones. Avoiding negative outcomes rather than approaching positive ones is a goal orientation associated with anxiety, hopelessness, and lack of autonomy. Students report that receiving grades activates feelings of shame and punishment, which are negative, deactivating emotions associated with low academic achievement. Even more alarming, written feedback accompanying grades is rarely incorporated into future work and is often not even read. Some students even report that they stop listening during the rest of the class session in which a poor grade is received.

Our Student Voices interviews confirmed many of these findings in the research literature. Students can feel a sense of self-efficacy only when the instructor's guidelines are clear and fair and their grading consistent. Students are clearly frustrated by a lack of such transparency and clarity for grading. One student, named Christopher, reflects:

> Not being transparent about the grading policy, that's one thing that really frustrates me sometimes. Additionally, it's not being consistent about it too. One thing that may have been wrong on one [quiz or project]

and then I do it again, it's not wrong or it is wrong, you know, the flip side of it. That really gets me angry a lot because it provides a lot of confusion. . . . When it does happen, it really demotivates me because I feel like there's no hope. Like, "What am I supposed to do?" you know? I don't know what my professor is thinking.

This student's self-efficacy was threatened. In a setting where his efforts were rewarded and punished inconsistently, his actions had a muted impact. He didn't feel competent. The grades were not just demotivating when they were low—they also failed to provide meaningful information about learning. This inconsistent grading obviously influenced his emotion and his motivation.

To tackle the dilemma of what to do about the demotivating nature of grading, I introduce you to this chapter's expert, Joshua Eyler. Josh is the director of faculty development and clinical assistant professor of teacher education at the University of Mississippi. He is author of *How Humans Learn: The Science and Stories Behind Effective College Teaching* and (even more relevant to our concerns here) the forthcoming *Scarlet Letters: How Grades Are Harming Children and Young Adults, and What We Can Do About It*. Josh and I have collaborated several times, including on a Pedagogies of Care project, in which we and a team of other higher education professionals developed and offered open resources to support practices of pedagogical care during the initial higher-ed pivot to online learning.

We announced our new book projects and our intention to interview each other for them on Twitter. To our amusement, fellow teaching-and-learning expert and podcaster John Kane reached out and said, "Hey, instead of interviewing each other quietly and on your own, do you folks want to take over my podcast for a day?" The podcast in question is called *Tea for Teaching* and is coproduced by Rebecca Mushtare, who codirects the Center for Excellence in Learning and Teaching with John at the State University of New York at Oswego. The podcast is a lively combination of discussing current pedagogy topics and tea drinking. Josh and I took over the podcast in October 2020, addressing this topic: What's in a grade? How should we think about grading as teachers and scholars ourselves in the science of teaching and learning?

Josh has been most moved by work in a field called critical pedagogy, a movement begun in the middle of the last century that challenges teachers to help their students identify the relative influences of power and inequality in everything they learn. The scholars most integral to this work are Paulo Freire and bell hooks, writers and activists who were instrumental in framing education as a practice of freedom. "For Freire," Josh said, "who was deeply invested in the political climate of Brazil, education as a practice of freedom means giving students agency, empowerment, and the tools to be able to remake the world that both benefits them and society at large." (Agency and empowerment sound a lot like autonomy here.) This liberation is achieved by freeing the classroom of controlling elements that prevent true education from taking place.

For bell hooks, this education as a practice of freedom meant breaking down the hierarchies of the traditional classroom, ceding a fair degree of control and direction of what happens in the classroom to the students themselves. She called upon instructors to cease seeing their classrooms as a "mini-kingdom" over which they rule. In reading this term I am reminded of an instructor I worked with at a previous institution. He objected to flexibly moving deadlines for students because he felt this diminished the intellectual rigor of the class, but he *also* objected to clearly laying out all deadlines for the semester in the syllabus. After all, life happens, and you can't predict how intellectual work will progress—he wanted that flexibility built in for himself. Mini-kingdoms, indeed. Hooks also argued that true education requires vulnerability on the part of the students and for the instructor to model such vulnerability for the students, a perspective that will be echoed by a famous acting coach in just a few chapters.

For Josh, critical pedagogy as informed by his study of Freire and hooks means grappling with the traditions that we have been handed about what education means and what teaching means. He sees grading as a core battleground in this work. He feels that it is a crucial space where innovative educators can remove emphasis on evaluation (How good is this work?) and instead focus on feedback (How close are you to your learning goals?).

Josh and I chatted for a bit about the story that opened this book, how for me the carrot of a good grade was a major moment in my willingness to try to conquer my fear of public speaking. I also shared with him that one of my great joys in life was taking high-stakes exams. It was one of the primary ways that I experienced a feeling of flow, a sense of self-efficacy, an awareness of competence. It was just me and the test, and I became pure intellect. All my hopes and fears and concerns, both petty and existential, melted away as I did what I do best. I often miss it. I have been known to threaten to take the GRE just for the pleasure of it.

Josh laughed at the idea of taking the GRE for fun, but he himself had similar experiences with grading and evaluation, where he felt that assessments were stimulating challenges to conquer. "I was an athlete in high school and college," he shared, "and I really approached grades in much the same way, that it was just one more competitor, one more opponent on the wrestling mat." But, critically, he pointed out that both of us had extensive early experiences in well-resourced school systems with supportive parents who were able and willing to help us navigate our educational experiences.

"Here I'm drawn to the work on inclusive pedagogy and on opportunity gaps," Josh said, "and what grades communicate to students who are coming to our colleges and universities from under-resourced schools where they have not had the same kind of educational opportunities." So many students don't have AP classes to prepare them for the demands of college work, don't have teachers with the bandwidth to provide individualized attention, don't have the right books, don't have the right materials. For students from well-resourced backgrounds, Josh thinks, a grade in an introductory level course could be a communicator: this information is important, pay attention to it. It could also communicate that a student has achieved a certain skill. For students from less resourced schools? Not so much. "I think what the research shows is that, more often than not," Josh said, "the grade is penalizing these students for what they didn't have, rather than being able to demonstrate what they know and can do at that point in their career." Grades thus become one more way that students with less support are short-changed by our educational system.

All this has led numerous scholars to rethink how we assess learning and how we give students feedback about their learning. Some approaches are pretty radical, such as completely throwing grades out the window, at least until the end of the course. Early calls to action were issued by

anthropologist Susan Blum and writer-educator Jesse Stommel, whose
essays and blog posts urged instructors to consider the practice of "ungrading." Ungrading is more of an orientation than a specific approach, as
its practitioners vary greatly in their methods. But most of these methods
have in common that they hold back letter or numerical grades until the
end of the semester, instead orienting student attention to feedback and
progress along the way. At a recent workshop, I put up a slide with various alternatives to traditional grading and one attendee raised her hand,
pointed at the term *ungrading*, and asked me to explain it. I did my best,
and she sat back, whistling through her teeth. "You just rocked my entire
world," she told me.

Early calls on blogs led to rapid adoption by faculty dismayed by the
effects of traditional grading. Just a few years after their first essays on
ungrading, Blum published an edited collection *UNgrading: Why Rating
Students Undermines Learning (and What to Do Instead)*, in which educators
share their experiences with various forms of alternative grading. In the
introduction she issues a clear challenge: "Though grading seems natural,
inevitable, a part of the very fabric of school, it isn't. It was created at a
certain moment, for certain reasons not entirely well thought out, and
then became embedded in the structures of schools for most students. But
because we invented it, we can uninvent it. We can remove it. And many
of us believe we should." The essays in the collection span different disciplines, from creative writing to math to chemistry, and the approaches of
the instructors vary as well, but all are infused with this rebellious energy
and with a fierce dedication to student learning.

Similarly, one of the things I like best about how Josh is approaching grading methods and alternatives is that he doesn't prescribe a one-
size-fits-all approach. He is currently organizing his thoughts and research on different approaches by degree of liberatory nature (modeling
this on Freire and hooks) and degree of complexity and logistics. Some
new approaches to grading such as that are called specifications grading,
involve numerous rubrics, tokens, and systems of mastery, and can be
difficult for students to understand and faculty to navigate. Some are
quite simple—such as contract grading, where students agree to a certain performance in return for a guaranteed grade—but are perhaps less

freeing. Josh encourages faculty to dip a toe in with the lower logistics, lower liberatory practices first, such as portfolio grading, in which students choose a number of projects in a portfolio for their final grade but receive traditional grades on each.

I love all of this work, and all of these arguments. On the other hand, when I think back to my daughter being discouraged by her automatically graded math assignment, it does occur to me that my daughter would never be intrinsically motivated to complete a math assignment without the extrinsic offering of a grade—any day of the week, let alone a Saturday night. In addition, grades don't just offer extrinsic carrots for students to complete work that is onerous but necessary for learning. They are also meant to provide feedback about progress toward learning goals, to communicate the relative distance between the student's learning and their proficiency, the degree of work or distance still to be bridged. In college classes, the grade distributions among different types of assessments (for example, your final grade is made up of 30 percent quizzes, 20 percent final project, and so on) are also key pieces of information for how students should allocate their effort in a course. The heavier-weighted parts of the course should take more time, more effort. In these ways grades are meant to be *information*, one tool among many to assist with the process of education.

I think it is a little unrealistic to expect our students to experience true intrinsic motivation for all their courses, in all their assignments. It seems also like sometimes educators conflate goal ends with goal means. We pursue goals important to our values, and for sure, there are times when our goals and the means to attain them are so closely related that it is thrilling, and we are intrinsically motivated to work hard. When you are training for a race and the final run before the big day gets you to your full mileage, your body in peak physical shape—those goal means have got to feel pretty great. Or when you are an undergraduate film major and you are working on a final project for your senior capstone and it is everything you ever thought filmmaking could be—that also has got to feel pretty great. Motivation scientists call this enjoyment of means a "fusion" of goals and means.

But so many of the means for achieving our goals are far from intrinsically motivating. The runner probably didn't feel all that exhilarated when they had to wake up two hours earlier than usual to get their run in. The filmmaker might not be thrilled having to solve calculus equations late on a Sunday night for their general education requirements. For these efforts, we might effectively apply some extrinsic motivators, like the thought of a big bowl of pasta after the run or a Netflix episode after the calculus. Or . . . a good grade for completing the calculus equations.

When deciding how much to rely on intrinsic motivation to engage students in difficult learning, another aspect of motivation science that is important to keep in mind is the idea of goal systems. We all are pursuing many, many goals at any given point in time—staying healthy, saving for retirement, maintaining relationships, being fit, successfully pursuing career aims, and so on. These goals, of course, sometimes can complement each other (eating well helps with fitness, for instance) but also often compete (your gym membership eats away at your savings, for instance). We have limited time, energy, money, and other resources. We must constantly figure out where to dedicate more and less energy, and extrinsic guideposts are often how we enact those decisions, a process motivation researcher Ayelet Fishbach dubs "goal juggling."

Kai, the student who spoke in the last chapter about reframing arousal as a motivating hand helping us out of the water, spoke very clearly about goal juggling. When we asked him about regulating emotions in education, he used an economic metaphor. He described an almost mathematical approach to how he decided how much effort to invest in a given class or a given assignment. You have a limited amount of energy, a limited amount of time. How much impact is a given assignment going to have on your GPA? How much sleep will you have to forsake to finish it? How much time will it take away from other courses—and what is the relative importance of each course, for instance a general education requirement versus something in your major?

Kai is someone that most student success departments would love to study, because early on in his college journey he left after failing several classes. He took a year off—but unlike many students in this situation, he also came back. He tested out different fields—biology, chemistry—but it wasn't until he explored electrical engineering that his intrinsic fire was lit. Here's a circuit, here's a PCB, here is a car that can follow a line without any programming. He was amazed. He described his early learning in electrical engineering as "wanting it." When he ran into past professors in the hallway and they asked how his classes were going, he told them he didn't want them to end. He found himself burning hours on YouTube, in books, learning more. Being graded in his electrical engineering courses didn't diminish his fire. But being graded in his other courses *did* mean that he put some time into them instead of dedicating 100 percent of his efforts to engineering.

I am moved by the principles, energy, and student-centered nature of the ungrading movement. I have begun ungrading myself. In my upper-level neuroscience seminar, it worked beautifully and was everything the leaders in the field promised. I offered frequent, elaborate feedback on student work throughout the semester but assigned no points or grades to it. We each met in my office around midsemester and talked about the degree of effort and progress demonstrated by the student and where we both felt they would be on a traditional grading scale. In all but one case, across multiple semesters, either we were in agreement or I nudged their grade estimate higher. We went through the same process at the end of the semester. Grading was easier, they didn't feel judged, and the focus was on learning. If I teach this course in the future, I will always teach it ungraded.

I've had less successful experiences attempting different iterations in more introductory courses. One student in a more introductory course was in a similar position as Kai and found a lack of grades distressing. She was working full time and caretaking for some family in her home. She had a limited budget of school time to direct to her various courses and wanted to titrate this time throughout the semester so that she'd end up with at least a B minus in all her courses. Not knowing exactly where she stood in my course at any given moment entirely confounded her ability to use this approach to her studies. This student might have been served better by a method called *contract grading* rather than by ungrading. Contract grading is just like it sounds: the instructor and students enter into a contract at the start of the semester about what sorts of work will result in which sorts of grades, and each commits to the practice. Writing in the *UNgrading* edited collection, educators Christina Katopodis and Cathy Davidson argue that "asking students to determine success for themselves, and to carefully review and agree to a contract as members of a community, affords them an opportunity to practice self-determination—one of the most important qualities a self-reliant adult needs in any career path or community." Contract grading can maximize both autonomy and a feeling of competence.

Practicing with ungrading, I also found it tricky to motivate students to memorize some of the scientific information in my introductory brain and behavior course without some traditional assessments and grades. Unlike some voices in education, I continue to believe that it is important to establish some foundational knowledge before doing more creative intellectual work. As James Lang writes in his book *Small Teaching: Everyday Lessons from the Science of Learning*, "Knowledge is foundational: we won't have the structures in place to do deep thinking if we haven't spent time mastering a body of knowledge related to that thinking. . . . One cannot get to the top levels of creative and critical thinking without a broad and solid foundation of knowledge beneath them." He asks us to consider a skilled lawyer making her case in a court of law. Of course her skills of analysis, public speaking, and argumentation will assist her in winning her case—but without a foundational knowledge of previous cases, rulings, and the idiosyncrasies of the law at her disposal, those skills will do little to advance her cause. Similarly, in my upper-level neuroscience seminar none of the work we do relates to memorization—but my students are able to thoughtfully debate the merits of peer-reviewed journal articles in neuroscience because they memorized quite a lot of brain terms, regions, and functions in their earlier classes. They can easily draw on this information at will when generating hypotheses and critiques in the much more advanced course.

What to do, then, if there are such problems with traditional grading, but the alternatives have their own drawbacks? I don't have a clear answer, but I do have a clear plan, and it involves Josh. For Josh agreed to serve on the steering committee for a grant I received from the National Science Foundation (with co-principal investigator Michele Lemons of Assumption University). Together with this steering committee, Michele and I have convened a national network of scholars to examine all these issues I've been discussing: the problems with traditional grading, the barriers and constraints to innovation, and possible solutions. The network is focusing on introductory biology classes in particular. Introductory biology is a key launching point into so many STEM fields and careers, from medicine to marine science to biotech. It is also notoriously plagued by something called weed-out culture. Students feel—not always inaccurately—that intro bio courses are designed to be incredibly difficult so that only the "best" students (which often translates into "the students with the most privileged preparation") make it through the funnel of intro bio to later STEM careers.

The beating heart of this project is the question, How can we educate students in biology classrooms in such a way that they are intellectually challenged and prepared for the demands of scientific study while also encouraged to further pursue education in science? And moreover, how can we be sure that the intellectual challenge is not by design set up to fail students who don't come to college with a very specific background and preparation? In other words, this is a question about compassionate challenge.

My best guess is that the conclusion of this work will have a lot in common with the suggestions of another important group of scholars working on grading reform. Mathematician Robert Talbert and physicist David Clark are working on their own book on grading called *Grading for Growth*, and they are generously sharing their developing thinking in a Substack newsletter. They compellingly argue that instructors shouldn't get overly fixated on specific labels and whether we're following the practices of various grading alternatives "correctly," but instead whether our grading practices meet four pillars of effective grading:

1. Clearly defined standards. Are your expectations for success clear to your students?
2. Helpful feedback. Do you give more information than a letter or numerical grade, and does said feedback help your students do better on subsequent assignments?
3. Marks indicate progress.
4. Students are allowed reattempts without penalty.

While much of the work of the grant still lies ahead of me, our conclusions will be grounded in this question: Which assessment, feedback, and grading practices enhance students' sense of competence and self-efficacy? These guidelines of Talbert and Clark's (clear standards, helpful feedback, a focus on progress, and an orientation toward developing proficiency) all seem designed to do just that.

Another way to frame the difference between compassionate challenge and what some have taken to calling "toxic rigor" is to return to a subject from the previous chapter: warmth versus chilliness in academic climates.

I AM COMPETENT: WARM DEMANDERS

Whether one uses grades or avoids them, it is important for students' sense of competence to have an instructor who expects success of them. If, motivated by compassion, an instructor or leader adopts a too passive, permissive stance, they actually risk reducing the students' sense of competence and thus their motivation. In her marvelous book *Culturally Responsive Teaching and the Brain*, educator Zaretta Hammond cites the work of psychologist Judith Kleinfeld on being a "warm demander." Kleinfeld worked with Indigenous children from rural schools in the United States and found that the most effective teachers of these children adopted a teaching style characterized by two elements: personal warmth and active demandingness. *Personal warmth* referred to what we'll consider in the next section as the importance of establishing community and connection in the classroom, and we have already begun this discussion of how to demonstrate warmth and engagement in the classroom. *Active demandingness* was not unyielding rigor but an insistence on effort and excellence. The opposite of these characteristics was *professional distance* (being cold and standoffish) and *passive leniency* (no insistence on excellence and effort).

In the absence of warmth or encouragement, intellectual challenge can be the opposite of motivating. Teri, a chemical engineering major at a highly selective private university, told us of a particular class in physical engineering that she and her classmates found to embody the chilly side of challenge. The course involved a weekly problem set that was not tied to the material in lecture or on the exams—the problems were a thing unto themselves. Since the problems were exceedingly difficult and the relevant material was not in the instructor's class lectures, the only road to success was to visit the teaching assistants' office hours every week to get a primer on the material, and then work on the problem sets with classmates in marathon sessions every Sunday evening. These sessions would often stretch from seven to ten hours at a time—some Sundays, they'd finish just before dawn and, blearily gazing at the sun rising, put on a change of clothes and go to class. It felt to Teri and her fellow students almost like they were being hazed by their professor, that he felt it was a rite of passage for students to get through this amount of work rather than it really having anything to do with their learning. After all, if the material was important, wouldn't he talk about it in class or include it on the exams?

In sharp contrast to this approach, warm demanders first explicitly build rapport and trust with their students before introducing high demand. They express curiosity about and interest in their students' personal lives. They are competent in the classroom—with teaching, and with technology. They have high standards for their students' performance but explicitly provide supports and scaffolding for learning and are transparent in their assessment. They inspire "productive struggle."

Hammond and I are far from the only voices encouraging instructors to challenge students in a warm or encouraging way. Karen Costa, the educational developer we met in chapter 4, has been offering workshops on "challenge-aware, trauma-informed" pedagogy. Tracie Addy, coauthor of *What Inclusive Instructors Do* and associate dean of teaching and learning at Lafayette College, calls this melding of warmth and demand *compassionate expectation* and identifies it as being sourced in the practices of relationship building, responsiveness, setting explicit learning goals and expectations, being adaptable within boundaries, and being willing to have hard conversations. A warm-demander approach is clearly becoming a common ground among many scholars thinking about how to best support student excellence.

Autonomy helps us shape our own futures, and perceived competence helps us believe that we have the skills to enact them. The third pillar of self-determination is belongingness, and it provides a solid grounding from which we can strive as well as visualizations of what success might look like for us.

BELONGINGNESS

What does home smell like to you?

Call it up, spend a few moments simmering in the sensations. To me, home smells like vinegar and garlic, gleaming glass vats of pickles releasing their steam into the air. Bubbling spaghetti sauce brewing from garden tomatoes, peppers sliced right over the giant pan with a paring knife by my mother. The sharp smell of pine combined with a crackling woodstove fire at the start of Christmas season. Basset hound grease (don't ask). Dad's Cabot cheddar on pumpernickel with onions burning in the oven, and don't you dare take them out before the cheese is bubbling and the bread is turning black and crisp.

Home is coded in sights, in turns of phrase, by whether you are frequently touched or left to yourself, whether voices rise in anger and enthusiasm or whether they stay soft and modulated. In whether the dogs are allowed on the couch or not. Or—god forbid—there are no dogs. Whether you answer "How are you?" with reassuring, peace-keeping platitudes or whether you tell the bracing truth. But *so much* of home is rooted in smell and taste, in the molecules that we take into our bodies to detect them. For unlike the light hitting our retinas or the sound waves hitting our ears, smell and taste are the few senses that involve the actual molecules of the exterior being taken into our interior. Literally made part of ourselves.

One question we asked all Student Voices participants was about whether they felt welcome on campus (and if so, in what ways and settings), and correspondingly, whether they ever felt isolated or alone on campus (and if so, in what ways and settings). I was struck by two answers to this question that spoke so clearly to each other and elegantly about the concept of home. Both involved food.

The first of these interviewees was Adam, the junior marketing major we met in the previous chapter. Adam was a Black student at a predominantly white institution. When we asked him about feeling welcome, he immediately told us all the ways he felt welcome on campus. He was a transfer student, and a sense of welcome was one of his primary reasons for transferring to the institution. He had started his intellectual journey at another college but had a close friend at this transfer institution and whenever he visited his friend, he was struck by how open and friendly everyone was on campus. After transferring, his impression of being welcome was continually reaffirmed, from the atmosphere his professors established in the classroom to students greeting each other across campus to the clubs he had joined. He was happy with his college.

But when we asked Adam about feeling isolated or alone on campus, he surprised us by focusing on food. He would enter the dining hall and stand in line with a plastic tray, watch as the servers would pile on bland, culture-stripped offerings of underseasoned stir-fries and mushy pasta. In these moments he would be swamped with a longing for home, for the tastes and traditions of his family. He would suddenly feel separate, different. On his own.

The second student who spoke of food and welcome was Jacinta, a senior mass communications student at a historically Black institution. When we asked about feelings of belongingness, she immediately thought of a weekly tradition on her own campus called What's Up! Wednesdays. On this day the cafeteria would focus on soul food, warm and nourishing and nostalgic. It wasn't just about the food, though—there would be great music, lots of people dressed up, and everyone would push the benches and chairs to the periphery of the room to allow for dancing. It was a tradition that made her feel at home, nourished body and soul, and made her feel one with her fellow students but also connected to her feeling of family.

Adam's and Jacinta's stories clearly illustrate our craving for belongingness. As we will see, belongingness is also critical to students' intrinsic motivation, to the extent to which they can determine themselves. One way that we can underscore a sense of belonging is to think about our classes as ensembles—we'll cover this idea in chapter 8 when we discuss play and improvisational learning. In this chapter, I'd like to consider how important it is to be sure that every student in our class feels welcome, feels like they belong. As we will see, establishing this welcome involves quality representation and inclusive teaching practices.

I BELONG: THE IMPORTANCE OF REPRESENTATION

In 2014, I brought my then eight-year-old to see the *Annie* reboot. I have a gigantic soft spot for both platonic love stories and melodrama, and *Annie* hits all the right notes. That night as I snuggled my daughter down to sleep, she lamented that she'd love to play Annie in a stage play someday and was sad that the role was closed to her. Confused, I asked why—*Annie* is a frequent choice for youth theaters, and several such groups and camps are available in the community where we live.

"Because," she responded, the implicit *duh* threaded in her tone, "I don't have the right hair or skin to play Annie." For in the reboot, Annie is played by Quvenzhané Wallis, who is Black. Just one single instance was able to convince my daughter that an entire realm of experience was closed to her—and one can imagine the decades of girls who thought *they* couldn't play Annie because they weren't freckled and redheaded.

Nnamdi Pole, a clinical psychologist at Smith College in Massachusetts, shared with me two compelling stories about representation in an interview. While in graduate school at Berkeley, he was at a party when a fellow partygoer, a Black man who was in the law school (let's call him Ben), approached him. Ben asked what department Nnamdi was in and was confused when Nnamdi told him psychology. Ben asked, "Were you a teaching assistant?" Nnamdi confirmed that yes, he was. Ben said, "Really? Because I was an undergrad at Cal Berkeley taking psychology classes a few years ago and was looking everywhere for Black folks, because I didn't see any. And so I decided psychology wasn't for me."

Just like that.

Nnamdi personally can't imagine making such a huge decision based solely on representation, but this wasn't the only time this issue came up for him. In his graduate program there was a bulletin board with pictures of all the graduate students and their names, and there was space for undergraduates to leave interesting questions for the graduate students pinned under their profile. Multiple times across his graduate training, he would receive a note from a total stranger saying, "My name is X. I'm Black. I see that you are at Berkeley. Would you meet me for coffee and tell me how you got there?" He asked his white colleagues if they had ever in their life had someone approach them in this way and they all said no.

"It's very much what you're saying, this Annie thing," Nnamdi said. "It seems that people literally do decide, this is not a path for me unless I see someone that looks in some way like me in that role. Of course, it's not just race—I'm sure this happens to women professors of all races in math and engineering, for instance—but it does seem to be one way that people choose their path in life, and it demonstrates how important it is to have representation."

It is *particularly* important that students from traditionally underrepresented groups see people who belong to their social groups in front of their classrooms, leading labs, and making policy decisions on campus, because these students are most likely to have paid the biggest cost in social embeddedness by removing themselves from their existing social networks in order to come to college in the first place. In her moving and important book *Moving Up Without Losing Your Way: The Ethical Costs of Upward Mobility*, philosopher Jennifer Morton from the City College of New York writes that those students who do the difficult work of engaging in higher education despite the many practical and economic barriers that face them have a whole additional level of barriers to surmount. That "in order to succeed, [they] will have to prioritize their own path over important relationships, over obligations to their family, and over maintaining their ties to their community. In so doing, they risk sacrificing important and meaningful aspects of their lives and identities." If they are then greeted by institutions that make little to no effort (or poorly executed good efforts) to welcome them with potential new ties and groups with which they can share meaning, then this cost will be doubled.

In the Student Voices project, we talked to Krystan, a junior psychology major at a small institution. She has a disability that creates some challenges for her in pursuing her degree. When we asked her about a sense of belonging and some of her most positive learning experiences in college, she told us at length about a certain professor. He was an engaging lecturer and cared about developing relationships with his students, telling her all about his cousins and siblings in office hours. But critical for this student was the fact that this instructor was blind. He explicitly drew a connection between his disability and hers, sketching out a path to success for her. "I could do it," he told her, "and so can you." He didn't minimize the difficulties along that path, the greater effort required of them than of abled students and colleagues, the setbacks and the struggles. But he expressed an abiding faith that she could achieve whatever she wanted, that she had a rich life and good fortune ahead of her. He told her, "You inspire me." Krystan shared that her parents and other abled professors had expressed this faith to her, but that she never believed it in her bones until she heard it from this particular professor. Someone who had traveled a similar road.

Philosopher Zena Hitz writes of the human need to see what one wants to be: "It is images and models that we need: attractive fantasies to set us in a certain direction and to draw us on, reminders of who we once were and who or what we might be." It is harder to immerse yourself in this future-based fantasy if all the mentors and scholars who surround you don't look like or talk like you, if they, in fact, look and talk like people who have always had more opportunities in your society. How do we create communities that welcome all members? The clearest and most simple answer is to hire and promote a diversity of faculty.

I am willing to bet that nearly every college and university in the United States has written in its latest strategic plan, its recent job announcements, and its mission that hiring and promoting faculty from underrepresented genders, races, and ethnicities is of the utmost priority.

But in practice, these policies rarely translate into action.

Recently on Twitter someone shared a GIF of one of those cutesy recipe videos where, in sped-up frames, you see a pair of hands tossing ingredients in a pan, whisking them up, and creating a mouthwatering masterpiece in a few seconds. The tagline of this one was "Every university enacting their diversity policy"—and amusingly, there were no ingredients. The hands went through a show of tossing, stirring, basting, but the ingredients were invisible, missing, and the result was nothing but air.

As an academic who has sat on many search committees and has many academic friends who sit on their university search committees, I can attest that, all too often, diverse faculty and women *do* make it through the early hoops of the byzantine application process to rise to the top of the short list. But at the end of the day, the position so often goes to a white male from a graduate program at an elite school with a high publication count and a wife at home. The other candidates were good, but they didn't have as many publications. Or they weren't in journals with quite the right impact factors. Or they just didn't speak as "intellectually" about the religious mission of the college. Or the diverse candidate makes it to the top slot, but the administration is unwilling to commit the supportive resources required to recruit them, and the job is taken by the majority candidate one down on the list.

I truly believe that in most cases, the deciding parties think that they are being objective, that they are sifting through the candidates and honoring diversity but in the end feel compelled to award the position to someone who they feel is the most "meritorious" candidate. They are simply blind to the ways in which the allure of someone who thinks like them, writes like them, and prioritizes the varied demands of an academic job like them leads them to the perception that people like them are more "objectively" deserving. Which is problematic not only for reasons of inequity of opportunities, as elite, educated white people award opportunities to other elite, educated white people, but also because it cheapens the entire intellectual endeavor that is education. For as improv expert Kelly Leonard writes, "Like-minded individuals from like-minded backgrounds will produce like-minded results," leading to impoverished outcomes, stale versions of what would be possible with truly diverse voices. But this is even more reason why people in administrative roles must consciously override these biases, or the system will ever perpetuate itself.

I BELONG: INCLUSIVE TEACHING PRACTICES

At the institutional level, we can support belongingness with fully actualized representation rather than equity policies that are mere promise. What can we do at the classroom level? Viji Sathy and Kelly Hogan are a psychologist and a biologist, respectively, at the University of North Carolina at Chapel Hill. Of like mind and like teaching practices, they teamed up a few years ago and formed the consulting group InclusifiED. They write, teach, and speak together about honoring all the many identities students bring with them to college campuses, and Sathy and Hogan work with faculty to change their practices in the classroom so that they are reaching all their students. In their book *Inclusive Teaching:*

Strategies for Promoting Equity in the Classroom, they write that "inclusive teaching includes the intentional ways instructors interact with students, provide multiple opportunities to practice the work in a discipline, and demonstrate care." Sathy and Hogan define inclusive teaching as practices that intentionally invite participation and engagement from all learners, regardless of their identities, degree of introversion/extraversion, previous learning experiences, strengths, and weaknesses.

An aspect of Hogan and Sathy's model of inclusive teaching that I most appreciate is how high levels of intentional structure in teaching benefits all students, and students coming to the classroom from less well-resourced secondary education experiences most of all. This is a bit counter-intuitive. You might think that a looser, more free-flowing class structure would be more inclusive. But as discussed earlier, students from elite and privileged high schools have had extensive training in the expectations of teachers. Many have taken Advanced Placement courses explicitly designed to replicate college classes. They have greater access to the meaning, traditions, and expectations undergirding college courses and are more easily able to intuit the intentions of the instructor. By crafting syllabi, participation, assignments, and class policies to explicitly call out these expectations and invisible assumptions, educators can create more welcoming and equitable classrooms. Such practices might include giving examples of past completed assignments, sharing grading rubrics ahead of time, including explanations for common terms and policies (e.g., office hours), and including "tips for success" on assignments.

Providing structure is just one way to teaching inclusively. In the book *What Inclusive Instructors Do: Principles and Practices for Excellence in College Teaching*, Tracie Marcella Addy, Derek Dube, Khadijah Mitchell, and Mallory SoRelle break inclusive teaching into the design of courses, demonstrating welcome to all students, and conducting the class inclusively. They highlight practices such as sending a "who's in class?" survey to students in advance of the semester to get to know the individual strengths and challenges of a given class of students, including diverse perspectives in readings and assignments, and incorporating student feedback into the course.

A final way to be inclusive and reinforce students' sense of belongingness is to explicitly welcome them into the life of the mind and show them that they, too, can contribute to the world's collection of insight and knowledge. In *The Narrow Road to the Deep North*, writer Richard Flanagan's character is looking for a copy of *The Aeneid* in a dusty library with slanted light when he is struck by a particular atmosphere he feels around certain books:

> an aura that both radiated outwards and took him inwards to another world that said to him that he was not alone. And this sense, this feeling of communion, would at moments overwhelm him. At such times he had the sensation that there was only one book in the universe, and that all books were simply portals into this greater ongoing work—an inexhaustible, beautiful world that was not imaginary but the world as it truly was, a book without beginning or end.

In higher education we are writing this collective book of insight together, and what greater motivation could there be than feeling connected to this endless pursuit of knowledge? Biologist and educational developer Bryan Dewsbury writes beautifully of wanting to convince students to see their transcripts, college credits, and degrees as "artificial endpoints that restrict the unbridled pursuit of knowledge." He wants his students instead to feel limited by the classroom, to ache to stretch beyond it. "I want my pedagogy to encourage students to demand more of the moment and themselves, aspiring in every waking second to this ideal. I want this ideal to hang like a guiding star above the classroom, reminding all involved of our collective responsibility to each other and the common good." Welcoming students to work on independent research with faculty members, innovative assignments that ask students to create their own scholarship, and even just highlighting past contributions from previous students at the institution can underscore this welcome to a life of the mind.

So there we have it, the three pillars of self-determination theory—autonomy, competence, and belongingness—applied to adolescent mental health and their education. Setting up their learning environments to fulfill these basic psychological needs (compassion) may encourage youth to funnel their future-directed energy and arousal into motivated pursuits rather than anxious rumination (challenge).

But what happens when our social structures undercut autonomy, competence, belongingness, and sense of purpose?

DRIVE TO THRIVE REVISITED: SELF-DETERMINATION WORKS ONLY WHEN FABRICS SUPPORT YOU

You might recall that in chapter 3 I discussed at length Wai Kai Hou's "drive to thrive" theory. Hou makes the argument that resilience lies not in the individual and their personality and coping mechanisms but rather the routines of their lives, a person's "interwoven psychosocial and communal activities, procedures, and practices," and the degree to which they are or are not disrupted by stress and trauma. These routines are shaped by our individual choices, by our families, by our neighborhoods, and on and on—we can keep broadening the social circles that shape the communal activities, procedures, and practices that are possible, that are open to us, and that are encouraged. In a way, these interwoven, overlapping fabrics make up our societies. What this means is that, to a large degree, the constructions of our fabrics are out of our hands.

You can only determine yourself in circumstances that allow for self-determination. You can't feel autonomous if you have no power to make meaningful choices about your life. You can't feel competent if your schooling is set up to discourage your efforts. You can't sense belongingness if you look around you and don't see communal activities, social support, and people you identify with who have achieved success. You can't choose a life of purpose if you are boxed by precarity and scarcity into making choices that pay your rent rather than feed your soul or change the world.

In the excellent book *Sedated: How Modern Capitalism Created Our Mental Health Crisis*, psychologist James Davies powerfully documents how a series of changes to social structures—such as the decimation of the social safety net,* the rise of the service field, and cultural support for individual over collective solutions to problems—has led to sharp declines in mental

---

*It is fascinating to me that a net is, of course, a type of fabric.

health. Moreover, these same forces have created cultural support for the idea that malaise that is actually related to the collective problems of low self-determination (e.g., overwork, meaningless work, wage stagnation, income inequality, lack of social support, racism, ageism, and so on) is both the fault and the responsibility of the individual. Following the logic of this mistaken idea, if it is flaws within the individual (whether neurochemical, flawed thinking, lack of resilience) that are causing mental health problems, then the solutions should also be individual. A pill, perhaps, or an employer-mandated wellness program. But a pill or a wellness program can never battle problems like income inequality or racism.

Davies believes that true change can only happen in changing these societal structures and providing actual support for the needs of a country's citizens. In the meantime, he believes youth in particular need supportive relationships. "In the end," he writes, "it is the ability of mental health interventions to obscure the social roots of distress that perhaps casts their longest shadow. . . . We must accept that for many children, the truest and most effective therapy won't be found in a pill, a consultancy room or a classroom intervention, but in loving and meaningful human relationships that endeavor to mitigate the harsher social forces and impacts that they neither perceive nor understand." Mitigating harm is a good first step—but again, a more powerful intervention would be tackling these problems at their root.

CONCLUSION

Human beings are naturally driven to determine ourselves, to carve out lives of meaning that we choose, where we are effective actors in our efforts, and where we feel embedded in a social landscape of shared meaning. We are also drawn to contribute to something bigger than the small lives we are granted.

As the neuroscientist and gifted science writer Oliver Sacks wrote in his book *Hallucinations*:

To live on a day-to-day basis is insufficient for human beings; we need to transcend, transport, escape; we need meaning, understanding, and explanation; we need to see overall patterns in our lives. We need hope, the sense of a future. And we need freedom (or at least the illusion of freedom), to get beyond ourselves, whether with telescopes and microscopes and our ever-burgeoning technology or in states of mind which allow us to travel to other worlds, to transcend our immediate surroundings. We need detachment of this sort as much as we need engagement in our lives.

By establishing compassionate environments that support and nourish the psychological needs of autonomy, competence, and belongingness, our youth are likely to challenge *themselves*.

So far we have considered how compassionate challenge works at the level of the body and brain and now at the level of beliefs. Next up: behaviors.

PART FOUR

BEHAVIORS

CHAPTER SEVEN

AROUSAL, ACTION, AND UNCERTAINTY

PAUSE FOR A MOMENT and run your fingertips over the landscape of your life to find its most tender moments—times when your heart skipped a beat and the world seemed suddenly fresh and new again, open to possibility.

I am willing to bet that these moments all involved a certain degree of uncertainty, physiological arousal, and psychological vulnerability. We can follow all the other advice in this book and smooth out our life rhythms and tapestries so that our days follow a steady and predictable flow, we can shore up the internal budgets of our bodies with good sleep and exercise, and we can work hard to pin down the future by following a path of self-determination. But at some point, life is going to break that all open, for better or for worse. A diagnosis, a job offer, a pandemic, the birth of a child. Life's most beautiful and most tragic moments are rarely predicted, and they are intense. We must rise and meet them.

Importantly, we don't have to passively wait for life to jar us out of our complacency with these unexpected moments—we can lean into vulnerability, into discomfort, to learn something new about the world or ourselves, to stretch our capabilities, and to shake the dust of daily living from our eyes. For most of the book so far, we've considered ways to help our youth control the settings and rhythms in their lives to feel safe, to be healthy and achieve balance, to belong, and to be excited for rather than terrified of the future. But at long last we are prepared to be challenged, to be provoked, to be pushed a bit beyond our so-called comfort zone, because we know we are starting from a secure base. We have compassion, and now we need to add in challenge.

For as we have considered from the beginning, this exposure to discomfort in a safe setting is crucial for reducing states of heightened anxiety and nipping in the bud the spread of anxiety into more situations. We need to help young people become comfortable with heightened states of arousal and interpret that arousal in nonthreatening ways so that they can focus on their learning and their well-being.

But as it turns out, arousal is not just integral to good mental health. It is also critical for learning itself.

"ANGST REQUIRED": AROUSAL AND LEARNING

Learning is a change in understanding, skills, or behavior based on experience. Human beings are biological creatures who are not mired in the present moment. Through the processes of memory and learning, the past lives with us still—and through imagination, ambition, and anxiety, we strive to stretch ourselves into the future. But while learning means carrying the past into the present, we do not learn everything. In fact, there is an important role for forgetting in the process of efficient memory, which raises the question: How do organisms select what to remember and what to forget?

The last few decades have seen a burgeoning of attention paid to this question in secondary and higher education, and the data point to a somewhat surprising role for emotions and other affective processes in learning. For as students decide how much attention to pay and effort to apply to their studies, they are guided by their emotions—what they are interested in, what they are fascinated by, what they are outraged about, and what they see as important for their future lives or careers. As neuroscientist Mary Helen Immordino-Yang, a pioneer in this work, often says, we only think deeply about things that we care about.

In chapter 6, we considered Reinhard Pekrun's control-value theory of achievement emotions, which has had an enormous influence on the study of student motivation and learning. He categorizes the types of emotions that arise during the process of learning into four quadrants, classified by both their *valence* (how pleasant to unpleasant they feel) and their *arousal* (degree to which they energize or activate). Studies reveal that positive activating emotions like curiosity and pride are most associated with good outcomes, and negative deactivating emotions like shame and disgust are the least. More complex are the relationships between positive deactivating (maybe relief will result in a motivational slump?) and negative activating (might not being frustrated or angry sometimes spur hard work?) emotions during learning and the quality of said learning. There is evidence that even though these positive states feel pleasant and the negative ones unpleasant, they nonetheless impact learning.

Because what might be critical here is not the valence element, whether things are pleasant or unpleasant, but rather the arousal one. An activated nervous system is one that is primed for learning, as these states arise when something important is happening in our environment. It is also when our brains get jarred out of their autopilot, because a prediction has gone awry. Something new has happened, and the system needs to be updated to accommodate this new information. A previously reliable friend has ghosted you, your morning commute is doubled by a new construction project, your usual lunch spot gives you a belly ache—these unexpected developments provoke the arousal of emotions and also new learning and changes in behaviors. You turn to a new friend, find a new route to work, and pack your lunch.

We have better memory for emotional information and events than neutral information and events. These effects seem to be linked to the fact that emotions are physiologically arousing, and part of this arousal involves the hormonal release of epinephrine (adrenaline) and also norepinephrine, which cues the brain to consolidate those memories more thoroughly. In my book *The Spark of Learning: Energizing the College Classroom with the Science of Emotion*, I have taken this body of work and applied it to the practical work of college educators in the classroom, considering both the implications for our teaching practices and the communities that we build in the classroom.

Studies of memory, stress, and anxiety in the classroom reveal a familiar refrain: stress results when there is both an external stressor like an exam or interpersonal conflict *and* a perception that coping resources are low—both appraisals are necessary for a stress response. When such a combined perception arises, then two systems come online—first, a fast autonomic response (think elevated heart rate and skin sweating) and, second, a slower hormonal response (involving the HPA axis, HPA standing for hypothalamus-pituitary-adrenal). The fast response prepares us for fight or flight and affects brain regions involved in learning and memory through the release of catecholamines like dopamine and adrenaline. The slower response affects the same brain areas but through the release of stress hormones like cortisol. All this means that in examining the impact of stress on memory in the classroom, asking *when* is important.

Researchers Susanne Vogel and Lars Schwabe write in a review of this literature that, worryingly, "by altering the balance between memory systems, stress may lead to strong, rigid memories and the retrieval of habits rather than creative and complex solutions to new problems, which may again lead to an underestimation of the students' abilities." Like so many other experiences and behaviors, arousal and memory are related in an inverted-U way—low levels of arousal lead to poor, shallow memories and skill acquisition, but so, too, do extremely high levels of arousal. You want to hit the sweet spot in the middle.

In the Student Voices project, many students discussed how anxiety can disrupt learning, and most of them framed it in terms of its effects on their attention. Anxiety-based arousal seems to dominate all available cognitive resources, almost to the level where it appears that such high levels of arousal shut down processing of the external environment to focus on the changes in one's body and the worries skittering around one's mind.

For instance, Student Voices participant Andre, a senior cybersecurity major at a small liberal arts university, told us that he would experience states of "panic" in classes where he wasn't able to follow along or understand the content. *What am I doing wrong, do I need extra help, what is the problem here?* would occupy his thoughts, and he'd find afterward that not only had he experienced a moment of struggle with the material but also the effects were such that, following these moments, he had blanked out for a significant portion of the class.

So, how to hit the right note, land right in one's ideal level of arousal? This seems like an exceedingly difficult question, so let's check in with an expert.

EPISTEMIC VEXATION: EMBRACING "NOT-KNOWING"

Ayanna Kim Thomas is a professor of psychology and dean of research for arts and sciences at Tufts University in Medford, Massachusetts. She is also the editor in chief of the renowned psychology journal *Memory and Cognition*, where she applies her expertise in memory retrieval and bias to shape the trajectory of our understanding of human cognition, learning, and memory, and doing so in a way that supports better equity and diversity in cognitive science.

In some of her current work, she is teaming up with colleagues in the Education and Engineering Departments at Tufts to explore the dual impact of physiological arousal and beliefs about learning on student success. They are starting with the study of math, both because the subject is a notorious trigger of anxiety for so many students and because it is required as a core underpinning for most of the STEM disciplines. Math instruction is thus an important moment to understand. Many students trip up early in their study in STEM fields, their future aims of being a doctor or an engineer dashed on the rocks of discouraging early experiences in some of these formative classes.

In terms of beliefs about learning, Ayanna and her collaborators are targeting how students think about their own emotional experiences during the process of learning. Her colleague David Hammer, a learning scientist, calls these thinking-about-learning emotions "meta-affect." How do students think and feel about their own feelings? David was inspired in part by a student in his introductory physics class whom he observed physically shaking during exams. He and some co-authors published a case study of this student's progress and their reflections about her journey, calling her by the pseudonym Mayra. He and his teaching assistants worked closely with Mayra over the course of a semester, attempting to persuade her to see *not-knowing* as an experience inherent to the study of physics rather than a failing on her part, and to even enjoy that feeling. He and his colleagues view meta-affect as necessary for the enjoyment of otherwise negative learning experiences—only by acknowledging that the feeling is present and only in *settings that are safe*, can one enjoy frustration or confusion or dismay. In the paper, David and colleagues quote several famous educators and scientists about these feelings of joy commingled with confusion and frustration: the "joy of going at it," "the pleasure of finding things out," the "torment of the unknown," the "angst required to motivate the search," and the possibility of "finding pleasure in mystery."

These epistemic (having to do with the process of knowing) feelings were frequently endorsed by Student Voices participants. Aditya, a junior computer-science major at a selective private university on the East Coast, discussed this quest for resolving not-knowing as even more important to his enjoyment of classes than anything to do with the professors themselves or the activities they chose in classes. When we asked him about his best learning experiences in college, he framed his response in terms of classes that contained coding assignments that were like puzzles whose solutions were accessible but difficult, creating in him a mental itch to solve them. He particularly liked when the coding assignment would keep him up at night, buzzing in his mind as he fell asleep—and he would sometimes awaken with solutions in mind and leap out of bed to scribble them down. Chuckling and leaning forward, he told us that during these times when a coding puzzle was pestering him, his friends would often get annoyed because he wouldn't be able to stop talking about the problem, and his behavior would become erratic; he was "jumpy" and excited. He identified it as a "fun frustration, not a negative frustration." David's collaborator, physicist Jennifer Radoff, calls this feeling "epistemic vexation."

In David and his colleagues' analyses of multiple sources of data, which included extensive interviews with Mayra, they concluded that her transition from feeling apprehensive about physics to excited about it was tied to two key transitions—first, how she experienced uncertainty personally and, second, how she interpreted uncertainty as an integral part of doing physics. It became, in her own words, "about the journey and the question" rather than getting the correct answer.

Intriguingly, many Student Voices participants also mapped for us a journey of feeling panicked by this sense of not-knowing early in their college careers, but over time (exposure again!) learning that epistemic vexation is part of the journey of becoming a scholar and to embrace it. Some even developed clever strategies for managing the tension of not-knowing. Sakura, a junior health sciences major at a small liberal arts college in New England, reported that early on in her educational career she would get very anxious in class when she didn't understand the material. The anxiety would make her "blank out" on what was happening in class, disrupt her attention, and shift it to her worries and her physiological arousal—which of course, would interfere with her learning of the material even further. Over time, she came up with the solution of drawing a little star in the margins of her notes whenever she felt this not-knowing feeling arise. Later, she would revisit the starred places while doing her reading, while having study groups with friends, or in office hours with her instructors. Knowing these solutions would be in place meant she could note the feeling of not-knowing and calmly move on without disruption.

In conversations with David and other collaborators, Ayanna became fixed on the question of what was driving these students' distraction, the underlying mechanisms by which anxiety interferes with learning and with performance on assessments. Were they blanking out because of the rumination (thinking, worrying) or because of the physiological response that was orienting all their attention to their bodies rather than to the content of the exam?

In the study that she is launching with David and others, Ayanna and her team are trying their best to address this question by tracking student reports of their emotions, their physiological arousal, and their learning of the material, in real time. Through the combination of these multiple measurements and some pretty complicated statistics, they hope to untangle the contributions of these variables to learning and to map their relationships as they unfold in actual classrooms. On the team are not just psychologists like Ayanna and educators like David but also mathematicians and engineers and critical race theorists, and everyone has a theory and a pet variable of interest. "Ooh, we can put sensors on the teeth to get a constant measure of cortisol," Ayanna said. "And oh wait, maybe we can look at brain activity using EEG! I mean we just keep going and going and going and the engineers want to just keep going and going and . . . wow." Ayanna's excitement about the possibilities is infectious, and in her excitement, she recalls Aditya talking about his coding puzzles.

This point isn't lost on her, that in conducting this experiment the scientists are experiencing the very effects they seek to study in their students—like a Mobius loop of epistemic excitement. *This* is what we need to help youth experience, this self-propelling seeking energy that feeds on itself and pushes the boundaries of how hard one is willing to work and to invest oneself. Both being anxious about one's performance in a class and being excited about the sense of being on a journey to solve a puzzle will result in heightened physiological arousal—what's essential is the interpretation, the appraisal. Ayanna thinks that students misidentify this bewilderment of not-knowing as the enemy, the monster. They want to conquer it, to rub it out. (If you want to know what she sees as the true monster, hold on for a bit—we'll get there.) They instead need to reinterpret, or reappraise, the not-knowing as pleasant instead of unpleasant.

"You know," Ayanna said, "it's like how we love horror movies—but Heather and Keith do not." Ayanna and I bond over our shared love of horror, but we frequently rope some mutual friends into the experience—friends who love us very much but very much do not love horror. When a new horror movie comes out, Heather and Keith trek along for the social experience, and we bribe them with dinner first. As Ayanna and I become progressively gleeful over the course of dinner in anticipation of the jumps and the unsettled feelings to come, Heather and Keith become progressively apprehensive. It is the same external situation—dinner and a movie. In many ways, it is also the same *internal* experience—of heightened excitement and sudden bursts of adrenaline. But because the appraisals are different, so, too, is the interpretation of pleasure versus dismay, and so, too, is the physical experience of excitement versus anxiety.

This individual difference between loving versus loathing recreational horror is probably, like most individual differences one could probe, the result of a complex blend of genetics, childhood experiences, parenting, and personality. But I believe it also probably relates to a trait that is a key underpinning to both our understanding of anxiety and our ability to appreciate *not-knowing*. This trait is called *uncertainty intolerance*.

THE TERRIFYING UNKNOWN: UNCERTAINTY INTOLERANCE

My mother hates New Year's Eve. She's not much better sold on anniversaries or milestone birthdays. She stands at the present moment and looks at the unfolding future—the next year, the next five, the next ten—and then she turns and looks behind her at the same set of years and sees their losses, their deaths, their hardships. She can't help but wonder, what's next? What's in store? The certainty that there will be terrors combined with the uncertainty of their exact shape unmoors her. She'd rather not think about it. My little brother, in contrast, can never understand her in these moments. He reasons that you can't do anything about all that uncertainty, so why even think about it? So he just doesn't. Like some sort of practical-person magic trick. He just faces forward without looking back.

Clearly, some people are better at managing uncertainty than others. Critically, how well you do or don't respond to uncertainty predicts a lot about your mental health. Uncertainty intolerance is often measured with a paper-and-pencil self-report scale that asks respondents to rate items like "I should be able to organize everything in advance," and "A small unforeseen event can spoil everything, even with the best of planning." One researcher calls it a "trait-like disposition that reflects a fundamental fear of the unknown and negative beliefs about uncertainty and its associated implications." This definition of uncertainty intolerance should sound a lot like our repeated definition of anxiety as the dual perception that the future is threatening and that one lacks the resources to cope. Uncertainty intolerance is believing that the unknown is scary, and that one might not be able to cope with whatever the future holds.

Research has shown that intolerance of uncertainty can occur both in the present moment ("This ambiguous moment is intolerable") and regarding the future ("I can't predict what's coming, and that's terrible"). Both types of uncertainty intolerance are highly associated with each other, and both share the "same core fear of the unknown." Interestingly, uncertainty intolerance is associated with heightened startle responses, even when you control for the degree to which someone is consciously worrying, suggesting that it is a physiologically based phenomenon and involves a hyperactivity of the body. People who are intolerant of uncertainty are more likely to interpret all ambiguous information as potentially threatening, and this interpretation is associated with significant elevations of biological processes such as heart rate, blood pressure, and startle response—little revs of the fight-or-flight system.

Uncertainty intolerance was originally studied in the context of generalized anxiety disorder, in which a person chronically worries across multiple different realms of life over long periods of time. Subsequent research has demonstrated that uncertainty intolerance is actually a "transdiagnostic" construct serving as a correlate of and a vulnerability factor for multiple forms of anxiety disorders and also depression. Uncertainty intolerance can manifest itself both in how a person interprets uncertainty and in how they behave in response to it—which is usually to withdraw or at least become apprehensive. Many people high in uncertainty intolerance attempt to control the future as a method for dealing with the discomfort that future uncertainty introduces. As I discussed in the previous chapter, some attempts to control the future can be adaptive, if the person throws themselves into goal pursuit and other healthy behaviors. Too often, though, people high in uncertainty intolerance come to believe that merely by worrying about possible negative outcomes, they can control said outcomes, which reinforces the worrying and makes it worse. Alternatively, they avoid situations that are uncertain, which can spiral into a greater withdrawal from social contact and opportunities for growth.

While it is true that this trait can be transdiagnostic, spanning multiple disorders, the flavor of how uncertainty intolerance manifests also varies by disorder type. In generalized anxiety disorder, it manifests as worry. Fear of the judgment of social others is how uncertainty intolerance expresses itself in social anxiety disorders. A sense of inflated responsibility for outcomes of the uncertainty is the focus for obsessive-compulsive disorder. Finally, uncertainty intolerance in panic disorder manifests as catastrophic interpretations of bodily signals and agoraphobic tendencies. Intriguingly (maybe just from my perspective, since it is self-relevant), while all these disorders are associated more strongly with their particular subtypes of uncertainty intolerance than the others, they also share robust relationships with a more generalized uncertainty intolerance—except for panic disorder, which seems to specialize more than the rest. People with panic disorder are highly focused on the possible meaning of their internal body signals but seem to manage other forms of uncertainty relatively well.

Many researchers conceptualize uncertainty intolerance as a vulnerability factor, predicting future elevation in symptoms or diagnostic flare-up in response to life stress. But at least one study of college freshmen over a year found that it was more of a component of distress than a predictor of future stress. Namely, while uncertainty intolerance tracked with symptoms of anxiety and depression (both uncertainty intolerance and mental distress elevating and dipping in concert), there was no evidence that uncertainty intolerance came first and mental distress second. So maybe it is less that people prone to uncertainty intolerance are more susceptible to anxiety and more that uncertainty intolerance is an important element of anxiety itself.

Uncertainty is core not just to anxiety but also to our definitions of the monstrous. Monsters are defined by what writer Jeffrey Jerome Cohen calls "a genetic uncertainty principle, the essence of the monster's vitality, the reason it always rises from the dissection table as its secrets are about to be revealed and vanishes into the night." Much of horror storytelling in general centers on the ambiguous, the uncertain. These stories explicitly raise questions about whether certain horrors are real or instead figments of the protagonist's imagination, or about whether the narrator can be trusted. We are often left uncertain about the exact nature of the creatures who spend most of the movie skittering or slithering around the corners of the film frame. Writer Simon Strantzas argues that these ambiguities are essential to the structure of horror: "What frustrates about ambiguity is our certainty that those answers do exist but are unreachable—we see the shape of them in the void but cannot make them out." As in life, we want the uncertainty resolved. As discussed previously, monsters *also* have a whole lot to do with uncertainty and unpredictability at the level of our bodies.

Usually fear involves the most unpleasant type of uncertainty—the kind that spells peril. We feel fear when our lives are under threat, or our livelihoods, or our loved ones. Our flesh crawls, our stomachs drop, our

breathing is either sucked out of us completely or sped into some carica-
ture of itself. We don't know what might happen next, but whatever it is,
it must be avoided at all costs.

So why do so many of us *seek it out*?

OPTING INTO UNCERTAINTY: RECREATIONAL HORROR

Many of us purchase overpriced movie tickets, buy overpriced pop-
corn, and sit in sticky seats for the privilege of being terrified by violent
shape-shifting clowns, murderous doppelgängers of ourselves, or a masked
man with a machete. Each October these same folks gather some friends
and pile onto bales of hay in the back of a rickety truck (or tiptoe into
mansions) where decomposing zombies grab at us and men with chainsaws
chase us. With our media streaming behavior and merchandise purchasing,
we make *The Walking Dead* one of the most successful television franchises
of all time.

Why do so many of us choose to expose ourselves to intentionally up-
setting material in the name of entertainment? What is the deal with what
some psychologists call recreational horror? Exploring that motivation
may help us preview the remaining content of this book. It has to do with
uncertainty, bodily arousal, and a sense of play.

Behaviors like horror movie watching, bungee cord jumping, and riding
roller coasters may be forms of benign masochism, intentional exposure to
arousing, potentially threatening experiences in settings that are technically and reassuringly safe. It is a type of play that is relatively low in risk
and allows the individual to toy with a feeling of uncertainty and danger
without experiencing harm. It also again involves that U-shaped curve
and "just right" level of stimulation and arousal.

In one experiment supporting these ideas, participants wore heart rate
monitors as they walked through a haunted house in Denmark called
Dystopia Haunted House. The house consisted of forty-two thematically
connected rooms and was an immersive, live-action theatrical horror
production. The researchers videorecorded the goings-on at three separate locations where jump scares took place—a mad scientist kicking
over a metal bucket and reviving a zombie who jumped out, a pig-man

chasing people with a loud chainsaw, and a cluster of zombies grasping at the attendees from underneath a stairwell—and were able to sample heart rates specifically from these junctures in the haunted experience. Participants were also asked to rate how afraid they anticipated being during the haunted house. At the end of the evening, they were asked to rate their enjoyment and fear, both overall and at the three videorecorded junctures (mad scientist, pig-man, and zombies, for those keeping track). The researchers also used the videotapes to code the emotional expressions of the participants at these moments.

The results indicated that self-rated fear was associated with large-scale elevations in heart rate, but that the relationship between fear and enjoyment revealed the expected upside-down U-shaped relationship. Small amounts of fear were not enjoyable, but neither were quite large doses. There was, however, an enjoyable level of arousal in between. There was also an inverted-U relationship between enjoyment and smaller-scale fluctuations in heart rate, indicating that there was also a pleasant degree of small elevations of heart rate. These results led the authors to conclude that "enjoyment appears to be related to smaller just-right physiological deviations from whatever state the organism currently inhabits." Our sweet spot strikes again.

Hilariously, when listing the limitations of the study, the authors noted that "the rather carnivalesque atmosphere in the waiting area, with dim lighting, guests and haunted-house workers milling about, and disturbing background sounds such as screams and roaring chainsaws, appears to have promoted some participants to forget to fill out the required questionnaires." Whoops.

In addition to her job teaching and researching and working on grant panels and editing a major journal, Ayanna also serves as an expert witness on the (un)reliability of memory in the judicial system, experiences in which she feels simultaneously physiologically aroused *and* confident. "You can ask me one thousand questions about memory and you're never going to stump me," she said—but her smartwatch reports that during these times her heart rate is so elevated it thinks she is engaged in cardiovascular exercise, running or doing jumping jacks. She once testified in an Innocence Project case in which the person on trial had already served twenty years in prison, but who may have done so as the result of memory confusion and poor trial dynamics. It could be that all those years of living in a cage were a mistake.

Let's linger here for a moment, in this courtroom. Ayanna is on the stand. A man's freedom is on the line. She is a Black woman applying her expertise in a predominantly white institution, being challenged by people whose job it is to discredit her credentials and testimony, for five hours straight. It is hard to imagine higher stakes than this. But she is confident in her skills, invested in the importance of the moment, and has had past experiences that were similar and which had good outcomes. Though her heart is pounding, thundering blood through her veins, she reads this arousal as her body rising to the challenge rather than as her body panicking at the threat. She prevails.

We often hear about the fight-or-flight system in contexts that emphasize the flight, that emphasize danger and threat. But it is easy to forget that the term starts with "fight" for a reason—and not all fights are inauspicious. Sometimes we fight reluctantly to protect our resources or our loved ones from danger. But sometimes we enthusiastically battle for a better tomorrow, we gear ourselves up for a self-chosen challenge like a race, or we decide that this MCAT is going *down*. In these contexts, our same autonomic nervous system that gets us running away from cheetahs or active shooters energizes us to move, to grab, to tussle, to get what we want. "I think that we humans often have to perform under high stakes," Ayanna says, "and to do so successfully we have to learn to recognize our strengths and weaknesses. The only way to really come to an understanding of that is to *experience* it." We have to live through it to know that we can live through it.

THE TRUE MONSTER

Earlier in this chapter Ayanna said that students believe that the bewilderment of not-knowing is the monster they need to conquer, but she disagrees. Surprising no one who read the last chapter, she believes that the true monster is instead the effects of anticipating evaluation. Ayanna explains that students do and should take different approaches to solving the same problems, but too often this practice is discouraged in traditional Western education. "In math, for instance, the US education system traditionally has tried to eliminate or reduce individualized approaches on the part of students and instead pushed conformity of approach," she told me. "That push towards conformity is a real driver for anxiety in the classroom, as it results in a constant sort of worrying rumination about *how* you're doing something." It leads the student to question "Am I doing this right or wrong? How is this going to affect long-term outcomes in terms of my grade?" rather than asking curious questions about the material. What is called *achievement-goal theory* separates mastery goals (understanding, competence) from performance goals (I can show you my skill), and then adds a layer of approach and avoidance. Unsurprisingly, focusing on avoiding failure is associated with the worst outcomes in terms of learning and motivation, and focusing on achieving competence is associated with the best outcomes, as it supports deep conceptual processing and engagement. Like many of the scholars we reviewed in the last chapter, Ayanna believes we need grading reform.

But she is not opposed to all forms of grading. Ayanna sees performance-based motivation as important at the beginning of education, a stepping stone to developing a more mastery-focused approach to the work of the classroom. She jokes that she may have become mastery oriented only in the last year or so, as she approaches fifty. She is also serious—a mastery focus didn't come early in life. But she points out that performance goals almost always precede mastery goals. With performance goals, you need external motivators to "push and guide you" before you learn that competence can have its own rewards. Mentees will ask how Ayanna got to where she is, so intellectually comfortable, and she tells them that when she read her first psychological scientific paper, her reaction was "shock and agony." It didn't make sense, and she didn't understand it. But maintaining a certain GPA was important to her, and so she stuck with it—and "at some point the ship rights itself and you realize that you have the foundation to start building mastery." But in getting there "you need a little carrot." Ayanna's description of becoming a proficient scientist exactly matches my own experience shared earlier where it was grade-based carrots for participation in my women's studies classes (again, a safe and welcoming environment) that served as motivation for me to engage in my own self-designed exposure therapy for speaking in class.

It might strike you that every single topic we have covered this chapter involves a delicate balance—the just-right level of arousal, of physiological activation, that could tip either into terror or into excited motivation depending on context and interpretation: Being cognizant of but not overly reactive to the unknown. Being vulnerable without being naive or exposed. Offering enough performance incentives to nudge students into a superior mastery orientation. As such, *how* to hit this precise balance is not obvious, and both prescriptions and proscriptions are going to vary widely by student, instructor, parent, discipline, identity, and social context. I don't have any tidy solutions to offer.

We all just have to forge forward—into the uncertain future—and do our best, being light on our feet, and above all, open to the experience.

BUT FIRST: A CAVEAT

One afternoon during a year of record-breaking snowfalls in New England, I took my older brother up on his invitation to join him and his family for some ice skating, sledding, and skiing. We planned to meet at Wendell State Forest, a lovely spot in western Massachusetts with a warming hut, ice rinks, and cross-country ski trails. I loaded up my Honda CRV with ice skates and cross-country skis and my then eight-year-old and plugged the address for the park into my GPS.

Once we got out to Wendell though, our cell signal was spotty, and the GPS grew unreliable. Worse, it kept insisting that we take a right onto a path that looked too small and unkempt to be the correct turn. Ignoring the repeated robotic entreaties to turn right, I circled the base of the forest three or four times, wondering if I was just overthinking things as usual and what other options I had, since my brother wasn't responding to texts. Finally, one of these times around my daughter shouted from the backseat, "For Pete's sake, just turn!" and I did.

This was a terrible mistake.

It was quickly obvious that this was not the correct turn, as the already-sketchy path became increasingly narrow and bumpy, and worse, intensely uphill. Everything that winter was covered in snow and ice, and so we slid a bit from side to side and a bit backward. I paused briefly, wondering if I should reverse direction—but the thought of sliding backward down that hill, on ice, onto the busy main road, was more terrifying than the thought of what could lie ahead. I plunged forward.

This was another terrible mistake.

We breached the hill and ended up at a four-way crossroads. Though *road* was a generous term—it was obvious at this point that we were on trails meant for skis and hiking poles and not a road at all. I said quick words of gratitude that we had taken my partner's small SUV and not my tiny sedan. I took a shaky breath to try to settle my racing heart, churning stomach, and crawling skin.

And then, more helpfully, I took a Xanax.

Which was a good thing, because my daughter was excitedly shouting in the backseat, I was having a hard time deciding whether it was better to leave the car and get on the skis and snowshoes and find help (at this point we had no cell service at all), and, little did I know, still ahead of us was a trip down a path with a sharp cliffside to our right that we easily could have tumbled down, car and all. I needed settled nerves to sort this all out and to survive it, and I very much needed to avoid a spell of vomiting into the snowy bushes or, worse, losing consciousness.

I chewed the pill rather than swallowed it—a trick my doctor taught me to maximize the speed of its effects, as my bodily panic drops upon me so abruptly—and within minutes I could feel my stomach begin to quiet, my hands stop their shaking, and my thoughts become slower and more logical. We got through it, eventually finding a path that broadened into an actual road and led us out of the woods. We didn't tumble down the cliff or have to abandon a vehicle on top of some mountainside, I sang to my daughter as the car scraped through branches to calm us both, and we eventually joined our family on the skating rink for some winter exercise and handfuls of homemade granola. My dad taught my daughter how to ice skate the same way he taught me—by skating behind her, with her, arms under her arms, the tempo of his long legs teaching her much shorter ones how to fly over the ice.

Therapy is great. Exposure is effective. Cognitive reappraisal works. But in certain situations and for certain extremities of experience, a helping hand is warranted, whether that helping hand is medication, academic accommodations, or saying no to a certain experience. There is no one-size-fits-all to any of this. Our youth must know themselves and find their own way. Any of us who struggle with unruly bodies and minds are going to need help at times.

In recent decades, I have done things that college-age me would have shrunk from for fear of a panic attack. I go camping (reluctantly). I ride giant racehorses through the forest for my cousin's bachelorette party. I parasail and scuba dive and speak in front of large audiences and plan bustling parties. Having learned the importance of exposure for my own personal struggles and growth, I now use the power of future planning to intentionally put myself in situations that push my boundaries, that force me to grapple with some disquietude and come out the other side stronger, infused with purpose.

But at the same time, I also give myself accommodations. As in the woods, I sometimes get a pharmaceutical helping hand through the more challenging of these experiences. I now rent an "introvert cabin" or hotel room on family vacations, because while I know I can *survive* a week of vacation in a crowded noisy house with lots of other people constantly pulling at my emotions, I'd much rather *enjoy* vacations, and the combination of rambunctious meals and ocean or mountain time followed by quiet escape makes all the difference in the world. For long trips that I anticipate getting anxious before, I intentionally plan flights and vacation departure times such that if I experience some bodily distress right before, there is time for it and it doesn't disrupt my plans. Moreover, there are certain things I'll likely never experience—like sleep overnight on my friend's sailboat, or take the incredibly long flight to Australia, or go to another amusement park. I've made my peace with all that.

Part of compassionate challenge is compassion for yourself and a deep understanding of your values and goals. Finding one's best comfort-but-stretch zone, identifying those behaviors and situations that are key to our values and those we can just skip, the personal match between compassion and challenge, is a lifelong journey. Young people will need the careful, individualized guidance of their parents, guidance counselors, therapists, and campus support staff to find their best path.

CONCLUSION

A certain degree of physical arousal may be required for learning, for the changes in neural pathways and consolidation of memory involved in nudging your view of the world to something that is slightly different than it was before learning took place. Uncertainty, too, is not all bad—some of life's most beautiful moments may exist in those fraught times when you aren't quite sure what comes next. Some people—people who enjoy recreational horror or those who are drawn to the roller coaster of falling in and out of love with new people—may know this lesson better than others. Pushing the boundaries of what is known and comfortable is where true learning occurs. As Ryan Glode stated back in the beginning of this book, all of life is a series of exposure therapies. But at the same time, we can most effectively be vulnerable in settings where security is assured. Where being vulnerable won't risk life, limb, or academic standing, and in settings related to our values.

Any remaining worries or tension you might have surrounding the idea that youth need to be challenged might turn out to be for naught, because in our final chapter we are going to consider a form of compassionate challenge that is the furthest thing from aversive or discouraging. It is time for play.

CHAPTER EIGHT

PLAY AND
IMPROVISATIONAL LEARNING

O NCE UPON A TIME when I was in elementary school, my school participated in the DEAR program. That's not a misspelling of Nancy
Reagan's infamous antidrug campaign but rather a literacy and reading
initiative. Some schools still celebrate it once a year in April on beloved
childhood author Beverly Cleary's birthday.

In my recollection, the program could be triggered at any time of day,
any day of the week. The intercom noise would buzz, and the principal
would clear her raspy voice in preparation for the announcement.

My skin would prickle with anticipation.

The words would then come: Drop! Everything! And! Read!

And whatever we were doing—math drills, verb conjugations, review-
ing the parts of a cell—we would indeed drop it. I would pull out from the
caverns of my desk a treasured, weathered paperback, crack its spine, and
in the resulting quiet, enter a world of dragons and wizards and romantic
swooning.

In a similar spirit, some campuses have experimented with sudden days
off from classes to invite students to engage in wellness and campus spirit
activities. One such campus is Hiram College, a small liberal arts college
in Ohio. Jennifer Herman, executive director of Simmons University's
Center for Faculty Excellence,* is an alumna. She shared with me that

---

* Now my boss!

when she was an undergraduate at Hiram, they called this sudden day off Campus Day. Information was withheld from the students about which day would be Campus Day until the last minute. Speculation would abound about when it would occur, and when it finally arrived it did so with events like barbecues and dips in hot tubs. She recalls that its arrival felt a bit like being a small child again, waking up to the expectation of another day of school drudgery but instead peeking outside and seeing the world blanketed in deep snow and realizing it would instead be a day of hot chocolate and sledding. A free day, a day in which anything was possible.

What both DEAR and Campus Day have in common is that they step outside the rhythms and conventions of usual life. They break the appraisal that one's educational responsibilities are dire, serious, and necessary. They communicate that long division can be interrupted by a trip to Narnia. Organic chemistry can be replaced by a hot tub full of laughter.

While the work of the classroom and higher education is important, it isn't life or death. We aren't on battlefields or running from sabertooth tigers intent on our throats.

We can stop.

We can breathe.

We can play.

Intentional interruptions like DEAR and Campus Day are just one method of helping our youth see that the monsters of constant stress and competition are not inevitable, that one can stop to play. In this chapter we will visit the science, the scholars, the entertainers, and the student-scholars who are arguing for the benefits of playfulness and improvisation for both student mental health and learning. For as we'll see, the practice of improv is at the heart of what I mean by compassionate challenge.

THE POWER OF IMPROVISATION FOR SHIFTING APPRAISALS AND EXPOSURE THERAPY

In the third section of this book, we considered at length the power of beliefs to shift both our bodily responses and our choices of behaviors. Appraisals are the little stories we humans tell ourselves about our challenges, about our anxiety, about our autonomy and competence and belongingness and purpose. These appraisals are all critical for determining our emotions, our motivation, and our actions. Anxiety is rooted in a perception that the future is frightening and you don't have the resources to cope. Appraisals that fuel depression are those that suggest global, stable, internal negativity, which demonstrate catastrophic thinking and which are intolerant of uncertainty. Depression tells us: "This stress is permanent, across life settings, my fault, will set me up for lifelong failure, and I'll never be secure or know true happiness."

Additional negative automatic appraisals that can interfere with student well-being are those of scarcity, precarity, and intense competition. Scarcity refers to the perception that resources are scarce—that if you don't snap them up, someone else may do so and you will be left empty-handed. Appraisals of precariousness lead you to believe that whatever resources you might have could be snatched away from you at any moment, that whatever status you have built up could be toppled in a strong wind. Intense competition is both a response to perceptions of scarcity and precarity and the method by which you protect your resources in situations marked by these appraisals.

In her landmark book *Improvisation for the Theater*, actor and mother-of-improv Viola Spolin notes that competition is deadly for good ensemble work. When a player feels that the performance is a competition and the players will be judged against each other, "energy is spent on this alone; a player becomes anxious and driven, and fellow players become a threat." The college experience works best as a collaborative endeavor, where students in classrooms, athletes on teams, and players in performing arts work with their instructors, coaches, and mentors to reach new heights of learning. An environment that promotes competitive appraisals is likely to diminish the beneficial effects of learning ensembles.

To support student mental health, we need to not only compassionately challenge them, but also help them to adjust their appraisals to ones that are hopeful and associated with well-being, willingness to take risks, and exploration. One promising candidate set of appraisals are playful ones, interpreting the work of the classroom through the framework of openness to experience, possibility, social connection, and the freedom to take risks.

Playful appraisals can help reduce anxiety but also open one's thinking to more creativity.

Playful appraisals are positive ones that encourage feelings of safety and freedom—much like panic and relaxation are biologically incompatible, so are interpretations of danger and safety, threat and whimsy. Indeed, psychologist Gordon Bermant presents a review of improv activities and their effects on psychological functioning. Improv activities are brief, invented-on-the-spot theatrical exercises, and Bermant argues that they have much in common with applied psychology practices such as therapy. Both improv and exposure therapy include a focus on body awareness, present-moment mindfulness, interpersonal attentiveness, and the development of trust. He also notes that improv activities are "unavoidably social." Indeed, social anxiety is among the most common sort of anxiety in college students, and so socially based improv activities are literally exposure to a common feared stimulus.

Improv may thus serve as a therapy of sorts and help us address the vast number of students who are struggling with excessive levels of fear, hopelessness, and sadness. But it turns out that improvisational learning doesn't just benefit emotion—it also benefits cognition.

IMPROVISATIONAL LEARNING IS CREATIVE LEARNING

Several researchers have explored whether brief improv exercises can improve creativity in undergraduate students. In a well-controlled example published in 2020, scientists from Stony Brook University teamed up with scientists from the University of Michigan to see whether randomly assigning participants to complete either a series of improv exercises or a series of more scripted social interactions would impact student's divergent thinking and ability to tolerate uncertainty. Both sets of tasks took about twenty minutes. The improv activities were famous ones, like co-constructing a story in rounds, each person adding a single word. The social interactions mirrored the improv ones in terms of structure, movement, and discussion but required no spontaneity or performance. Divergent thinking was measured using a task that directly tested the ability to think outside the box, whereas uncertainty intolerance was measured using a questionnaire in which higher scores were indicative of greater worry and dislike of undetermined situations.

Across two studies, the authors found evidence that engaging in these improvisational activities improved student scores of divergent thinking and reduced intolerance of uncertainty. They speculate that the mechanisms underlying this learning were those practices already discussed at length in this book and that are consistent with exposure therapy. Students were initially fearful but then learned new, positive, safety-related associations between being creative and speaking out in class that they hopefully could now draw on in other contexts. As creativity is pivotal for the work of the classroom and increasing tolerance of uncertainty can be beneficial for reducing depression and anxiety, these are promising findings for both education and shoring up student well-being.

In an even more recent investigation, some motivation scientists tested whether encouraging students to adopt a positive appraisal of discomfort for learning would motivate personal growth. The researchers conducted five different studies involving over two thousand student participants. For the first study, they teamed up with improv expert Kelly Leonard, whom we'll meet in just a few pages as this chapter's expert. They gave some students instructions to seek discomfort ("feel awkward, uncomfortable") and some students a vaguer instruction ("feel skills developing"). The students then all completed an improv activity called "Give Focus." In this activity, one person has "focus" and is free to move about the room, acting in whatever way they want, while all other students remain frozen in place. The person's turn ends when they decide to pass the focus on to another student using touch or gestures. Coders who were not aware of the study's hypotheses or which instructions students were given measured first how long each person maintained focus and also how many risks they took in their performance. As hypothesized, the instruction to seek discomfort led to significantly longer persistence of holding focus and greater risk-taking during one's turn—suggesting that these students were more tolerant of the baleful light of social attention and more creative in their efforts. These results suggest that we can reframe our resistance to discomfort, our intolerance of uncertainty. We can learn to play.

In his book *Impro: Improvisation and the Theater*, legendary acting coach Keith Johnstone argues that the reason improv activities spur creativity is because what holds us back from creativity is fear of the censure of others—as he says, "laughter is the whip that keeps us in line." He argues that teachers should adopt a new view of their students, that "instead of seeing people as untalented, we can see them as phobic, and this completely changes the teacher's relationship with them." He offers numerous examples of students being "stuck," unwilling to engage in a creative enterprise until Johnstone takes away their responsibility for the creation. For instance, in one story-based activity there is a questioner (Johnstone) and a respondent (student). The questioner operates under the assumption that the respondent has a creative story within their psyche that needs to be elicited. They tell the respondent that, rather than telling a story, the respondent must guess a story that is in the questioner's head. This immediately relaxes the respondent because they no longer have to fear being responsible for creativity. The questioner then asks a series of questions of the respondent that can be answered with only yes, no, or maybe—and the story is slowly revealed by the interaction of these creative partners. In one example a student inadvertently spins a story about giant insects that aim to destroy the world, but they become too large to fit into the buildings where people are hiding because they eat everything they find, and thus are conquered. Of course, the actual story comes from the respondent, not the questioner.

Johnstone was writing about these ideas decades before the invention of functional magnetic resonance imaging (fMRI) and related techniques began pulling back the curtain on how our brains operate. But with all these years of neuroscience under our belts, his ideas about how to unleash creativity have a new resonance all their own. Neuroimaging research reveals that much of brain function involves the kinds of seesaws discussed earlier when we considered how to address anxiety—but here, instead of arousal and relaxation, much of the vacillating activation has instead to do with inhibition and control on the one hand (being focused on tasks and ignoring distractors) and processing memories and associations on the other (disconnecting from the present and daydreaming). We might need to dial down inhibition and control to release creativity.

Recent research has revealed that people are most creative when drifting between wake and sleep states, and this is no surprise—in these liminal states of consciousness, the more inhibitory control regions are entering quiescence. As you begin to fall asleep, your brain generates what are called hypnagogic hallucinations. These are brief images that bloom and fade and are likely precursors to a dreaming state. For instance, last night as I fell asleep I experienced three such hallucinations. The first image was the tiny shack-turned-storefront in my favorite seaside town where the proprietor creates jewelry inspired by the ocean's moods. This hallucination was first the outside of the shack, then a ring of iridescent greenish blue, like the gentle waves of the sea on a quiet summer morning. Next, a portobella mushroom, a chef's knife in my right hand, a clump of dirt clinging to the side of the mushroom that would need to be brushed away. Finally, a red bicycle upside down, its wheels spinning. The tension between neural modes exists even here—as I examined each image in order to commit them to memory to write these words, the effort roused my conscious, controlled circuits. I climbed the ladder to wakefulness and had to calm myself again to return to the blooming sights.

There is some speculative evidence, too, that our brains are doing this associative work *all the time*, that during ordinary wakefulness we just don't have access to these associations and mini-hallucinations because ordinary wakeful sensations and perceptions from the world override them and slip them under the hood of conscious awareness. One cannot help but wonder if creative sorts—artists, musicians, novelists—have some genetic advantage that gives them greater access to the more intuitive, associative aspects of their brains even while awake and aware. The idea is consistent with the lived experiences of such individuals. My aunt Eliza, a pianist, novelist, and poet, always talked about the people having full conversations in her mind, that their noisiness was at times incredibly distracting. There is an entire online support movement for people prone to almost pathological daydreaming, those who struggle to rein in their constant creative associations. They call themselves "wild minds."

Many of Johnstone's improv activities intentionally shut down the controlled circuits of our minds and try to elicit insights from the spontaneous circuits. The more you can shut down the self-judging, moderating, inhibitive sides of yourself, the more creative your ideas might be. Neuro-imaging studies of musicians generating new music demonstrate a strong role for regions of the brain involved in spontaneous thought and making connections between ideas.

The great David Lynch, writer and director of classics like *Dune* and *Blue Velvet*, observes, "Ideas are like fish. If you want to catch little fish, you can stay in the shallow water. But if you want to catch the big fish, you've got to go deeper. Down deep, the fish are more powerful and more pure." But as anyone who has struggled through one of Lynch's more free-wheeling works knows, it pays to combine deep intuition with logic and planning, to use the strengths of both modes of your brain. I most enjoy Lynch's collaborative works, like *Twin Peaks*, where you can see his uncanny insights and striking combinations of ideas paired with a more linear thinker's narrative structure. Musical improvisation similarly seems to involve not just those regions involved in spontaneous thought but also those involved in control and planning.

Decreasing anxiety and increasing creativity are laudable goals for higher education and both may increase concrete learning of material and new skills. But all educators want students to be capable of more than just thinking calmly and creatively. We also want to educate them to be able to handle any future situation, to think lightly on their feet, and to deal with all the unexpected obstacles life throws their way—both the comedic and the tragic. Doing so successfully is also key to mental health.

SLINGS AND ARROWS, COMEDY AND TRAGEDY

During a hectic trip in which I was keynoting a big conference, I dashed back to my hotel room for a podcast interview about my second book. The interview was to be aired on longtime creative executive and writer Kelly Leonard's show *Getting to Yes, And*. It was such a busy weekend that I didn't have time to do a lot of research before the interview, and so I was delighted when the interview turned out to be one of my favorite conversations about the content of my book—Kelly was warm, responsive, and thoughtful. He made me feel like my work was better than it was by weaving together my thoughts and ideas with his own insights and intuitions.

I was so impressed by Kelly that after the trip I ordered a copy of the book he wrote with his friend and colleague Tom Yorton, *Yes, And: How Improvisation Reverses "No, But" Thinking and Improves Creativity and Collaboration — Lessons from The Second City*. I discovered that I had unknowingly had this most marvelous discussion with one of the greats of early improv. Reading the book, I learned that the Chicago-based Second City was the birthplace of a modern comedy movement, employing the improvisational techniques of actor and academic Viola Spolin and her son (and Second City founder) Paul Sills. The outfit served as a career launcher for an astonishing number of comedy greats from Bill Murray to John Belushi to Amy Poehler. For thirty years Kelly worked his way up the leadership ladder at the Second City, rubbing elbows with the likes of Stephen Colbert and Keegan-Michael Key. Kelly now serves as executive director of insights and applied improvisation and is highly involved in Second City Works, the arm of the organization that conducts training and in-services for businesses, colleges, and other organizations.

I also began following Kelly on Twitter. A few months in, during the dizzying interim between the end of the Christmas holiday and New Year's Day, he posted a picture of a girl about my daughter's age opening presents on Christmas morning, with the simple line "I miss you."

It stopped me in my scrolling tracks.

Half not wanting to know, I clicked over to Google and read. About his daughter Nora's diagnosis of liver and lung cancer in tenth grade. About how he and his wife and fellow performer Anne Libera battled to save her life and her spirits through a #TeamNora campaign that included contributors like Ben Affleck, Tina Fey, and Steve Carrell. How after her death Kelly became involved in a movement that replaces cemeteries with memory parks, where people can gather and play and celebrate the memories of the ones they have lost rather than mourn.

With such a rich history embedded in the world of applying improvisational insights outside the theater world, as well as being someone who can speak to how improv helps one weather the slings and arrows (and full-fledged traumas) that life flings at us, I was moved and honored when Kelly agreed to talk with me about the ideas in this book. He helped me to see that not only do improvisational activities in the classroom and setting up situations of play help students confront and overcome feelings of anxiety and competition; they also have numerous other cognitive and instructional benefits.

We begin with how improv and play can help us build communities of learning in the classroom.

THINKING AS AN ENSEMBLE

In the field of the scholarship of teaching and learning, one of the biggest movements in the last five years has been increased attention to community building within the classroom. After a long history of viewing students purely as individuals and a classroom as a room full of such individuals that do independent work and should be educated as such, scholars of teaching and learning have begun to focus on the interconnections among students and how to shape the entire collective. We began to consider the power of attending to community in chapter 6, in discussing the role of belongingness in self-determination. Here the power of improvisational learning shines, because all improv assumes ensemble work rather than individual work. Fittingly, the word *ensemble* refers to both a group of performing artists and a group of individual units that work collectively.

Instructors need to accept that as much as they are leading the class, so is the class leading them—and each other. As educational developer Richard Bale writes in his book *Teaching with Confidence in Higher Education: Applying Strategies from the Performing Arts*: "The key message for us as teachers is that we should learn not to fear the unexpected, but to view teaching and learning as semi-structured experiences which can, and will, develop according to ongoing dialogue and negotiation with our students." Awareness of this cocreation not only acknowledges a reality but also allows the instructor to capitalize on existing classroom dynamics to the benefit of all.

How to do it? The most well-known improv activity and really the underpinning of the whole philosophy is the one that shares a title with Kelly's book: "Yes, And." As an activity, you create a story with your ensemble partners by building off whatever your partner just said using just those words, "yes, and"—then this next thing happens. Person A: "A dog walks into a barbershop." Person B: "Yes, and—he has a lollipop in his mouth!" As a philosophy, it means never shutting down people's ideas or trying to compete with them; rather, finding something to value in everyone's contribution and then building upon it. It means not saying no. It means being open to experience, vulnerable to the unexpected, and accepting of the imagination.

"I love the term *ensemble*," Kelly said, "because I think the word *team* sometimes implies competition." An ensemble, on the other hand, works together as one unit for the success of all—and its success often hinges on the individuals' ability to help each other out. It also deeply honors the diversity of members that make it up and does not traffic in status or power differentials.

Kelly started his career washing dishes at Second City and was astonished when Harold Ramis, the most serious of the Ghostbusters and writer and director of many iconic comedies (*Groundhog Day*, *Caddyshack*, *Animal House*) would regularly drop by and have conversations with him. During these chats, Ramis would often talk about the fact that individual success pales in comparison to shared success—a principle he lived by and one that Kelly was sure to carry through once he was in more of a leadership role at Second City. "But this does not come by creed," Kelly notes, "it comes through practice"—practice that Ramis amply demonstrated by checking in with the kid washing dishes as much as the actors on his stage or the bigwigs in his audience.

Once the ensemble is working together smoothly, it can handle anything thrown at it. For improvisation in particular and play in general involve training for the unexpected.

TRAINING FOR THE UNEXPECTED

Kelly's children attended Chicago Waldorf schools, where he says they were sent outside to play in almost every form of weather. Parents were told to send every item of clothing they could think of, because everything would get wet and torn. The children's bodies, too, often came home with bruises and bumps and skinned knees. Kelly called this practice a philosophy of playful risk (compassionate challenge!), in which both the play and the risk worked hand in hand to teach the students about the world and about their own skills. It reminds me of how my brothers and I have raised our children together, employing more of an American-1970s-era benign-neglect style of parenting than the helicopter approach so many of our contemporaries have adopted. Throughout their early childhood my daughter Noelle and her cousins ran pretty wild together on holidays and vacations. My favorite memory emblematic of this approach was at an Easter celebration when my daughter was around four years old. My brother squinted through the bay window to the yard beyond and said, "Is that Noelle in the fire pit . . . holding a hammer?"

Play is as ubiquitous as sleep across the mammalian kingdom. In a pivotal review in a major journal, biologists Marek Spinka, Ruth Newberry, and Marc Bekoff take a wide view of all the research and conclude that across species, whether it is kittens playing with balls of yarn, birds darting in and out of trees, or human beings playing dodgeball, the evolutionary purpose of play is to train for the unexpected. Specifically, unexpected moments that involve either loss of movement control (falling, being pushed over) or times of sudden stress and loss of usual resources (another human being is holding you captive). In playing, organisms voluntarily alternate between being in control and being quite out of control to develop reflexive and adaptive strategies to use when they are out of control in more dangerous circumstances.

In simpler animals, most play is movement oriented—nonhuman animals tackle, wrestle, jump out at each other, pretend a leaf or a pipe cleaner is prey. Play in dogs can get downright nerve-wracking, as they grab at each other's necks with their jaws and whip back and forth, but without the force of teeth or movement required to bring any harm to each other. Some of this play involves intentional "self-handicapping"—witness the puppy who tosses herself on the ground and displays her belly. Anyone spending time on social media has seen YouTube videos or GIFS of crows and dogs and other animals seeking out piles of snow, slippery slopes, or water to intentionally lose their balance in play.

As creatures become more complex, so does the play. For human beings, much of children's play involves miming social and emotional challenges and intentionally toying with social power or status differentials.

Spinka and colleagues note that play is distinguishable from exploration, in that exploration often involves seeking *ways out of trouble* or how to replenish low resources, whereas play intentionally *puts you in trouble* in order to then puzzle your way out of it.* Play seems to be evolutionarily preserved, because regaining control after losing it is inherently rewarding, and play results in an unusually appealing brew of excitement, pleasure, and then relaxation. This appealing brew of excitement, pleasure, and relaxation is often referred to by nonacademics as "having fun."

Play gets a bad rap as something that is more frivolous and less intellectually demanding than serious work. But in fact, improv and play are highly cognitively demanding. By definition, you don't know what might happen next and must prepare for any number of possible scenarios. You also must make estimations of your ensemble partners' interior mental states, which is one of the grandest feats of human cognition. You must also adjust your thinking and behavior on the fly as more information comes in. Moreover, you need to project yourself and your partners into the future, thinking several steps ahead.

Read any brochure for any liberal arts institution and you'll read that students will emerge from said institution ready for the complicated, constantly changing, technologically evolving world—adjusting on the fly, projecting into the future, understanding implications. As literature professor Paul Hanstedt writes in his book *Creating Wicked Students*, "If we've educated our students effectively, they move into the world as questioning, informed, thoughtful agents of positive change." Play may be just what students need to accomplish the mission of higher education.

"I'm looking at the increasingly complex world that we live in," Kelly said, "and what do we want for our kids? We want them to adapt and be agile and be change-ready. And you'll only learn that if you are experimenting with it. And how do you experiment with a mindset that's ready for that? That's called improvisation." He described for me an improv activity called Point and Untell, in which, instead of describing an object,

---

* Recall that in our early discussions of motivation, the neuroscientist Panksepp also distinguished what he called the play system and the seeking system (the latter being consistent with exploration).

you must describe what it is not, but in a way that leads the guesser to the right answer. He said it is one of the most difficult activities for novices to master, and that they have a sensation much like a muscle that hasn't been trained yet. But over time, as this creative muscle develops, one becomes capable of breaking outside the traditional box of thinking.

Kelly and I had our chat for this book during the middle of the first wave of the COVID-19 pandemic, when we were both under stay-at-home orders. My college, like all colleges, had pivoted suddenly to remote learning, and in my role as director of our Center for Teaching Excellence I was intimately involved in helping our faculty adjust to the current semester and also trying to guess the shape of future semesters. Kelly's son was a graduating senior in college, and so they were dealing with the loss of all the usual transition celebrations and grappling with what to do with the fall. Both of us knew people who were sick.

I had conceptualized this book before the crisis and asked Kelly about whether he thought communicating the need for play was still relevant in so much upheaval and stress. His answer was immediate.

"We have to," he said. "Because we don't survive otherwise."

Losing his daughter over the last year made him surer of the human need for play than ever before. "When we were dealing with Nora's illness and then her death," he said, "if I didn't have my play and my improvisation, I would not be here. I would not have been able to make it." We need meaning and purpose. Kelly and family found such meaning and purpose every day through playful improvisation with their daughter, with each other, with their caregiving team, and with their overall community.

Here we see the benefits of learning to improvise so clearly—to confront the unthinkable, to appraise even the most tragic circumstances as opportunities for connection and gratitude and play, to creatively think up solutions like their #TeamNora campaign, to solidify social connections and draw on one's web of social support, and to find a transcendent meaning in even the worst of life's circumstances. To meet the hardest challenges with compassion.

I cannot imagine having higher hopes for our students.

Tracing the origins of the word *play*, Diane Ackerman, poet and author of *Deep Play*, writes that all playful activities have in common that they "require daring, risk, concentration, the ability to live with uncertainty, a willingness to follow the rules of the game, and a desire for transcendence." Structuring higher education around such goals could be transformative for both student mental health and learning.

If I'm not advocating in this chapter that all professors host rotating series of traditional improv activities in their classes (and I'm not), how can we take the principles of improvisational play and bring them onto our campuses and into our classes? Below I provide some suggestions.

IMPROVISATIONAL LEARNING AT PLAY: CAMPUSES

I know I just said I'm not advocating all professors adopt improv practices in their classes (though it also couldn't hurt). But I *am* advocating that people organizing first-year orientations, residence hall activities, and student club activities all use a wealth of improv activities to invite our students to be brave and vulnerable from the very beginning of their academic careers. In fact, many already do.

Trinity, a Student Voices participant who was a psychology major at a small liberal arts university, immediately called out student groups that didn't engage in such activities. She was involved in athletics and student clubs in high school but quickly realized that she'd have to choose one or the other when she transitioned to college. She wasn't prepared to dedicate the amount of time that college-level athletics would require and so chose student clubs. And in characteristic overachiever fashion, she didn't choose just one—she participated in a remarkable eight clubs her first year of college. Right away she could see differences among them. Some passed out to-do lists and put her right to work. She was taken aback—she had expected that all these clubs would require some elbow grease from her, but she also anticipated having some fun and developing new friendships. The clubs that instead spent some time shoring up a sense of play and cohesion with improv-like activities were the clubs that she continued to be involved with as the years passed and are also the clubs that fostered deep relationships over time.

As reflected in Trinity's experiences, the transition to college is probably the most important time for these community-building improvisational activities, to help students find friends and support in the startling new world of college. That said, improv activities can also get stale. How many times have you had to answer the question "What's one strange thing no one would guess about you?" Mix it up. Resources are a'plenty, including three we have already cited: Kelly's book *Yes, And*; Viola Spolin's *Improvisation for the Theater*; and Keith Johnstone's *Impro*. If one has the funds, there are numerous groups offering applied improvisational training like Second City Works does.

IMPROVISATIONAL LEARNING AT PLAY: CLASSROOMS

A few years ago, some colleagues and I ran a one-day faculty training event in which we shared the research findings from a grant-funded experiment. To round out the day we also invited other speakers either to share related research or to lead the attendees in a practical activity that could benefit their pedagogy. One of the speakers was Paul Kassel, actor and current dean of the College for Visual and Performing Arts at Northern Illinois University. Paul is also author of the book *Acting: An Introduction to the Art and Craft of Playing*. Paul led us in a series of improv activities aimed at getting us to think more deeply about our work in the classroom.

In one activity, he demonstrated for us several types of social energy that he believes are common to all human interactions.* He argued that these energies vary both by person and by situation, but that understanding which energies you specialize in might give you insight into your teaching strengths or even interactions with friends and colleagues. The first is called *push*, and to demonstrate the physicality of this energy he asked us to break into pairs, meet palms with our partner, and push against them. Another was *hold*, which involved not pushing but remaining present and holding one's position. Another was *release*, which was just like it sounds—you suddenly release either the pushing or the holding you were

---

*As an experimental psychologist I must note that the mechanisms underlying this concept (personality? nonverbal behaviors? affective presence?) are entirely unknown—but would be fun to test.

just doing and relax. The final one was *pull*, and you were meant to pull the partner to you.

Push felt alienating to me. Hold felt boring. Release felt disappointing. When we moved to pull, I felt an explosion in my chest and a sizzling up my spine. "*This*," I thought. "This is my energy." The strength of the realization was startling, and immediately on its heels followed a series of other realizations about previously mystifying interactions with others. I realized that my pull energy is so strong that I've self-protectively learned to hold most people at arm's length—but when people cross a certain threshold of intimacy, the degree to which I pull sometimes gets me into trouble. I also realized that a friend who routinely confuses me with his energies was engaging in a strong pull and then a sudden last-minute push that would leave me disoriented and unsteady on my feet. A different friend who struggles with her relationships pulls *everyone* in and exhausts herself in the process, leaving no time to recuperate.

Much to my amusement, I was startled out of my reveries by Paul saying to the group, "You likely had the experience where some of these energy practices felt uncomfortable, but one really resonated with you." Indeed.

Thinking about your dominant energy is a fun new way to think about your personal style and strengths in the classroom. Though it is not my energy, push does not always involve avoidance or aggression. It can also take the form of challenge and excitement. Hold could be mindful, present, in the moment. And while your dominant energy could inform your dominant teaching style—I have always thought about teaching as an invitation to dance, a pull into intellectual play—it may be even better to cycle through the energies within a class. Provoke students to rise to a challenge, pull them in with an enticing idea, hold them there as you engage in the work of the class, and then release them to reflect.

Reflecting on movement-related energy can be a fun exercise that could improve one's teaching, but so is *actually moving*. So many classrooms involve sitting stock-still, and we have to our detriment trained students through more than a decade of elementary and secondary education that education involves sitting upright, immobile, facing forward. But this model is both stultifying to creativity and even physically unhealthy. In her book *Minding Bodies: How Physical Space, Sensation, and Movement Affect Learning*, literature professor Susan Hrach presents a compelling argument that students and teachers need to move more in our classes. She issues an impassioned plea for instructors to build courses "based on how to build knowledge and skills through physical movement, an attention to the spatial environment, and a sensitivity to the energy bandwidth of my students on any given day." Movement in the classroom can be as simple as asking students to contribute work on the whiteboard or providing discussion activities that require students to get up and join other students in another part of the classroom, whether to discuss, brainstorm on large sheets of paper, or make comments on each other's work.

Movement in the classroom can also be more creative. Theater instructor Phil Smith asks his students to adopt the stance of a zombie and shuffle around campus in groups without speaking in order to see the space anew, to understand symbols and their relation, and to immerse themselves in a new frame of being. The students reported suddenly being able to sense each other's needs and interests, to move together as one collective being. "We didn't need words because we were all thinking the same thing. . . . We didn't need to push our way through to get it, we all just gave way to everyone, so everyone could get it." The activity not only forced their perspective into a new light but also increased their sense of being an ensemble.

When I talked with Trinity about times when she was most engaged in her college classes, she immediately brought up two different experiences that both involved a reversal of expectations. One was a psychology class and one a class on genetics. She didn't really expect to enjoy either class, but from the very first moments the professors entered the class, she realized that this one was going to be different. Trinity said she could recall being so startled by their lighthearted demeanor and innovative takes on teaching that she sought out eye contact with other students to verify that, yes, this was something different for them too.

Trinity reports that these experiences were instantly engaging—in our video interview, she demonstrated for me a slumped posture and her head resting in her hand and then perking up. "[The psychology professor] didn't stop there. I thought she was just making a good first impression,"

Trinity said, "but it was the whole semester. Even in quarantine—like, she changed the syllabus to the *Syllabpocalypse*, and she'd send us videos about how she missed us with pictures of her cat. She really wanted to have that student-professor relationship with each and every one of us." These reversals of expectations are so effective because they immediately arrest attention, as they did Trinity's.

Acting educator Keith Johnstone claims, too, that all storytelling involves describing a routine and then interrupting it. Two families are at war and hate each other—but their children fall in love. A little girl visits her grandmother—who has been replaced by a wolf. It is the interruption of the routine that arrests our attention.

For instructors, part of how to weave this energy into your classroom is to not overplan, to challenge yourself, and to take your own risks. Leave some room in your class plan for going off-script, for making a different decision than usual, for it is the energy involved in the deciding that is invigorating. Paul Kassel likes to say that once someone jumps, everything afterward is boring—you know the person is coming down to earth. It is the *deciding* whether to jump that gathers an audience into a shared moment.

Especially once you've hit the groove in your semester, when everything is running smoothly and students now can anticipate everything that is going to happen in your classroom, you can shake things up. If you find that certain successful strategies prove less effective as the semester progresses, try a dramatic shift in routine.

PROFESSORS: THE FUCKING WORST (OR, RELEASE YOUR STATUS)

Acting educator Keith Johnstone also claims that every human interaction—every utterance, every smile, every text—involves one person elevating or lowering their level of dominance or submission with respect to the other. He calls this relative level of dominance and submission "status" and argues that all conversations act like a seesaw of status. Johnstone discovered this insight while brainstorming ways to get his acting students to converse more authentically. They kept delivering stilted, non-natural-sounding performances. It was only when he told them to deliver each line as if they were attempting to manipulate status that they began to deliver credible performances.

To test his theory, let's pluck a scene from a popular movie and see if we can dissect all the interactions through the lens of status: *Dirty Dancing*. The movie tells the story of a love affair between an idealistic upper-class heroine (Baby) visiting a country resort with her family and a working-class dancer (Johnny) who forces her to confront her privilege.

It is the end of the movie. Johnny has been fired (status demoted) for fraternizing with the clientele's daughter to the tune of "Hungry Eyes." Baby sits, dejected, at a table with her parents. She could not be lower status—a grown woman forced into a child's role, stuffed into a dark corner against the wall. Johnny strides in wearing his leather jacket and his delicious combination of pure masculinity and graceful vulnerability. He plays high status to Baby's parents by delivering the timeless line, "Nobody puts Baby in the corner." No one, in other words, makes Baby low status on his watch. He follows this bold statement by physically elevating her status—reaching out his hand for her to stand and join him on stage.

He always does the last dance of the season (high status). Someone tried to tell him not to (attempted to quash his high status), but he's going to do it anyway, and with his kind of dancing (nice try, he's still high status). In his speech he elevates Baby's status again by rechristening her with her given name—Miss Frances Houseman. It is hard to imagine a lower-status nickname than Baby, with its connotations of complete powerlessness and dependency. Frances Houseman, on the other hand, is stately, and we know from earlier in the movie that she was named after the first woman in the American government's cabinet, named for power.

Her father stands, about to play high status and put a stop to these shenanigans. Baby's mother, to this point in the movie having played low status to her husband, restrains him with a hand on his arm and unexpectedly pulls high status: "Sit down, Jake."

Baby and Johnny dance.

The dance ends with Johnny quite literally lifting Baby to the skies, above the crowd, above her parents, above her own self-doubts.

On high, she laughs. It is beautiful.

There are many ways in which we enjoy status manipulations, even make games out of them. Many of us delight in teasing our siblings about their incompetence and unattractiveness. Many others enjoy a vicarious status rush when our favored sportsball team wins its coveted trophy. We exult in sudden status reversals, underdogs winning in an upset, and high-flying celebrities and politicians brought low.

Both Johnstone and Spolin advise teachers to voluntarily release their high status in the classroom. Johnstone literally sits on the floor and speaks up to his students, apologizes to them when they make mistakes (for he must have failed them as a teacher), and regularly creates opportunities for them to lead the class. Spolin writes, "True personal freedom and self-expression can flower only in an atmosphere where attitudes permit equality between student and teacher and the dependencies of teacher for student and student for teacher are done away with." For our expertise as educators should not be in our demonstrated authority or power but rather in our ability to create learning situations in which the entire ensemble—students and instructor both—achieve new insights and develop new skills.

This releasing of status might be hard for some instructors to do. Many academics are quite in love with their intellectual authority. An elite institution that shall remain nameless once hired Second City Works for some faculty training.* "We came out and led a workshop for a bunch of professors," Kelly said. And then, deadpan, making me laugh: "They were the fucking worst." Kelly and his team were leading an improv exercise intentionally designed to demonstrate the team-building power of being receptive to ideas and sharing the floor, and how disruptive practices like interrupting and insisting on high status can be to team dynamics. While one of the Second City facilitators was explaining the exercise, a professor jumped up and said something along the lines of, "Yup, yup. No. Listen, we all know about this. Can we skip to the next exercise?" Kelly had to step in and explicitly point out the irony to the interrupter.

---

*It was Harvard.

Of course, whether the students perceive the instructor as high status to begin with varies quite a bit based on the identity characteristics of the instructor. In a collection of essays edited by historian Jessamyn Neuhaus titled *Picture a Professor: Interrupting Biases About Faculty and Increasing Student Learning*, Jessamyn and numerous other scholars tackle the racialized, gendered, and other biases about faculty that students bring into the classroom and offer solutions for dismantling them.

Summing up this section, three ways that we can tap directly into the power of improvisational learning are to (1) explicitly use improv activities in our student-focused community building exercises (for example, orientations, student groups); (2) pay attention to energy and movement in the classroom, interrupting routines and ruts; and (3) release our high status to encourage ensemble building.

CONCLUSION

For a while in the 2010s, everyone's attention was riveted to the concept of self-control. The ability to persevere, to delay gratification, to temper your desires was the key to everything. Tiger moms knew it. People with grit got it. Apps and life coaches and habit gurus promised they could hack it for you if you didn't come to it naturally. Research study after research study suggested that high self-control was linked to better grades, better marriages, better wages, and trimmer waistlines.

Leave that marshmallow on the table and the world was yours.

There were a few problems with all this research, though. Boring statistical problems, in that most of the research was correlational rather than experimental, and some researchers started having trouble observing the same effects in their own laboratories that originally got all the attention. There were also amusing (to me, anyway) problems like research indicating that maybe these glossy, high self-control people feel temptations less intensely than low self-control people. In other words, it isn't that high self-control people have these enormous powers of restraint but rather that when you're sort of dull and unmoved by things, it is super easy to turn away from marshmallows and pretty new boots and people with sparkly eyes in the bar.

But beyond these issues with the research, other problems with trying to get everyone on the self-control train is that self-control is difficult to train up in people who are naturally low in it, and it is also enormously effortful. As any dieter knows, the moment you stop constant vigilance, everything quickly falls apart and you're back to square one. One study that checked in on participants seven times a day over a week of their life found that participants reported feeling desires of some sort about half the time. The researchers concluded, "Desire pervades everyday life." Resisting impulses requires constant application of cognitive resources, which are limited. We also are terrible forecasters of our own future temptations, assuming that our capacity for restraint is much better than it is, and thus place ourselves in overly tempting circumstances, like joining friends on a smoke break soon after quitting smoking.

What is the solution to resisting temptation then? There may be many solutions, but one with quite a lot of research support is to avoid tempting situations in the first place. In other words, intentionally craft your situations ahead of time so that you don't end up experiencing the need for self-control. Quitting smoking? Try not to hang out with your co-workers during their smoke breaks—instead have a snack, or indulge in some Candy Crush, or take a walk around the block. Is your ex coming to town? Don't arrange to meet them for a candlelit dinner, instead arrange to meet them during the day in a crowded museum and cafe. Crafting the external situation so that your desired behavior is effortless is much less work and more oriented for success than attempting to self-control yourself through a tempting situation.

In much the same way, it is easier for colleges and universities to create settings that engender a sense of play, a willingness to enter uncertainty and respond to challenge, than it is to attempt to influence the internal efforts and interpretations of a very diverse student body. We should focus on the structures and situations that meet our students when they begin their college experience. As we saw in this chapter, playfulness can help all of us regulate our emotions, think divergently, cocreate, and respond to the unexpected with agility. We can certainly devise campus and class-room policies specifically designed at tapping into the art and practice of improvisation, or as Kelly Leonard calls it, "Human Being Practice." But before we can do so, and perhaps even more important than doing so, we need to set up environments that support a sense of play. By environments I explicitly mean classrooms, campuses, dormitories, and online spaces (for many students are taking their courses online). The first and arguably most important aspect of a learning environment that encourages a sense of playful risk-taking is safety. One cannot strive to play, to explore, to confront one's fears in situations where one does not feel safe. And here we are, circling back to where we began.

Young people—really, all people—need challenge, but first they need compassion.

THE MONSTER AT THE END
OF THIS BOOK

YOU KNOW THIS STORY. A little furry blue Muppet. His name is Grover. He spends the whole tale terrified of the monster at the end of it, begging the reader to stop turning pages. He uses tape, boards, and finally brick to wall up the pages, to delay the inevitable confrontation. He begs and he cries. But readers of the story, driven by our relentless curiosity, by our desperate desire to explore, to seek, ignore his entreaties and keep turning those pages—only for Grover (and us) to discover at the end that all along, *he* was the monster at the end of this book. Lovable, furry, neurotic Grover. Nothing to be feared, nothing to be dreaded.

The Monster at the End of This Book is a delight for young children and the adults who read it to them because of its twist ending. I imagine that you are feeling no such surprise at this point in this book, because we have been building up to this moment from our very first pages together—gathering evidence, talking to experts, conversing with students, considering science. The monsters that plague both us and the young people we care about are not external beasts to be vanquished. They are part and parcel of who we are. They represent the activity of biological systems that were designed to keep us safe and healthy—and as we have seen, well-being is integrally tied to health and the good functioning of our internal systems, and so in a way, they are also designed to keep us happy.

At the same time, living in a body where one of these monsters is rampaging is pretty dreadful. I do not recommend it. Importantly, these systems go out of whack when the environments our bodies are operating in are *cueing them* to overreact, when the setting itself is monstrous. When our jobs require us to burn out to be successful, or even just to keep them, and we neglect tending to all the systems that need tending for proper homeostasis (sleep, relaxation, social time). When systems of injustice mean you can't meet your basic needs and/or you are under constant threat, both real and perceived. When unresolved and untreated trauma in your past hasn't been woven into the landscape of your memories and instead torments you, front and center. When you feel like your entire self-worth is bundled up in what grades show up on your report card or what elite college you are accepted into, and both of those things feel somewhat arbitrarily determined. "Monsters, I've argued," Scott Poole writes, "are creatures of historical context and cultures get the monsters they deserve, the vengeful ghosts they have raised." We, the collective *we* as a society, have raised these monsters, and we are going to need collective changes to have any hope of addressing an epidemic.

But ultimately, collectives are made of the individuals that comprise them, and so we can consider the decisions and actions that individuals, parents, teachers, campuses, and societies can make. Let's do that now.

YOUTH NEED COMPASSIONATE CHALLENGE

To my mind, all the evidence we considered—voices, science, and solutions—underscores the importance of crafting learning environments for youth with the principles of compassionate challenge in mind. These principles can first of all be spelled out at the level of *bodies*. Physical health and well-being are integrally woven together with mental health and well-being—after all, the brain regulates both the body and the mind. Especially for those who have faced the unthinkable, we need learning environments that support students whose bodies may have learned to overreact even in safety. But an analysis of the effect of *beliefs* on our mental experience suggests that it is also important to communicate to our youth that they are strong, that they are resilient, that they have autonomy over their lives, that they are competent, that they belong, and that they can choose a life of purpose. By creating learning environments that encourage these key beliefs, we can help youth translate uncertainty about the future into motivation rather than anxiety. Once all these aspects of a compassionate learning environment are in place, we can nudge our youth to engage in *behaviors* that involve vulnerability and states of arousal, where they feel safe enough to play.

Writing in the mid-1990s, well before declarations of a student mental health crisis, bell hooks reflected on how many students she saw who were struggling and needing therapy:

> There are times when I walk into classrooms overflowing with students who feel terribly wounded in their psyches (many of them see therapists), yet I do not think they want therapy from me. They do want an education that is healing to the uninformed, unknowing spirit. They do want knowledge that is meaningful. They rightfully expect that my colleagues and I will not offer them information without addressing the connection between what they are learning and their overall life experiences.

Students should not want their college instructors to be therapists, and it would also be highly unethical for untrained instructors to attempt to provide therapy. With a few exceptions, college instructors are not that kind of doctor. But what we *can* do is craft learning environments in our classrooms and campuses that support the components of compassionate challenge, to provide the education that hooks describes—healing to uninformed, unknowing spirits, meaningful, and connected to their lives.

But providing learning environments of compassionate challenge will not be cheap. As a society, we need to invest in our youth.

MENTAL HEALTH—AND COMPASSIONATE CHALLENGE—WILL BE EXPENSIVE

It may have struck you (because it struck me) how so much of setting up these environments of compassionate challenge to support mental health requires personalized attention to individual students, and how much of it relies on deep care and work of individual instructors and school staff and administrators. Such attention is expensive. If teachers are to provide this level of focus to individual students, their class sizes will need to be smaller, and more teachers will be needed for fewer classes. If we follow Ryan Glode's encouragement to replace band-aid venting sorts of therapy with empirically supported exposure and cognitive behavioral therapies, we are going to need to hire more therapists and provide more sessions.

Establishing and maintaining environments of compassionate challenge are also emotionally expensive for the teachers, and so teachers are going to need more mental health support in terms of time off to replenish and reductions in other responsibilities to prevent burnout. So many institutions are hiring fancy consulting firms to tell them how to shore up admissions and retention, and we need to remember Karen Costa's words—we know what works. Deep, attentive relationships between students and faculty are what works. But providing them will be expensive.

But *not* supporting youth mental health? That carries its own costs, in myriad forms that are as easy to imagine as they are terrible to imagine. As a society we need to commit greater resources to the effort.

YOUTH NEED TO SEE THEMSELVES—AND TO SEE JOY

Human beings are aspirational creatures, and they are also highly visual ones. For students to expect success and visualize themselves into creative, fulfilling futures, they need models of success that are accessible to them, roles they can imagine inhabiting themselves one day. Recall Krystan, who didn't believe all her abled instructors when they told her to expect success despite the greater roadblocks in her path than other students—but she believed her instructor with a similar disability. Representation matters. Being taught by some instructors who share your gender, ethnicity, sexuality, disability status, first-generation status, and other characteristics can illustrate possibility.

Youth also need to look to the adults in their lives and see models of happiness. If they look around them and see unhappy, burnt-out adults who do not find delight in either their work or their home lives, it can be tough to aspire to joy. As a child I can remember so many times being frustrated at being shut out of adult fun. Sent to bed early while my parents played uproarious poker with my maternal grandparents and their neighborhood friends, the whole house smelling of stuffed grape leaves that I couldn't have until leftover in the morning, when they were cold instead of steaming the scent of tangy lemon. Other nights at my paternal grandparents' winter home in New Hampshire, where I laid in bed listening to joy that was more formal but no less intriguing—passionate arguments about politics and literature punctuated by laughter and the clink of cordial glasses. Adulthood seemed to be this time of freedom and high emotions and setting your own rules.

Supporting *adult* mental health would be the subject of a whole other book, but as essential as it is to invest in our youth, culturally we also need to invest in our adults, to provide them with the resources necessary to pursue their own mental health.

COLLEGE IS WORTH IT

I am the furthest thing from an unbiased perspective on this issue, but the message I took from all our student interviews and other research is, "College? It is worth it." The stories of the thirty-five students we interviewed were all so beautiful to me, each and every one. They varied so much, from type of institution to major to background of the student. Some came from well-resourced backgrounds and attended elite colleges. Some grew up in poverty and worked their way through the community college system. And on the flip side—some were first-generation students who were assisted through scholarships and internal programs to support their success at more elite colleges, and some were students from well-resourced backgrounds saving tuition dollars in a community college setting. But every story was of growth and discovery. All of them shared how close relationships with professors, community with their fellow students, and academic programs that offered opportunity and creative richness that expanded their horizons, guided them to their vocations, and helped them grow as people.

One of the pleasures of these interviews was at the conclusion of each one, when we asked the student participant to imagine giving a little brother or sister advice about the college experience—or their college administrators about how colleges should be run. Over and over, we heard stories about how they started their first year of college feeling alone and intimidated, getting to-go containers of food from the cafeteria and returning to eat in their dorm room by the lonely light of their phone. Over and over these same students found their niche, their clubs, their crowds. If they could offer advice to their past selves or future college students, it would be to just get out there. Attend the club meetings you see on flyers or splashed around your school's social media. You don't have to sign up for a leadership role; just showing up will be enough to begin the process of being embedded in a group.

Think about it: Attending college means starting adult life in an environment that is structurally designed for you to learn practical skills to carry into your future career but also to establish a network of cherished social partners. At the same time, you have opportunities to explore your creative passions and physical abilities, to develop networking relationships with professionals in your field, *and* to have fun along the way. These college years are such a gift for those who can access them. And for the increasing numbers of students who are returning to campus at other stages in life, college can similarly be an opportunity to change career directions, begin anew after a major life change like divorce, or explore possibilities that were closed in youth for one or another reason.

Saying college is worth it isn't the same thing as saying that it is worth taking on enormous amounts of debt to pursue it. For one thing, one needs to be wary of predatory for-profit colleges or even typically operating colleges that encourage students to take on more debt than they can handle with low chances of finishing the program or earning back the money one has spent. Moreover, it is not the case that students should always opt for the most "prestigious" or "elite" college that will accept them. While our team interviewed only a handful of people from each institution type, and so we can't draw large-scale conclusions, it was nonetheless intriguing to me that many of our interviewees from extremely selective colleges discussed being reluctant to approach their professors for fear of "wasting their time" and also of taking some courses with such heavy workloads that they felt hazed. The students at these institutions who didn't come from high-income families also reported feeling out of place in many conversations with their peers, almost like they were from different planets. In contrast, students across other institution types—community colleges, tribal colleges, historically Black colleges and universities, state universities, and small liberal arts colleges—all reported enjoying close, intimate mentoring relationships with their professors and feeling deeply supported by them. The best college for a given student is often not the college highest up on silly magazine lists.

The college-entrance and aid system is deeply flawed, especially for those not among the highest income brackets. But college is such a wonderful opportunity to craft learning environments of compassionate challenge to nurture future adults with good mental health that we cannot miss the opportunity. We need to make college accessible for all. Education writer John Warner provocatively argues for free public universities in his book *Sustainable. Resilient. Free.: The Future of Public Higher Education.*

Warner asks, "Who will believe with me?"

I will. Will you?

FINIS: LIFE IS DARK AND FULL OF TERRORS

One Halloween party, I confessed to chapters 1 and 2 expert Ryan Glode that when my prematurely born daughter was still very small, I would routinely become disturbed by the sight of roadkill on the highway. How could she stay safe, unharmed, when she was no bigger than these poor furry beings so casually and routinely smushed and left to rot? Ryan raised an eyebrow, took an imaginary clinician's notebook out of his costume's nonexistent pocket, and pretended to jot down (while speaking out loud), "Well, *that's* an automatic negative thought." We shared a laugh and then continued with the spooky merriment.

Listen: Life is terrifying. Monsters are real. The most horrifying moments of our lives lurk just around the corner. It is somewhat remarkable to me that we get up each day, don our armor, and face it all. It is even more remarkable to me that our youth do so, given how much more uncertainty they face day in and day out than those of us who are older and more settled. But of course, the most beautiful moments of our lives await around other corners, waiting for us to leave our sanctuaries and risk vulnerability and its multitudinous rewards.

The best way we can encourage our youth is to not push them out of the nest unaided. We must first create for them learning environments where they can experiment with risk in settings where they are safe, where they feel they belong, and where they can play.

Then, quite on their own, they can soar.

ACKNOWLEDGMENTS

L EARNING TO LIVE WITH—and sometimes love—one's monsters while not letting them rule the roost is a lifetime journey requiring much support. My journey was supported first and arguably best by my wonderful parents, Rosemary and William Cavanagh. They created a home built out of both compassion and challenge, where I experienced unconditional safety, nurture, and love, but where my brothers were also not allowed to help me open car doors until I figured it out myself (a task I found confounding until an embarrassingly late age). My brothers Andrew and Daniel certainly helped me out with lots of exposure therapy, including some very hands-off babysitting by the former and once duct-taping me into a coffee table box by the latter.

I owe deep gratitude to all my student and expert interviewees—Alison Cares, William Cavanagh, Karen Costa, Josh Eyler, Ryan Glode, Kelly Leonard, Esteban Loustaunau, Nnamdi Pole, Elly Romero, and Ayanna Thomas. I always am amazed by generosities involving time, but since these interviews mostly occurred during the monstrous early years of the COVID-19 pandemic, I feel such generosity particularly keenly.

To brother Dan, Laurie and Matt Spencer, Julie and Lisa Berube, Summer and Jeb Praetorius, and all the rest of our neighborhood gang who stayed out of our childhood houses for hours on end at very young ages swinging from tree vines in the woods, hurtling ourselves over reservoir gates twenty feet above concrete, and smacking bee nests out of swing-set pipes, thanks for helping me develop monster-fighting skills and confidence.

I deeply thank my wonderful literary agent, Jessica Papin, at Dystel, Goderich, and Bourett and attentive editor, Rachael Marks, at Beacon

Press for slaying imposter syndrome and doubt and providing such a bedrock of support, warmth, and positivity from which to create this work. Jessica's deft handling of finding a home for this book during the early phase of the pandemic was such a bright and reassuring spot in a dark time, and my monthly calls with Rachael through the entire process of writing were so enriching.

Thank you to my stalwart writers' group, Jim Lang and Mike Land, as always, for the patient reads of malformed early drafts, for helping me find the through line through the mess, and for still being alive in this world with me. I cherish each and every minute together.

I am further thankful for the team of collaborators who conducted the Student Voices project with me. Gary Senecal helped me navigate my first qualitative interview project with great patience and care, Heather Urry provided her usual keen insights, and Brigitte Manseau made so many thoughtful contributions. Most of all I am grateful to Jasmin Veerapen, who co-conducted all the interviews with me and shaped the questions we asked as part of her senior honors thesis. I can't wait to see all that your future holds.

To my alt-spouse/second-brain, Julie Sargent, who stands with me in the face of it all.

To my org-spouse/love, Brian Chandley, who knows all that he does and all that it means.

And to my bearnoodlefishface Noelle Margery, who has been braver than me since the moment she burst into the world five weeks early. May you have all the adventures you crave.

NOTES

PREFACE

Richard Peck, *Monster Night at Grandma's House* (New York: Dial Books for Young Readers, 2003).

"Young People's Mental Health Is Finally Getting the Attention It Needs," editorial, *Nature*, October 7, 2021, https://doi.org/10.1038/d41586-021-02690-5. A UNICEF report on the state of the world's children revealing the understudied, underfunded nature of the crisis and also that anxiety and depression are among the most common mental health struggles.

Shelli Avenevoli et al., "Mental Health Surveillance Among Children—United States, 2005–2011," *Morbidity and Mortality Weekly Report* 62, no. 2 (2013): 1–35.

Suicide rates among adolescents, worse for women, Black youth, and those on the LGBTQIA+ spectrum: Asha Z. Ivey-Stephenson et al., "Suicidal Ideation and Behaviors Among High School Students—Youth Risk Behavior Survey, United States, 2019," *MMWR Supplements* 69, no. 1 (2020): 47.

Russell B. Toomey, Amy K. Syvertsen, and Maura Shramko, "Transgender Adolescent Suicide Behavior," *Pediatrics* 142, no. 4 (2018).

Worsened depression following COVID-19: Catherine K. Ettman et al., "Prevalence of Depression Symptoms in US Adults Before and During the COVID-19 Pandemic," *JAMA Network Open* 3, no. 9 (2020): e2019686.

Interestingly, there were not increased depressive symptoms in Chinese students. Jiawen Deng et al., "The Prevalence of Depressive Symptoms, Anxiety Symptoms and Sleep Disturbance in Higher Education Students During the COVID-19 Pandemic: A Systematic Review and Meta-Analysis," *Psychiatry Research* (July 2021): 113863.

The idea that screentime, smartphones, and social media are responsible for raising rates of mental health struggles among adolescents is a perspective most associated with Jean Twenge and colleagues. See Jean M. Twenge, *Generation Me—Revised and Updated: Why Today's Young Americans Are More Confident, Assertive, Entitled—And More Miserable Than Ever Before* (New York: Simon & Schuster, 2014).

Greater care and concern for young people from an educational perspective is such an important idea that brings to mind so many scholars, but here are just two: Maha Bali's collected works can be found at https://www.aucegypt.edu/fac/mahabali, and Cate Denial's essay "A Pedagogy of Kindness" will soon be a book! See https://hybridpedagogy.org/pedagogy-of-kindness, retrieved October 22, 2021; a call for greater challenge is most associated with Greg Lukianoff and Jonathan Haidt, *The Coddling of the American Mind: How Good Intentions and Bad Ideas Are Setting Up a Generation for Failure* (New York: Penguin Books, 2019).

UNICEF report on the state of the world's children described by an online editorial in *Nature* revealing understudied, underfunded nature of the crisis and also that anxiety and depression are among the most common mental health struggles: "Young People's Mental Health Is Finally Getting the Attention It Needs."

Millennials and burnout: Anne Helen Petersen, "How Millennials Became the Burnout Generation," *AMASS* 23, no. 4 (2019): 16–21. Petersen has further developed these ideas into a book: Anne Helen Petersen, *Can't Even: How Millennials Became the Burnout Generation* (New York: Mariner Books, 2021).

Only 11% of college students are getting enough sleep: W. C. Buboltz et al., "Sleep Habits and Patterns of College Students," *Journal of American College Health* 50 (2001): 131–35.

Sex recession among young people: Kate Julian, "Why Are Young People Having So Little Sex?," *The Atlantic* 67, no. 12 (2018): 35–39.

Kevin Gannon wrote many more beautiful words about radical hope and education in his titular book *Radical Hope: A Teaching Manifesto* (Morgantown: West Virginia University Press, 2020).

CHAPTER 1: CRISIS AND COMPLEXITIES

Jeffrey Andrew Weinstock, ed., *The Monster Theory Reader* (Minneapolis: University of Minnesota Press, 2020).

Sigmund Freud, *The Uncanny*, trans. David McLintock, orig. pub'd. 1899 (New Delhi: Prabhat Prakashan, 1976).

W. Scott Poole, *Monsters in America: Our Historical Obsession with the Hideous and the Haunting* (Waco, TX: Baylor University Press, 2011), 15.

Patrick Ness and Siobhan Dowd, *A Monster Calls* (London: Walker Books, 2015).

Richard Peck, *Monster Night at Grandma's House* (New York: Dial Books for Young Readers, 2003).

James B. Twitchell, *Dreadful Pleasures: An Anatomy of Modern Horror* (New York: Oxford University Press, 1985).

John Edgar Browning, Sean Moreland, and Aalya Ahmad, "Towards a Monster Pedagogy: (Re) Claiming the Classroom for the Other," in *Fear and Learning: Essays on the Pedagogy of Horror*, ed. Sean Moreland and Aalya Ahmad (Jefferson, NC: McFarland, 2012), 40–55.

Asa Simon Mittman, "Teaching Monsters from Medieval to Modern," in *Monsters in the Classroom: Essays on Teaching What Scares Us*, ed. Adam Golub and Heather Richardson Hayton (Jefferson, NC: McFarland, 2017), 19.

Elizabeth A. Grosz, "Intolerable Ambiguity: Freaks as/at the Limit," in *Freakmaking: Constituting Corporeal and Cultural Others*, ed. R. G. Thomson (New York: New York University Press, 1997), 55–66.

Here, Mittman was talking more about the internet creating so many subcultures that there is less of an average or typical experience, but I think the splicing holds a similarity that applies the quote to both concerns. From Mittman, "Teaching Monsters from Medieval to Modern," 19.

Eric Goodman, *Your Anxiety Beast and You: A Compassionate Guide to Living in an Increasingly Anxious World* (Takapuna, New Zealand: Exisle, 2020).

Kelly J. Baker, *Final Girl—and Other Essays on Grief, Trauma, and Mental Illness* (Chapel Hill, NC: Blue Crow Books, 2020).

Escalations of mental health symptoms in adolescents in the 2010s: Jean M. Twenge, A. Bell Cooper, Thomas E. Joiner, Mary E. Duffy, and Sarah G. Binau, "Age, Period, and Cohort Trends in Mood Disorder Indicators and Suicide-Related Outcomes in a Nationally Representative Dataset, 2005–2017," *Journal of Abnormal Psychology* 128, no. 3 (2019): 185; Center for Collegiate Mental Health, *Center for Collegiate Mental Health 2018 Annual Report*, 2017.

The American Academy of Pediatrics, the Children's Hospital Association, and the American Academy of Child and Adolescent Psychiatry joined together to issue a warning about a mental health crisis among children and adolescents: AAP-AACAP-CHA Declaration of a National Emergency in Child and Adolescent Mental Health, https://www.aap.org/en/advocacy/child-and-adolescent-healthy -mental-development/aap-aacap-cha-declaration-of-a-national-emergency-in -child-and-adolescent-mental-health, retrieved October 22, 2021.

Lee Skallerup Bessette, "You Can Ask for Mental-Health Help, But Can You Find Any?," *Chronicle of Higher Education*, October 27, 2021.

Two-thirds of primary care clinicians report difficulty in connecting clients with psychiatric services: Steinberg Institute, "Fact Sheet: How Primary Care Providers Can Help Solve Our Psychiatrist Shortage," https://steinberginstitute.org/press -release/fact-sheet-primary-care-providers-can-help-solve-psychiatrist-shortage, accessed June 17, 2022.

Sixty percent of psychiatrists over age fifty-five: "Active Physicians by Age and Specialty, 2019," AAMC, https://www.aamc.org/data-reports/workforce/interactive -data/active-physicians-age-and-specialty-2019.

Concerns about anxiety epidemics since antiquity: Marc-Antoine Crocq, "A History of Anxiety: From Hippocrates to *DSM*," *Dialogues in Clinical Neuroscience* 17, no. 3 (2015): 319.

Changes in mental health symptoms globally over time: Dirk Richter et al., "Is the Global Prevalence Rate of Adult Mental Illness Increasing? Systematic Review and Meta-Analysis," *Acta Psychiatrica Scandinavica* 140, no. 5 (2019): 393–407.

Lucy Foulkes, *Losing Our Minds: What Mental Illness Really Is—and What It Isn't* (London: Bodley Head, 2021), 38.

Randy Glasbergen, "med19," 2002, www.glasbergen.com.

Jess Zimmerman, *Women and Other Monsters: Building a New Mythology* (Boston: Beacon Press, 2021).

Mental health struggles share similar etiology, neurobiology, and treatment: Avshalom Caspi and Terrie E. Moffitt, "All for One and One for All: Mental Disorders in One Dimension," *American Journal of Psychiatry* 175, no. 9 (2018): 831–44.

Credit to Lucy Foulkes's already cited book for the metaphor of moving goalposts for mental illness: Foulkes, *Losing Our Minds*.

Lisa Damour, *Under Pressure: Confronting the Epidemic of Stress and Anxiety in Girls* (New York: Ballantine Books, 2020), 27.

Thanks to psychologist Eiko Fried for the blood pressure analogy for mental health diagnoses. Eiko Fried, "Studying Mental Disorders as Systems, Not Syndromes," *Measurement, Modeling and Complexity of Mental Health* (blog), posted December 6, 2021.

John Warner, "Improving Student Mental Health Means Working from the Roots," *Educational Endeavors*, September 4, 2021, https://educationalendeavors.substack

.com/p/improving-student-mental-health-means?r=9v887&utm_campaign=post &utm_medium=web&utm_source=copy.

Songbirds learning tunes during a critical period: Ronald E. Dahl et al., "Importance of Investing in Adolescence from a Developmental Science Perspective," *Nature* 554, no. 7693 (2018): 441–50.

"Liddy, First to Fly" appears in Kim Fu's book of short stories: *Lesser Known Monsters of the 21st Century* (Portland, OR: Tin House, 2022).

Foulkes, *Losing Our Minds*, 118.

Human adolescence as a critical period needing intervention: Dahl et al., "Importance of Investing in Adolescence from a Developmental Science Perspective," 441–50.

Martha C. Nussbaum, *The Monarchy of Fear: A Philosopher Looks at Our Political Crisis* (New York: Simon & Schuster, 2019).

From Summer Praetorius, "The Climate Learning Tree," *Nautilus*, December 20, 2019, https://nautil.us/issue/79/catalysts/the-climate-learning-tree.

Imagining future threats involve judgments about how likely certain threats are (which is hard) and also assign value to the outcomes of such threats (which is also hard)— how good or bad would it be? From Eli R. Lebowitz, *Breaking Free of Child Anxiety and OCD: A Scientifically Proven Program for Parents* (New York: Oxford University Press, 2020).

Developmental timeline of anxiety and depression emergence in adolescence: Lisa R. Starr, Catherine B. Stroud, and Yihan I. Li, "Predicting the Transition from Anxiety to Depressive Symptoms in Early Adolescence: Negative Anxiety Response Style as a Moderator of Sequential Comorbidity," *Journal of Affective Disorders* 190 (2016): 757–63.

Anxiety precedes depression in research studies and patient perception: A. R. Mathew et al., "Co-Morbidity Between Major Depressive Disorder and Anxiety Disorders: Shared Etiology or Direct Causation?" *Psychological Medicine* 41, no. 10 (2011): 2023–34; and Paul A. Frewen et al., "Perceived Causal Relations Between Anxiety, Posttraumatic Stress and Depression: Extension to Moderation, Mediation, and Network Analysis," *European Journal of Psychotraumatology* 4, no. 1 (2013): 20656.

Negative response styles predict transition from anxiety to depression: Starr, Stroud, and Li, "Predicting the Transition from Anxiety to Depressive Symptoms in Early Adolescence," 757–63.

Neuroticism common underlying factor to most forms of mental illness, which lead to avoidance as a coping mechanism: David H. Barlow, Andrew J. Curreri, and Lauren S. Woodard, "Neuroticism and Disorders of Emotion: A New Synthesis," *Current Directions in Psychological Science* 30, no. 5 (2021): 410–17.

CHAPTER 2: OUR YOUTH NEED COMPASSIONATE CHALLENGE

For two excellent books summarizing the research on this topic as it applies to the college experience, see Peter Felten and Leo M. Lambert, *Relationship-Rich Education: How Human Connections Drive Success in College* (Baltimore: Johns Hopkins University Press, 2020), and Daniel F. Chambliss and Christopher G. Takacs, *How College Works* (Cambridge, MA: Harvard University Press, 2014).

Philip Roth, *American Pastoral* (1997) (New York: Random House, 2016).

Lisa Damour, *Under Pressure: Confronting the Epidemic of Stress and Anxiety in Girls* (New York: Ballantine Books, 2020).

Avoidance means never learning that previous learning was incorrect and that the situation is safe: Dan W. Grupe and Jack B. Nitschke, "Uncertainty and Anticipation in Anxiety: An Integrated Neurobiological and Psychological Perspective," *Nature Reviews Neuroscience* 14, no. 7 (2013): 488–501.

Importance of establishing new learning about safety rather than just extinguishing associations with fear and panic: Hyein Cho, Ekaterina Likhtik, and Tracy A. Dennis-Tiwary, "Absence Makes the Mind Grow Fonder: Reconceptualizing Studies of Safety Learning in Translational Research on Anxiety," *Cognitive, Affective, and Behavioral Neuroscience* (2021): 1–13.

Growth versus fixed mindset: Carol S. Dweck, *Mindset: The New Psychology of Success* (New York: Random House Digital, 2008).

Growth mindset about anxiety: Hans Schroder, "Set Yourself Free by Developing a Growth Mindset Toward Anxiety," *Psyche*, June 22, 2021, https://psyche.co/ideas/set-yourself-free-by-developing-a-growth-mindset-toward-anxiety.

Christopher Emdin, *Ratchetdemic: Reimagining Academic Success* (Boston: Beacon Press, 2021), 30.

CHAPTER 3: INFUSED WITH EROS–EMBODIED MENTAL HEALTH

Emotion and cognition in the brain both part of survival circuits: Joseph LeDoux, "Rethinking the Emotional Brain," *Neuron* 73, no. 4 (2012): 653–76.

It's right there in the title: Joseph Cesario, David J. Johnson, and Heather L. Eisthen, "Your Brain Is Not an Onion with a Tiny Reptile Inside," *Current Directions in Psychological Science* 29, no. 3 (2020): 255–60.

Lisa Feldman Barrett, *7 1/2 Lessons About the Brain* (New York: Mariner Books, 2020).

Bessel A. van der Kolk, *The Body Keeps the Score: Brain, Mind, and Body in the Healing of Trauma* (New York: Penguin Books, 2015), 56.

Drive to thrive theory of resilience: Wai Kai Hou, Brian J. Hall, and Stevan E. Hobfoll, "Drive to Thrive: A Theory of Resilience Following Loss," in *Mental Health of Refugee and Conflict-Affected Populations: Theory, Research, and Clinical Practice*, ed. Nexhmedin Morina and Angela Nickerson (Cham: Springer, 2018), 111–33.

Drive to thrive theory applied to the COVID-19 pandemic: Wai Kai Hou et al., "Regularizing Daily Routines for Mental Health During and After the COVID-19 Pandemic," *Journal of Global Health* 10, no. 2 (2020).

Social others as ways to regulate our body budgets: David Sloan Wilson and James A. Coan, "Groups as Organisms: Implications for Therapy and Training," *Clinical Psychology Review* (2021): 101987.

A representative article on the importance of supporting students in transition to college: Anne Duffy et al., "Mental Health Care for University Students: A Way Forward?" *Lancet Psychiatry* 6, no. 11 (2019): 885–87.

On the challenges presented to first-generation students in particular: Lisa A. House, Chelsea Neal, and Jason Kolb, "Supporting the Mental Health Needs of First Generation College Students," *Journal of College Student Psychotherapy* 34, no. 2 (2020): 157–67.

Special collection on supporting youth mental health in journal *Nature*, collection:, https://www.nature.com/collections/ciiabjeice; "Young People's Mental Health Is Finally Getting the Attention It Needs," editorial, *Nature* 598 (October 7, 2021): 235–36, https://doi.org/10.1038/d41586-021-02690-5; and Wellcome report summarizing it all, *What Science Has Shown Can Help Young People with Anxiety and Depression*, Wellcome Trust, London, 2021, https://cms.wellcome.org/sites/default /files/2021-10/What-science-has-shown-can-help-young-people-with-anxiety-and -depression.pdf.

The report also covers some active ingredients related to the body that there isn't time for in this book, for instance the microbiome (the research literature on this topic is pretty limited at the moment) and use of psychiatric medication (because this book focuses on encouraging mental health rather than treating mental illness).

Sara Goldrick-Rab, *Paying the Price: College Costs, Financial Aid, and the Betrayal of the American Dream* (Chicago: University of Chicago Press, 2021).

Hope Center's report on differential impact of COVID-19 infections: Sara Goldrick-Rab et al., *August 2021 Research Brief: Self-Reported COVID-19 Infection and Implications for Mental Health and Food Insecurity Among American College Students*, Hope Center for College, Community, and Justice, 2021, https://hope4 college.com/wp-content/uploads/2021/08/COVID19-Infection-Implications.pdf.

Maslow's hierarchy influenced by his time with the Blackfoot Nation: Rodger E. Broomé, "Review of Transformation Beyond Greed: Native Self-Actualization," *Humanistic Psychologist* 45, no. 4 (2017): 397.

Jennifer S. Hirsch and Shamus Khan, *Sexual Citizens: A Landmark Study of Sex, Power, and Assault on Campus* (New York: W. W. Norton, 2020).

Hirsch and Khan, *Sexual Citizens*, 255–56.

Teri.Zin, "My Genre Makes a Monster of Me," *Uncanny*, 2018, https://uncanny magazine.com/article/my-genre-makes-a-monster-of-me.

Zin E. Rocklyn, *Flowers for the Sea* (New York: Tor, 2021).

Sara Hendren, *What Can a Body Do? How We Meet the Built World* (New York: Penguin, 2020), 14.

Arley Cruthers, "An Incomplete History of My Teaching Body," *Voices of Practice* (2021).

Olivia Laing, *Everybody* (New York: Macmillan, 2021), 179.

Laing, *Everybody*, 199.

Anxiety sensitivity and its relation to panic: Johanna H. M. Hovenkamp-Hermelink et al., "Anxiety Sensitivity, Its Stability and Longitudinal Association with Severity of Anxiety Symptoms," *Scientific Reports* 9, no. 1 (2019): 1–7.

Physical activity to reduce anxiety sensitivity (though note that many of these studies also showed that physical activity did not decrease distress tolerance: Mark B. Powers, Gordon J. G. Asmundson, and Jasper A. J. Smits, "Exercise for Mood and Anxiety Disorders: The State-of-the-Science," *Cognitive Behavioral Therapy* (2015): 237–39.

Kelly McGonigal, *The Joy of Movement: How Exercise Helps Us Find Happiness, Hope, Connection, and Courage* (New York: Penguin, 2019), 212.

Physical activity to reduce depressive symptoms in young people: Report from Wellcome summarizing it all: Alan Bailey et al., *What Science Has Shown Can Help Young People with Anxiety and Depression* (London: Wellcome Trust, 2021).

Lisa Damour, *Under Pressure: Confronting the Epidemic of Stress and Anxiety in Girls* (New York: Ballantine Books, 2020), 88.

Systematic review of college student sleep: João Dinis and Miguel Bragança, "Quality of Sleep and Depression in College Students: A Systematic Review," *Sleep Science* 11, no. 4 (2018): 290.

Two-thirds of college students meeting criteria for "poor sleep": Stephen P. Becker et al., "Sleep in a Large, Multi-University Sample of College Students: Sleep Problem Prevalence, Sex Differences, and Mental Health Correlates," *Sleep Health* 4, no. 2 (2018): 174–81.

Sleep trackers in college students suggest that sleep is directly tied to academic performance: Kana Okano et al., "Sleep Quality, Duration, and Consistency Are Associated with Better Academic Performance in College Students," *NPJ Science of Learning* 4, no. 1 (2019): 1–5.

Narrative literature review of research on sleep-wake disturbances and depression in young people: Jacob J. Crouse et al., "Circadian Rhythm Sleep-Wake Disturbances and Depression in Young People: Implications for Prevention and Early Intervention," *Lancet Psychiatry* 8, no. 9 (2021): 813–23.

Barbara Fredrickson's broaden-and-build theory of positive emotions: Barbara L. Fredrickson, "The Role of Positive Emotions in Positive Psychology: The Broaden-and-Build Theory of Positive Emotions," *American Psychologist* 56, no. 3 (2001): 218.

Additional research support for broaden-and-build: Annette Bolte, Thomas Goschke, and Julius Kuhl, "Emotion and Intuition: Effects of Positive and Negative Mood on Implicit Judgments of Semantic Coherence," *Psychological Science* 14, no. 5 (2003): 416–21; Barbara L. Fredrickson and Marcial F. Losada, "Positive Affect and the Complex Dynamics of Human Flourishing," *American Psychologist* 60, no. 7 (2005): 678.

Motivational intensity and the broadening/narrowing of attention: Philip Gable and Eddie Harmon-Jones, "The Motivational Dimensional Model of Affect: Implications for Breadth of Attention, Memory, and Cognitive Categorisation," *Cognition and Emotion* 24, no. 2 (2010): 322–37; Philip Gable and Eddie Harmon-Jones, "Approach-Motivated Positive Affect Reduces Breadth of Attention," *Psychological Science* 19, no. 5 (2008): 476–82.

Literature review on the benefits of time in nature: Gregory N. Bratman, Hector A. Olvera-Alvarez, and James J. Gross, "The Affective Benefits of Nature Exposure," *Social and Personality Psychology Compass* (2021).

Langdon Cook, *The Mushroom Hunters: On the Trail of an Underground America* (New York: Ballantine Books, 2013), 229.

Japanese forest-bathing: Bum Jin Park et al., "The Physiological Effects of Shinrin-Yoku (Taking in the Forest Atmosphere or Forest Bathing): Evidence from Field Experiments in 24 Forests Across Japan," *Environmental Health and Preventive Medicine* 15, no. 1 (2010): 18–26.

Michelle N. Shiota, "Awe, Wonder, and the Human Mind," *Annals of the New York Academy of Sciences* 1501, no. 1 (2021): 85–89.

Susan Hrach has wonderful ideas for getting outside with your students in her book *Minding Bodies: How Physical Space, Sensation, and Movement Affect Learning* (Morgantown: West Virginia University Press, 2021).

Blair Braverman, *Welcome to the Goddamn Ice Cube: Chasing Fear and Finding Home in the Great White North* (New York: HarperCollins, 2016); Blair Braverman's essay on supporting sled dogs as a metaphor for resilience during the pandemic: "What My Sled Dogs Taught Me About Planning for the Unknown," *New York Times*,

September 23, 2020, https://www.nytimes.com/2020/09/23/sports/sled-dogs
-mushing-unknowns-planning.html.

CHAPTER 4: UNRULY BODIES IN AN UNPREDICTABLE WORLD
Psychiatry's diagnostic bible is the *DSM-5*; "American Psychiatric Association, *Diagnostic and Statistical Manual of Mental Disorders* 5th ed. (2013), 591–643.
Research article from my time in Lisa's lab: Lisa M. Shin et al., "A Functional Magnetic Resonance Imaging Study of Amygdala and Medial Prefrontal Cortex Responses to Overtly Presented Fearful Faces in Posttraumatic Stress Disorder," *Archives of General Psychiatry* 62, no. 3 (2005): 273–81.
A research article by Lisa Shin and colleagues on the topic of using brain function in PTSD to predict treatment response: Lisa M. Shin et al., "Neuroimaging Predictors of Treatment Response in Anxiety Disorders," *Biology of Mood and Anxiety Disorders* 3, no. 1 (2013): 1–11.
Quote from Lisa Shin about moving into research on predicting treatment response in PTSD from brain function: Kalimah Redd Knight, "The Pain of PTSD— and Hope for Help," *Tufts Now*, June 25, 2019, https://now.tufts.edu/articles/pain-ptsd-and-hope-help.
It's right there in the title: Isaac R. Galatzer-Levy and Richard A. Bryant, "636,120 Ways to Have Posttraumatic Stress Disorder," *Perspectives on Psychological Science* 8, no. 6 (2013): 651–62.
Grinding teeth during pandemic: D. Dadnam, C. Dadnam, and H. Al-Saffar, "Pandemic Bruxism," *British Dental Journal* 230, no. 5 (2021): 271.
Bessel A. van der Kolk, *The Body Keeps the Score: Brain, Mind, and Body in the Healing of Trauma* (New York: Penguin Books, 2015), 1.
American Psychiatric Association, *Diagnostic and Statistical Manual of Mental Disorders* (3rd ed., revised) (Washington, DC: American Psychiatric Publishing, 1987).
Definition of trauma: Abuse, Substance, Trauma and Justice Strategic Initiative, *SAMHSA's Concept of Trauma and Guidance for a Trauma-Informed Approach*, US Department of Health and Human Services, July 2014, s.v. "abuse, substance," https://ncsacw.samhsa.gov/userfiles/files/SAMHSA_Trauma.pdf.
A review of Bonanno's many studies of trajectories of functioning following trauma (as well as that of others): Isaac R. Galatzer-Levy, Sandy H. Huang, and George A. Bonanno, "Trajectories of Resilience and Dysfunction Following Potential Trauma: A Review and Statistical Evaluation," *Clinical Psychology Review* 63 (2018): 41–55.
DSM-IV's requirement that "fear, helplessness, and horror" be part of the reaction to the traumatic event: Thomas A. Widiger et al., *DSM-IV Sourcebook*, vol. 3 (Washington, DC: American Psychiatric Publishing, 1997).
The defensive circuit underlying fear involving behavioral inhibition: Joseph E. LeDoux, *Anxious: Using the Brain to Understand and Treat Fear and Anxiety* (New York: Penguin, 2015).
Van der Kolk, *The Body Keeps the Score*.
Van der Kolk, *The Body Keeps the Score*, 37.
Adverse childhood experiences associated with poor physical and mental health, e.g., Elizabeth Crouch et al., "Assessing the Interrelatedness of Multiple Types of

Adverse Childhood Experiences and Odds for Poor Health in South Carolina Adults," *Child Abuse and Neglect* 65 (2017): 204–11; and Robert F. Anda et al., "The Enduring Effects of Abuse and Related Adverse Experiences in Childhood," *European Archives of Psychiatry and Clinical Neuroscience* 256, no. 3 (2006): 174–86.

Economic hardship affecting nearly a quarter of the sample of US youth: Elizabeth Crouch et al., "Prevalence of Adverse Childhood Experiences (ACES) Among US Children," *Child Abuse and Neglect* 92 (2019): 209–18.

Dena Simmons, writing about overachievement as a trauma response: "The Trauma We Don't See," ASCD.org, 77, no. 8 (2020), https://www.ascd.org/el/articles /the-trauma-we-dont-see.

The Onion satirizing the idea of safe spaces: "Parents Dedicate New College Safe Space in Honor of Daughter Who Felt Weird in Class Once," *The Onion*, July 15, 2015, https://www.theonion.com/parents-dedicate-new-college-safe-space-in-honor -of-dau-1819578004.

Animals drop play under harsh conditions: Marek Spinka, Ruth C. Newberry, and Marc Bekoff, "Mammalian Play: Training for the Unexpected," *Quarterly Review of Biology* 76, no. 2 (2001): 141–68.

Importance of establishing new learning about safety rather than just extinguishing associations with fear and panic: Hyein Cho, Ekaterina Likhtik, and Tracy A. Dennis-Tiwary, "Absence Makes the Mind Grow Fonder: Reconceptualizing Studies of Safety Learning in Translational Research on Anxiety," *Cognitive, Affective, and Behavioral Neuroscience* (2021): 1–13.

John Warner argues that maybe a large part of the debate about safe spaces is semantic rather than true disagreement: "What If Everyone Actually Agrees About Safe Spaces?" *Inside Higher Education*, September 6, 2021, https://www.insidehighered. com/blogs/just-visiting/what-if-everyone-actually-agrees-about-safe-spaces.

Karen Costa's contribution to an edited collection on trauma-informed pedagogy appears in *Trauma-Informed Pedagogies: A Guide to Responding to Crisis and Inequality in Higher Education*, ed. Phyllis Thompson and Janice Carello (New York: Palgrave Macmillan, 2022).

Substance Abuse and Mental Health Services Administration's report on trauma-informed approaches: Trauma and Justice Strategic Initiative, *SAM-HSA's Concept of Trauma and Guidance for a Trauma-Informed Approach*.

Universal design for learning is well described (with tips for implementation!) by Kirsten Behling and Thomas Tobin in their *Reach Everyone, Teach Everyone: Universal Design for Learning in Higher Education* (Morgantown: West Virginia University Press, 2018); a wonderful overview of culturally responsive teaching is Zaretta Hammond's *Culturally Responsive Teaching and the Brain: Promoting Authentic Engagement and Rigor Among Culturally and Linguistically Diverse Students* (Thousand Oaks, CA: Corwin Press, 2014).

Alex Shevrin Venet, *Equity-Centered Trauma-Informed Education* (New York: W. W. Norton, 2021).

School counselors are missing in many schools, especially those that serve low income students and students of color: School counselors: Education Trust and D. Cratty, "Fact Sheet: School Counselors Matter," Education Trust, February 1, 2019, https://edtrust.org/resource/school-counselors-matter.

Mays Imad's essay "Leveraging the Neuroscience of Now," *Inside Higher Education*, June 3, 2020, https://www.insidehighered.com/advice/2020/06/03/seven -recommendations-helping-students-thrive-times-trauma.

Peter Felten and Leo M. Lambert, *Relationship-Rich Education: How Human Connections Drive Success in College* (Baltimore: Johns Hopkins University Press, 2020).

Instructor-student relationships key to "humanizing" online learning: Michelle Pacansky-Brock, Michael Smedshammer, and Kim Vincent-Layton, "Humanizing Online Teaching to Equitize Higher Education," *Current Issues in Education* 21, no. 2, "Shaping the Futures of Learning in the Digital Age" (2020).

Trigger warnings started online in the feminist blogosphere: Amanda Marcotte, "The Year of the Trigger Warning," *Slate*, retrieved November 7, 2021, https://slate .com/human-interest/2013/12/trigger-warnings-from-the-feminist-blogosphere -to-shonda-rhimes-in-2013.html; Brenda D. Phillips, "Teaching About Family Violence to an At-Risk Population: Insights from Sociological and Feminist Per- spectives," *Teaching Sociology* 16, no. 3 (1988): 289–93.

Students with PTSD more likely to report low GPA and leave institution: Rachel L. Bachrach and Jennifer P. Read, "The Role of Posttraumatic Stress and Problem Alcohol Involvement in University Academic Performance," *Journal of Clinical Psychology* 68, no. 7 (2012): 843–59; and Güler Boyraz et al., "Posttraumatic Stress, Effort Regulation, and Academic Outcomes Among College Students: A Longitu- dinal Study," *Journal of Counseling Psychology* 63, no. 4 (2016): 475.

Catherine Denial writes about the experience of being triggered in an essay: "On Being Triggered," *Cate Denial* (blog), March 9, 2017, https://catherinedenial.org/ blog/uncategorized/on-being-triggered.

Richard McNally, "If You Need a Trigger Warning, You Need P.T.S.D. Treatment," *New York Times*, September 13, 2016, https://www.nytimes.com/roomfordebate /2016/09/13/do-trigger-warnings-work/if-you-need-a-trigger-warning-you-need -ptsd-treatment.

Greg Lukianoff and Jonathan Haidt, "The Coddling of the American Mind," *The Atlantic*, September 2015, https://www.theatlantic.com/magazine/archive/2015/09 /the-coddling-of-the-american-mind/399356. See also Greg Lukianoff and Jon- athan Haidt, *The Coddling of the American Mind: How Good Intentions and Bad Ideas Are Setting Up a Generation for Failure* (New York: Penguin Books, 2019).

Essay against using trigger warnings that includes (in my mind) an endorsement of trigger warnings: Anna Khalid and Jeffrey Aaron Snyder, "The Data Is In—Trig- ger Warnings Don't Work," *Chronicle of Higher Education*, September 15, 2021, https://www.chronicle.com/article/the-data-is-in-trigger-warnings-dont-work?cid2 =gen_login_refresh&cid=gen_sign_in&cid2=gen_login_refresh.

Review of research literature on experimental tests of trigger warnings on distress and mental health: Payton J. Jones, Benjamin W. Bellet, and Richard J. McNally, "Helping or Harming? The Effect of Trigger Warnings on Individuals with Trauma Histories," *Clinical Psychological Science* 8, no. 5 (2020): 905–17.

Faculty use of trigger warnings research by Alison Cares: Alison C. Cares et al., "For or Against? Criminal Justice and Criminology Faculty Attitudes Toward Trigger Warnings," *Journal of Criminal Justice Education* 32, no. 3 (2021): 302–22; Ali- son C. Cares et al., "'They Were There for People Who Needed Them': Student

Attitudes Toward the Use of Trigger Warnings in Victimology Classrooms," *Journal of Criminal Justice Education* 30, no. 1 (2019): 22–45.

Major trigger warning study referenced by Alison Cares: G. A. Boysen et al., "Trigger Warnings in Psychology Classes: What Do Students Think?" *Scholarship of Teaching and Learning in Psychology* 4, no. 2 (2018): 69–80, https://doi.org/10.1037 /stl0000106.

For a wonderful overview of faculty burnout, its consequences, and what we can do to ameliorate it, see Rebecca Pope-Ruark, *Unraveling Faculty Burnout: Pathways to Reckoning and Renewal* (Baltimore: Johns Hopkins University Press, 2022).

Words create worlds: I had heard this saying before, but for due diligence I want to note that Karen quoted it during our interview. Some research into its origins reveals many people who have been attributed with first saying these words, but no definitive attribution.

The academic article that resulted from the study of surgical amputation and its psychological effects: Sarah R. Cavanagh et al., "Psychiatric and Emotional Sequelae of Surgical Amputation," *Psychosomatics* 47, no. 6 (2006): 459–64.

George A. Bonanno, *The End of Trauma: How the New Science of Resilience Is Changing How We Think About PTSD* (New York: Basic Books, 2021).

Didier Fassin and Richard Rechtman, *The Empire of Trauma: An Inquiry into the Condition of Victimhood* (Princeton, NJ: Princeton University Press, 2009).

Fassin and Rechtman, *The Empire of Trauma*, 279.

Bonanno quote on flexibility mindset from his book: Bonanno, *The End of Trauma*, 151.

For an account of some of the dangers of assuming everyday experiences are actually markers of repressed trauma, see Richard J. McNally, *Remembering Trauma* (Cambridge, MA: Harvard University Press, 2005).

CHAPTER 5: SEEKING ONESELF

Neda DeMayo's quote about "passion, followed by correct action" is from an interview with journalist Mike Land, referenced later in the chapter. You can read Mike's blog post about the interview here: "Passion—and Action," *Serving . . . The Story* (blog), November 22, 2016, https://servingthestory.com/2016/11/22/strong -passion-and-correct-action.

First mention of motivation in the written record: Johnmarshall Reeve, *Understanding Motivation and Emotion* (Hoboken, NJ: John Wiley & Sons, 2014).

Highest levels of cortisol in the morning: Sue Edwards et al., "Association Between Time of Awakening and Diurnal Cortisol Secretory Activity," *Psychoneuroendocrinology* 26, no. 6 (2001): 613–22.

Link between *higher* waking cortisol outcomes and poor mental health or life situation: Deborah E. Polk et al., "State and Trait Affect as Predictors of Salivary Cortisol in Healthy Adults," *Psychoneuroendocrinology* 30, no. 3 (2005): 261–72; Sabine R. Kunz-Ebrecht et al., "Differences in Cortisol Awakening Response on Work Days and Weekends in Women and Men from the Whitehall II Cohort," *Psychoneuroendocrinology* 29, no. 4 (2004): 516–28; and Else Refsgaard, Anne Vibeke Schmedes, and Klaus Martiny, "Salivary Cortisol Awakening Response as a Predictor for Depression Severity in Adult Patients with a Major Depressive Episode Performing a Daily Exercise Program," *Neuropsychobiology* (2022): 1–10.

Link between *lower* waking cortisol outcomes and poor mental health or life situations: Gregory E. Miller et al., "Clinical Depression and Regulation of the Inflammatory Response During Acute Stress," *Psychosomatic Medicine* 67, no. 5 (2005): 679–87; Nalini Ranjit, Elizabeth A. Young, and George A. Kaplan, "Material Hardship Alters the Diurnal Rhythm of Salivary Cortisol," *International Journal of Epidemiology* 34, no. 5 (2005): 1138–43; and Megan R. Gunnar and Delia M. Vazquez, "Low Cortisol and a Flattening of Expected Daytime Rhythm: Potential Indices of Risk in Human Development," *Development and Psychopathology* 13, no. 3 (2001): 515–38.

Higher waking cortisol on workdays than weekends: Kunz-Ebrecht et al., "Differences in Cortisol Awakening Response on Work Days and Weekends in Women and Men from the Whitehall II Cohort," 516–28.

Morning cortisol tracks stress only on weekdays, not workdays: Wolff Schlotz et al., "Perceived Work Overload and Chronic Worrying Predict Weekend–Weekday Differences in the Cortisol Awakening Response," *Psychosomatic Medicine* 66, no. 2 (2004): 207–14.

Blunting of cortisol response in depression: Katarina Dedovic and Janice Ngiam, "The Cortisol Awakening Response and Major Depression: Examining the Evidence," *Neuropsychiatric Disease and Treatment* (2015).

Tracy Dennis-Tiwary, *Future Tense: Why Anxiety Is Good for You (Even Though It Feels Bad)* (New York: Harper Wave Books, 2022).

Declines in intrinsic motivation when offered a reward: E. L. Deci, R. Koestner, and R. M. Ryan, "A Meta-Analytic Review of Experiments Examining the Effects of Extrinsic Rewards on Intrinsic Motivation," *Psychological Bulletin* 125, no. 6 (1999): 627.

Defining intrinsic motivation: Stefano I. Di Domenico and Richard M. Ryan, "The Emerging Neuroscience of Intrinsic Motivation: A New Frontier in Self-Determination Research," *Frontiers in Human Neuroscience* 11 (2017): 145.

Human intrinsic motivation is underpinned by systems governing exploration and play in other mammals: Di Domenico and Ryan, "The Emerging Neuroscience of Intrinsic Motivation," 145.

Seeking system in the brain: Jaak Panksepp, *Affective Neuroscience: The Foundations of Human and Animal Emotions* (New York: Oxford University Press, 1998).

Anticipatory euphoria: Jaak Panksepp and Lucy Biven, *The Archaeology of Mind: Neuroevolutionary Origins of Human Emotions*, Norton Series on Interpersonal Neurobiology (New York: W. W. Norton, 2012).

Behavioral activation system is part of Jeffrey Gray's model: "A Critique of Eysenck's Theory of Personality," in *A Model for Personality*, ed. Hans J. Eysenck (Berlin: Springer, 1981), 246–76; approach motivation: Eddie Harmon-Jones, Cindy Harmon-Jones, and Tom F. Price, "What Is Approach Motivation?" *Emotion Review* 5, no. 3 (2013): 291–95.

Sarah Waters, *The Paying Guests* (London: Hachette UK, 2014), 36.

Waters, *The Paying Guests*, 86.

As quoted in Keith Johnstone, *Impro: Improvisation and the Theatre* (1979) (London: Routledge, 2012).

Autopoetic feedback loop: Erika Fischer-Lichte, *The Transformative Power of Performance: A New Aesthetics* (London: Routledge, 2008).

Affective crossover in teaching: Eva Susann Becker et al., "The Importance of Teachers' Emotions and Instructional Behavior for Their Students' Emotions—An Experience Sampling Analysis," *Teaching and Teacher Education* 43 (2014): 15–26.

Education as moving from romance to precision to generalization: Alfred North Whitehead, *Aims of Education* (New York: Simon & Schuster, 1967).

Jessica Lahey, interview with Teller, "Teaching: Just Like Performing Magic," *The Atlantic*, January 21, 2016, https://www.theatlantic.com/education/archive/2016/01/what-classrooms-can-learn-from-magic/425100.

College students choose their majors based on experiences with certain introductory instructors is backed up by qualitative research presented in Daniel F. Chambliss and Christopher G. Takacs, *How College Works* (Cambridge, MA: Harvard University Press, 2014).

Emotional synchrony in the classroom: Anne C. Frenzel et al., "Emotion Transmission in the Classroom Revisited: A Reciprocal Effects Model of Teacher and Student Enjoyment," *Journal of Educational Psychology* 110, no. 5 (2018): 628.

Teacher immediacy: Paul L. Witt, Lawrence R. Wheeless, and Mike Allen, "A Meta-Analytical Review of the Relationship Between Teacher Immediacy and Student Learning," *Communication Monographs* 71, no. 2 (2004): 184–207.

bell hooks, on classroom community: *Teaching to Transgress* (New York: Routledge, 2014), 8.

Warm versus chilly academic climate: Alexander S. Browman and Mesmin Destin, "The Effects of a Warm or Chilly Climate Toward Socioeconomic Diversity on Academic Motivation and Self-Concept," *Personality and Social Psychology Bulletin* 42, no. 2 (2016): 172–87.

Varieties of how motivation affects energy and direction: R. G. Geen, *Human Motivation: A Social Psychological Approach* (Pacific Grove, CA: Thomson Brooks/Cole, 1995).

Esteban E. Loustaunau and Lauren E. Shaw, *Telling Migrant Stories: Latin American Diaspora in Documentary Film* (Gainesville: University Press of Florida, 2018).

Esteban E. Loustaunau, "*Imaginarte*: Unaccompanied Refugee Minors Tell their Stories of Belonging Through Photography," *Latino Studies* 17 (2019): 269–77.

Paul J. Wadell, "Ethical Considerations in Mentoring for Vocation," St. Norbert College, November 11, 2010.

Horizons of significance: Charles Taylor, *The Ethics of Authenticity* (Cambridge, MA: Harvard University Press, 1992).

Mike Land's "The Whole Service Trip" is an unpublished manuscript in author's possession."

CHAPTER 6: DETERMINING ONESELF

Quote from Ryan, Deci, and co-authors on self-determination theory: Richard M. Ryan et al., "Building a Science of Motivated Persons: Self-Determination Theory's Empirical Approach to Human Experience and the Regulation of Behavior," *Motivation Science* 7, no. 2 (2021): 97.

Brain circuits that activate and deactivate during intrinsic motivation: Human intrinsic motivation is underpinned by systems governing exploration and play in other mammals. See Stefano I. Di Domenico and Richard M. Ryan, "The Emerging Neuroscience of Intrinsic Motivation: A New Frontier in Self-Determination Research," *Frontiers in Human Neuroscience* 11 (2017): 145.

Meta-analysis of self-determination theory's relation to various student outcomes: Joshua L. Howard et al., "Student Motivation and Associated Outcomes: A Meta-Analysis from Self-Determination Theory," *Perspectives on Psychological Science* (2021): 1745691620966789.

Autonomy improves quality of life across domains and cultures: Richard Koestner and Anne Holding, "A Generative Legacy: SDT's Refined Understanding of the Central Role of Autonomy in Human Lives," *Motivation Science* 7, no. 2 (2021): 111.

Control-value theory of achievement emotions: Reinhard Pekrun and Raymond P. Perry, "Control-Value Theory of Achievement Emotions," in *International Handbook of Emotions in Education*, ed. Reinhard Pekrun and Lisa Linnenbrink-Garcia (New York: Routledge, 2014), 130–51.

Goalsetting works: E. A. Locke and G. P. Latham, eds., *New Developments in Goal Setting and Task Performance* (New York: Routledge/Taylor & Francis Group, 2013).

Computerized goal setting study of college students experiencing academic difficulty: Dominique Morisano et al., "Setting, Elaborating, and Reflecting on Personal Goals Improves Academic Performance," *Journal of Applied Psychology* 95, no. 2 (2010): 255.

Jessica Lahey, *The Addiction Inoculation: Raising Healthy Kids in a Culture of Dependence* (New York: Harper-Collins, 2021).

Grades associated with a goal orientation involving anxiety, hopelessness, and lack of autonomy: Caroline Pulfrey, Céline Buchs, and Fabrizio Butera, "Why Grades Engender Performance-Avoidance Goals: The Mediating Role of Autonomous Motivation," *Journal of Educational Psychology* 103, no. 3 (2011): 683.

Grades activate feelings of shame and punishment: Nancy Rost Goulden and Charles J. G. Griffin, "Comparison of University Faculty and Student Beliefs About the Meaning of Grades," *Journal of Research and Development in Education* (1997); Reinhard Pekrun et al., "Academic Emotions in Students' Self-Regulated Learning and Achievement: A Program of Qualitative and Quantitative Research," *Educational Psychologist* 37, no. 2 (2002): 91–105.

Written feedback accompanying grades not even read: Susan M. Brookhart, *How to Give Effective Feedback to Your Students* (Alexandria, VA: Association for Supervision and Curriculum Development, 2017); Ross B. MacDonald, "Developmental Students' Processing of Teacher Feedback in Composition Instruction," *Review of Research in Developmental Education* 8, no. 5 (1991).

Stop listening after negative grades are received: Ruth Butler, "Enhancing and Undermining Intrinsic Motivation: The Effects of Task-Involving and Ego-Involving Evaluation on Interest and Performance," *British Journal of Educational Psychology* 58, no. 1 (1988): 1–14.

Joshua R. Eyler, *How Humans Learn: The Science and Stories Behind Effective College Teaching* (Morgantown: West Virginia University Press, 2018); *Scarlet Letters* forthcoming from the University of West Virginia Press.

This Pedagogies of Care project was helmed by Thomas Tobin and Victoria Mondelli, https://sabresmonkey.wixsite.com/pedagogiesofcare.

Sarah Rose Cavanagh and Josh Eyler, "Takeover," *Tea for Teaching*, October 14, 2020, https://teaforteaching.com/157-takeover/.

Paolo Freire, *Pedagogy of the Oppressed*, rev. ed. (New York: Continuum, 1996); hooks, *Teaching to Transgress*.

Both Susan Blum and Jesse Stommel have written extensively about ungrading, but some of their most popular and early essays on the topic are Blum, "Ungrading," *Inside Higher Education*, November 14, 2017, https://www.insidehighered.com /advice/2017/11/14/significant-learning-benefits-getting-rid-grades-essay); Stommel, "Why I Don't Grade," *Jesse Stommel* (blog), October 26, 2017, https:// www.jessestommel.com/why-i-dont-grade; and Stommel, "How to Ungrade," *Jesse Stommel* (blog), March 11, 2018, https://www.jessestommel.com/how-to-ungrade.

Susan D. Blum (ed). *UNgrading: Why Rating Students Undermines Learning (and What to Do Instead)* (Morgantown: West Virginia University Press, 2020).

Blum, *UNgrading*, 2.

Specifications grading: Linda B. Nilson, *Specifications Grading: Restoring Rigor, Motivating Students, and Saving Faculty Time* (Sterling, VA: Stylus, 2015).

Contract grading: Christina Katopodis and Cathy N. Davidson, "Contract Grading and Peer Review," in *UNgrading: Why Rating Students Undermines Learning (and What to Do Instead)*, ed. Susan Blum (Morgantown: West Virginia University Press, 2020), 105–22.

Portfolio grading: Kathleen Blake Yancey, "Grading ePortfolios: Tracing Two Approaches, Their Advantages, and Their Disadvantages," *Theory into Practice* 54, no. 4 (2015): 301–8.

Ayelet Fishbach, *Get It Done: Surprising Lessons from the Science of Motivation* (New York: Little, Brown Spark, 2022).

Blum, *UNgrading*, 106.

James M. Lang, *Small Teaching: Everyday Lessons from the Science of Learning* (New York: John Wiley & Sons, 2021), 15.

Zaretta Hammond, *Culturally Responsive Teaching and the Brain: Promoting Authentic Engagement and Rigor Among Culturally and Linguistically Diverse Students* (Thousand Oaks, CA: Corwin Press, 2014).

Jennifer Morton, *Moving Up Without Losing Your Way: The Ethical Costs of Upward Mobility* (Princeton, NJ: Princeton University Press, 2019).

Morton, *Moving Up Without Losing Your Way*, 150.

Zena Hitz, *Lost in Thought: The Hidden Pleasures of an Intellectual Life* (Princeton, NJ: Princeton University Press, 2020), 48.

Like-minded people get like-minded results: Kelly Leonard and Tom Yorton, *Yes, And: How Improvisation Reverses "No, But" Thinking and Improves Creativity and Collaboration—Lessons from The Second City* (New York: Harper Business, 2015).

Kelly Hogan and Viji Sathy, *Inclusive Teaching: Strategies for Promoting Equity in the Classroom* (Morgantown: West Virginia University Press, 2022).

Tracie Marcella Addy, Derek Dube, Khadijah A. Mitchell, and Mallory SoRelle, *What Inclusive Instructors Do: Principles and Practices for Excellence in College Teaching* (Sterling, VA: Stylus Publishing, 2021).

Bryan Dewsbury, "The Soul of My Pedagogy," *Scientific American*, January 23, 2018, https://blogs.scientificamerican.com/voices/the-soul-of-my-pedagogy.

Drive to thrive theory of resilience: Wai Kai Hou, Brian J. Hall, and Stevan E. Hobfoll, "Drive to Thrive: A Theory of Resilience Following Loss," in *Mental Health of Refugee and Conflict-Affected Populations: Theory, Research, and Clinical Practice*, ed. Nexhmedin Morina and Angela Nickerson (Cham: Springer, 2018), 111–33.

James Davies, *Sedated: How Modern Capitalism Created Our Mental Health Crisis* (London: Atlantic Books, 2021).

Davies, *Sedated*, 185–86.

Oliver Sacks, *Hallucinations* (Basingstoke: Pan Macmillan, 2012), 90.

CHAPTER 7: AROUSAL, ACTION, AND UNCERTAINTY

Mary Helen Immordino-Yang's pivotal work on emotions and learning may be best represented by her collection of essays on the topic, *Emotions, Learning, and the Brain: Exploring the Educational Implications of Affective Neuroscience*, Norton Series on the Social Neuroscience of Education (New York: W. W. Norton, 2015).

Control-value theory of achievement emotions: Reinhard Pekrun and Raymond P. Perry, "Control-Value Theory of Achievement Emotions," in *International Handbook of Emotions in Education*, ed. Reinhard Pekrun and Lisa Linnenbrink-Garcia (New York: Routledge, 2014), 130–51.

Emotional material is more memorable because it is arousing: Larry Cahill and James L. McGaugh, "Mechanisms of Emotional Arousal and Lasting Declarative Memory," *Trends in Neurosciences* 21, no. 7 (1998): 294–99.

Sarah Rose Cavanagh, *The Spark of Learning: Energizing the College Classroom with the Science of Emotion* (Morgantown: West Virginia University Press, 2016).

Susanne Vogel and Lars Schwabe, "Learning and Memory Under Stress: Implications for the Classroom," *NPJ Science of Learning* 1, no. 1 (2016): 1–10.

See, for example, a recent research article by Ayanna Kim Thomas et al., "How Prior Testing Impacts Misinformation Processing: A Dual-Task Approach," *Memory and Cognition* 48, no. 2 (2020): 314–24.

Meta affect: Jennifer Radoff, Lama Z. Jaber, and David Hammer, "Meta-Affective Learning in an Introductory Physics Course," in *Physics Education Research Conference 2016 Proceedings*, vol. 10, ed. Dyan L. Jones, Lin Ding, and Adrienne Traxler (Sacramento, CA: PERC, 2016).

Meta affect and the case study of a student in physics named Mayra: Jennifer Radoff, Lama Ziad Jaber, and David Hammer, "'It's Scary But It's Also Exciting': Evidence of Meta-Affective Learning in Science," *Cognition and Instruction* 37, no. 1 (2019): 73–92.

Quote about uncertainty intolerance being about a fundamental fear of the unknown: Sarah Shihata, Peter M. McEvoy, and Barbara A. Mullan, "Pathways from Uncertainty to Anxiety: An Evaluation of a Hierarchical Model of Trait and Disorder-Specific Intolerance of Uncertainty on Anxiety Disorder Symptoms," *Journal of Anxiety Disorders* 45 (2017): 72–79.

An overview of the research on uncertainty intolerance can be found here: R. Nicholas Carleton, "The Intolerance of Uncertainty Construct in the Context of Anxiety Disorders: Theoretical and Practical Perspectives," *Expert Review of Neurotherapeutics* 12, no. 8 (2012): 937–47.

Study examining order of uncertainty intolerance and anxiety over time in college students: Mary O. Shapiro et al., "Prospective Associations Between Intolerance of Uncertainty and Psychopathology," *Personality and Individual Differences* 166 (2020): 110210.

Jeffrey Cohen quote about monsters and uncertainty from his "Monster Culture (Seven Theses)" essay in *The Monster Theory Reader*, ed. Jeffrey Andrew Weinstock (Minneapolis: University of Minnesota Press, 2020).

Simon Strantzas, "The H Word: Ambiguity—What Does It Mean?" *Nightmare* 119 (2022).

Recreational horror study in a haunted house: Marc Malmdorf Andersen et al., "Playing with Fear: A Field Study in Recreational Horror," *Psychological Science* 31, no. 12 (2020): 1497–1510.

CHAPTER 8: PLAY AND IMPROVISATIONAL LEARNING

Viola Spolin's landmark book on improv: *Improvisation for the Theater: A Handbook of Teaching and Directing Techniques* (Evanston, IL: Northwestern University Press, 1999), 11.

Gordon Bermant, "Working With (Out) a Net: Improvisational Theater and Enhanced Well-Being," *Frontiers in Psychology* 4 (2013): 929.

Experiment on improv for college students: Peter Felsman, Sanuri Gunawardena, and Colleen M. Seifert, "Improv Experience Promotes Divergent Thinking, Uncertainty Tolerance, and Affective Well-Being," *Thinking Skills and Creativity* 35 (2020): 100632.

Research study using changes in appraisal to encourage students to embrace discomfort during improv: Kaitlin Woolley and Ayelet Fishbach, "Motivating Personal Growth by Seeking Discomfort," *Psychological Science* 33, no. 4 (2022): 510–23.

Most recent version of Keith Johnstone's famous tome: *Impro: Improvisation and the Theatre* (London: Routledge, 2012).

Johnstone, *Impro*, 31.

Oliver Sacks writes of these theories in his trade book *Hallucinations* (Basingstoke: Pan Macmillan, 2012), 90.

Roger E. Beaty, "The Neuroscience of Musical Improvisation," *Neuroscience & Biobehavioral Reviews* 51 (2015): 108–17.

David Lynch, *Catching the Big Fish: Meditation, Consciousness, and Creativity* (New York: Penguin, 2016), 1.

Kelly Leonard and Tom Yorton, *Yes, And: How Improvisation Reverses "No, But" Thinking and Improves Creativity and Collaboration—Lessons from The Second City* (New York: Harper Business, 2015).

Richard Bale, *Teaching with Confidence in Higher Education: Applying Strategies from the Performing Arts* (New York: Routledge, 2020), 105.

Review of mammalian play: Marek Spinka, Ruth C. Newberry, and Marc Bekoff, "Mammalian Play: Training for the Unexpected," *Quarterly Review of Biology* 76, no. 2 (2001): 141–68.

Paul Hanstedt, *Creating Wicked Students: Designing Courses for a Complex World* (Sterling, VA: Stylus Publishing, 2018), 3.

Deep play: Diane Ackerman, *Deep Play* (New York: Vintage, 2011), 9.

Paul Kassel, *Acting: An Introduction to the Art and Craft of Playing* (Boston: Pearson Allyn and Bacon, 2007).

Susan Hrach, *Minding Bodies: How Physical Space, Sensation, and Movement Affect Learning* (Morgantown: West Virginia University Press, 2021), xi.

Phil Smith's zombie movement activity is described in Adam Golub and Heather Richardson Hayton, eds., *Monsters in the Classroom: Essays on Teaching What Scares Us* (Jefferson, NC: McFarland, 2017), 151.

Viola Spolin, *Improvisation for the Theater: A Handbook of Teaching and Directing Techniques* (Evanston, IL: Northwestern University Press, 1999), 9.

Jessamyn Neuhaus, ed., *Picture a Professor: Interrupting Biases About Faculty and Increasing Student Learning* (Morgantown: West Virginia University Press, 2022).

Wilhelm Hofmann, Roy F. Baumeister, Georg Förster, and Kathleen D. Vohs, "Everyday Temptations: An Experience Sampling Study of Desire, Conflict, and Self-Control," *Journal of Personality and Social Psychology* 102, no. 6 (2012): 1318.

CONCLUSION: THE MONSTER AT THE END OF THIS BOOK

Autumn B. Heath and Jon Stone, *The Monster at the End of This Book: An Interactive Adventure Starring Lovable Furry Old Grover* (San Diego, CA: Studio Fun International, 2019).

W. Scott Poole, *Monsters in America: Our Historical Obsession with the Hideous and the Haunting* (Waco, TX: Baylor University Press, 2011).

bell hooks, teacher well-being, and students not wanting therapists but empowering education: bell hooks, *Teaching to Transgress* (New York: Routledge, 2014), 19.

The danger of predatory colleges: Tressie McMillan Cottom, *Lower Ed: The Troubling Rise of For-Profit Colleges in the New Economy* (New York: New Press, 2017).

John Warner, *Sustainable. Resilient. Free.: The Future of Public Higher Education* (Cleveland: Belt, 2020), 177.

INDEX